# Skepticism in Ethics

# Skepticism in Ethics

PANAYOT BUTCHVAROV

*Indiana University Press*

BLOOMINGTON AND INDIANAPOLIS

Manufactured in the United States of America

**Library of Congress Cataloging-in-Publication Data**

Butchvarov, Panayot, 1933-
  Skepticism in ethics.

  Includes index.
  1. Ethics.    2. Skepticism.    I. Title.
BJ1012.B76    1989    170    88-45103
ISBN 0-253-35321-1

1 2 3 4 5 93 92 91 90 89

*To David John and*
*Catherine Suzanna*

# CONTENTS

## 5. The System of Goods / 82

## 6. The Quantities and Degrees of Good and Evil / 123

## 7. Our Knowledge of Good / 137

## 8. Our Knowledge of Right / 161

# ACKNOWLEDGMENTS

I have included in this book revised portions of my articles "That Simple, Indefinable, Nonnatural Property *Good*," *The Review of Metaphysics* 36 (1982), and "Realism in Ethics," *Midwest Studies in Philosophy* 12 (1987). I thank the publishers of these periodicals for allowing me to do so.

Early versions of parts of the book were presented as a series of four lectures (the 1984 inaugural Jerome S. Simon Lectures) at the University of Toronto, and as individual lectures at the University of Miami, the University of Missouri, the State University of New York at Geneseo, The University of Iowa, the University of Akron, East Carolina University, and the University of Texas. I am indebted to many philosophers at those institutions for their valuable questions and comments.

A draft of the manuscript was read by Professor Albert Casullo, who convinced me that some topics I had discussed only briefly required extended discussion. I am grateful to him.

I am also indebted to Dennis Bradshaw, Susan Brennan, Rex Clemmensen, Daniel Holbrook, Huo-Wang Lin, William O'Brien, and Mary Ella Savarino for many useful discussions. As graduate students at The University of Iowa, they wrote, or are writing, dissertations on topics (not all belonging in ethics) considered in this book.

An outside reviewer of the manuscript for Indiana University Press made numerous suggestions for which I am deeply grateful.

The University of Iowa granted me a Senior Faculty Fellowship in the Humanities for the spring semester of 1983, and a Faculty Developmental Leave for the spring semester of 1986. One of the many admirable policies of The University of Iowa is its enlightened program of research leaves for its faculty.

# Skepticism in Ethics

# CHAPTER ONE

# Introduction

At the end of the earliest exposition of his emotive theory of ethics, Charles L. Stevenson acknowledged that the obvious response of many would be: "When we ask 'Is X good?' we don't want mere influence, mere advice. . . .We want our interests to be guided by . . . truth, and by nothing else. To substitute for such a truth mere emotive meaning and suggestion is to conceal from us the very object of our search." To this Stevenson replied: "I can only answer that I do not understand. What is this truth to be *about*? . . . I find no indefinable property, nor do I know what to look for."[1] Perhaps Stevenson might be excused for not trying harder to "find" the property in question. But no excuse is available for the failure of recent moral philosophy as a whole to do so.

G. E. Moore, whom presumably Stevenson had in mind in the last statement I quoted, and whose *Principia Ethica* determined the course of twentieth-century British and American ethics, claimed to be aware of an objective simple, indefinable, and nonnatural property *good*, in terms of which we could understand what ends are worthy of pursuit and therefore what actions we ought to perform. Is there such a property? Are we aware of such a property? Obviously, the answer would depend in part on the relevant phenomenological data, though not on a bare appeal to them, but on an appeal informed by a sufficiently subtle understanding of what it is for something to be a phenomenological datum. The answer would depend in part on purely metaphysical considerations about the sort of property goodness would be if there were such a property, and then about the very possibility of there being such a property. And the answer would, clearly, depend in part also on our success or failure in satisfying ourselves that such a property is, or at least can be, known, in the sense that we do or at least can know that there is such a property and that certain things have it and others do not, an issue by no means settled solely on phenomenological or metaphysical grounds.

In view of its subject matter, perhaps it is ultimately a tautology to say that ethics is the most important branch of philosophy. But certainly it is not the most fundamental. Little in it can be done that would be of value except on the basis of an adequate phenomenology, metaphysics, and epistemology. The fate of Moore's ethics, well exemplified by the passage from Stevenson with which we began, was to a great degree due to his failure to provide in detail the necessary phenomenological, metaphysical, and epistemological explanations in terms of which it would need to be understood. One specific purpose of this book is to provide such (long overdue) explanations, at times engaging even in fairly detailed exegesis. But this is not a book about Moore; some of the explanations to be offered might not have been acceptable to him. And its general purpose is much more ambitious: to provide, insofar as this can be done in one book, the phenomenological, metaphysical, and epistemological foundations of an ethical theory that can withstand the challenge of skepticism, insofar as this can be done, a theory that indeed resembles in some important respects Moore's (as well as Hastings Rashdall's and, less so, also H. A. Prichard's and W. D. Ross's), but in others is closer to the ethical theories of the major twentieth-century continental moral philosophers Max Scheler and Nicolai Hartmann, and in still others to the mainstream of classical Greek and medieval ethics. The reader should therefore expect phenomenological, metaphysical, and epistemological discussions much more detailed than those usually found in a book in ethics. For skepticism is, in part, a metaphysical position and, in part, an epistemological position, and, insofar as metaphysics and epistemology involve phenomenological considerations, in part also a phenomenological position. But our inquiry may also be regarded, more simply, as concerned with the question, Do we, or at least can we, know what is good and what is right? since the phenomenological and metaphysical discussions will be motivated by the epistemological goal. To answer this question we shall consider a number of views, all of which may be described as varieties of skepticism in ethics.

By skepticism in ethics I shall mean the general view that we have no knowledge of ethical facts, of facts that may be the subject matter of ethical judgments and statements, of the goodness of some things or the rightness of some actions, or of virtue, or of duty. The more familiar versions of this view rest on the claim that we have no such knowledge because there are no such facts, that so-called ethical judgments and statements are neither true nor false, have no cognitive content, and therefore, strictly speaking, are not judgments or statements at all. These versions may be said to be opposed to ethical realism. But the skeptic may also rest his case on a very different claim: that while there are ethical facts and therefore genuine ethical judgments and statements, possessing determinate truth-value, we do not, perhaps cannot, have knowledge of those facts, of the truth-value of those judgments and statements. In this book I shall explore the extent to which both kinds of ethical skepticism are justified, and indeed will concede that there is a respect in which each is justified. I believe that the second kind, which is the one opposed to cognitivism proper, is much more serious than the first. But it is the first, which is opposed to realism, that has received most attention, and I shall devote the first six chapters to it.

The *general* topic of realism is, once again, trendy. It dominated philosophy in the later decades of the nineteenth and early decades of the twentieth centuries. That realism was contrasted then with idealism and contrasted now with just irrealism (or antirealism) is of less significance than it may seem, since what the idealists meant by "mind" or "spirit" included what is meant today by "our conceptual scheme." And, like the idealism of the earlier period, contemporary irrealism rests on one or both of two assumptions that are not necessarily related (both evident, for example, in Hilary Putnam's recent writings). The first is representationalism, the view that we are encircled by our sensations, ideas, and beliefs (whether these are understood as mental, or neural, or linguistic states or events), which at most *represent* an independent reality. If so, then it becomes plausible to suggest that we have no reason to suppose they represent anything at all, or that even if they do, they could be taken to represent any one of a great variety of possible realities. G. E. Moore (and, later, Sartre) denied this assumption by arguing that to have, say, a sensation (understood as a mental state or event) is already to be outside the circle, to be in direct epistemic contact with something other than a sensation. (Hilary Putnam rejects such a view as magical,[2] presumably because it does not fit the scientific picture of perception. Yet, in his later works, he himself deplores the scientism and physicalism characteristic of current analytic philosophy.)[3] The second assumption is that we can have no epistemic access to an unconceptualized reality. H. H. Price, in the chapter on the given in *Perception*, in effect argued (I take some liberties with the text) that the very idea of our conceptualizing something presupposes that there is something (to be) conceptualized and that this presupposition is coherent only if we allow for an independent, unmediated by concepts, epistemic access to the thing. That this is so is especially plausible if we think, as most philosophers do today, that conceptualization involves the employment of language. Usually, it takes years to learn to talk.

As with any trendy topic, the first rule a discussion of realism must enforce is: distinguish! Michael Devitt has recently argued[4] that realism must not be confused with a theory of truth, or a theory of meaning, or a theory of knowledge, though it may be dialectically connected with such theories. It is a metaphysical theory.

Very roughly, I shall mean by unqualified realism with respect to $x$ the view that (1) $x$ exists and has certain properties, a nature, and (2) that its existence and nature are independent of our awareness of it, (3) of the manner in which we think of (conceptualize) it, and (4) of the manner in which we speak of it. Obviously, a great variety of views can be called realist or irrealist. One principle of classification would be what meanings are attached to the terms "exists" ("real"), "awareness," "independent," "conceptualize," and how conditions 3 and 4 are distinguished (as they should be by any phenomenologically sensitive philosophy of mind), crucial questions to which recent discussions of the topic accord very little attention. Another principle of classification would be which (if not all) of the four conditions are accepted. This question becomes even more complicated if we distinguish, as Meinong did, between the two parts of (1) and thus between realism with respect to the existence of $x$ and realism with respect to the nature (properties) of $x$. It should be noted that the conditions are largely independent of one another. Perhaps (3) entails (4), but not vice versa; Meinong held that the second part of (1), as well as (2), (3), and (4), may be satisfied even if the first part of (1) is not; Moore held that almost nothing fails to satisfy (2); Berkeley held that almost everything does.

A third principle of classification, which is especially relevant to our purposes in this book, would be the subject matter of the view, the value of the variable $x$ with respect to which one or more of the four conditions are accepted or rejected. In addition to what may be called unqualified global realism (more plausibly stated

as "Whatever exists satisfies conditions 2, 3, and 4," rather than as "Everything
satisfies conditions 1, 2, 3, and 4") and unqualified global irrealism (more plausibly
stated as "Whatever exists satisfies none of conditions 2, 3, and 4," rather than
"Nothing satisfies any of conditions 1, 2, 3, and 4"), and the many possible qualified
but still global realisms and irrealisms between those extremes (qualified by excluding only one or two of conditions 2, 3, and 4), there are theories distinguished
according to their specific subject matter, for example, realism or irrealism with
respect to numbers, realism or irrealism with respect to the theoretical entities of
physics, realism or irrealism with respect to the properties ethics is concerned with.
Just as there are important differences among the varieties of realism (irrealism)
distinguished according to the first two principles of classification, there are important differences among the varieties distinguished according to this third principle, differences that result from the differences in subject matter.[5]

Now there are at least three requirements, I suggest, genuine realism in ethics
should satisfy. (1) The alleged reality of ethical properties must be understood in a
straightforward, familiar, unsurprising fashion. What it is for something to be real
or to exist is perhaps the deepest philosophical problem, but one does realism in
ethics no service by resting it on highly dubious and unclear solutions to that
problem. (2) The argument for realism in ethics must not rest on definitions of all
ethical terms in nonethical terms. Of course, if it is obvious that the definitions
capture the senses of the ethical terms, this requirement would be unjustified. But
it should be commonplace by now that this is not obvious in the case of any
definitions so far proposed or that can even be conceived. For example, Gilbert
Harman's remark that "there are relative facts about what is right or wrong with
respect to one or another set of conventions"[6] cannot be regarded as an argument
for genuine realism. (3) The argument for realism in ethics must concern the realist
interpretation of an ethical *theory*, not of isolated, haphazardly selected reports of
alleged moral "intuitions." To take a familiar example, whether Hitler's moral
depravity is an irreducible moral fact cannot be judged in abstraction from a theory
of moral depravity, which itself must be a part of a whole ethical theory. The reason
is that we can have no genuine understanding of what moral depravity is without
such a theory. A vapor trail in a cloud chamber (another much-used example!) is
not a reason for concluding that a free proton has passed through the chamber
except in the context of a physical theory; we need such a theory even to understand
what a proton is. The case with ethics is quite similar, I suggest, and this is why
my discussion of skepticism in ethics will include the provision of an ethical theory.

There is also at least one requirement that genuine cognitivism (by which I
mean one that entails realism) in ethics must satisfy: that our alleged knowledge
of, or justified belief in, ethical facts be understood in a straightforward, familiar,
unsurprising fashion. One does no service to cognitivism by resting it on highly
dubious epistemologies. For example, even if some day someone will work out a
defensible purely coherentist theory of justification (one that is not wedded to a
coherence theory of truth, yet preserves and elucidates the connection between
justification as coherence and truth as correspondence),[7] to rest cognitivism now
on such a theory can only be described as misguided. The idea that "there is no

exit from the circle of one's beliefs"[8] would not be a promising start for a defense of cognitivism in ethics. Nor would be reliance on the view that the test of reality is explanatory necessity,[9] which usually itself rests on a commitment to "the scientific image of the world," a commitment that, philosophically, belongs in the century of the French *philosophes*, when science was still a wonderful novelty, not the century of Husserl and Wittgenstein, when, despite its enormous advances, the limits of its relevance to philosophy should have become a philosophical commonplace. Perhaps there was an excuse for Laplace to proclaim that he (that is, celestial mechanics) had no need for the hypothesis of God. But anyone today, whether theist or atheist, who thinks of the issue of God's existence in this way does not understand that issue. In this respect ethics is not unlike the philosophy of religion.

The above requirements, when combined, call for what may be described as a highly conservative approach to the issues of realism and cognitivism in ethics. We must defend realism and cognitivism by showing that a standard, traditional type of ethical theory describes ethical realities as these would be understood in a standard, traditional manner, and that (at least in part) it can be known to be true in ways that can be understood in a standard, traditional way. The rationale for this approach has to do with philosophical strategy. A proposed solution to a philosophical problem is far more valuable if it does not depend on a change in the conditions in terms of which the problem arose and was originally understood. This is especially true in ethics. Unlike most other branches of philosophy, it is firmly rooted in everyday thought, in which often its subject matter is understood better than by academic philosophers, and from which it derives its identity, interest, indeed life. This is why the topics of realism and cognitivism in ethics differ importantly from those of realism and cognitivism with respect to some other subject matters. Realism in mathematics may allow severely reductive definitions. Cognitivism with respect to some of the "theoretical entities" of science can be defended, perhaps, only by substantive modifications in our ordinary conception of knowledge. Not so with ethics. Only utter despair over finding a defense of realism and cognitivism that satisfies the above requirements could justify tampering with them. The time for such despair, I suggest, is not yet upon us.

It may seem that skepticism in ethics is far less common now than it was thirty or forty years ago. And, indeed, its more primitive versions are seldom defended today. But to some extent appearances in this respect are deceptive. For, as I have just argued, it is not sufficient to say that ethical statements have truth-value, of which we can have knowledge. It is also necessary to have a clear view of what such truth-value and such knowledge amount to. They may well be so unlike truth and knowledge as ordinarily conceived as to render the claim to realism and cognitivism empty. I proceed to give some examples from the recent literature, but merely to explain my approach further, not to engage in detailed criticism of the views of others. I shall therefore be succinct, even at the risk of appearing unfair.

John Rawls tells us that the justification of ethical propositions "is a matter of the mutual support of many considerations, of everything fitting together into one coherent view."[10] But that he can appeal (in a footnote) to Quine's view and (in another footnote) to Goodman's view that this is the nature of justification in general hardly suffices to make clear that such a notion of justification accords with what we ordinarily understand by justification, knowledge, and truth. As I pointed out earlier, the relationship of justification-as-coherence to truth is quite opaque, and this violates the ordinary notion of justification. If the relationship is made transparent by accepting a coherence theory of truth, then this violates the ordinary notion of truth. It is worth noting that a conception of justification such as Rawls's (or Quine's or Goodman's) when applied to science is a major motive for irrealism with respect to science. As a motive for irrealism with respect to ethics, it would be almost irresistible, given the striking differences between science and ethics, such as the role of observation and experimentation and the incomparably greater extent of agreement and progress in the former.[11] I shall return to the coherentist theory of justification in chapter 7. Suffice it here to say that the appeal to coherence, whether in the theory of justification or in the theory of truth, rests on the belief that there is nothing else to which we can appeal. In this book I shall try to show that this belief is false, that our ordinary, noncoherentist, indeed foundationalist notions of justification and truth have a clear application in ethics, whatever the case with science may be.

Richard B. Brandt defines ethical notions in terms of those of cognitive psychology and regards the justification of ethical propositions as of the same nature as the justification of the propositions of cognitive psychology. For example, he defines good as what is rationally desired and claims that a desire is rational if and only if it is not extinguishable under cognitive psychotherapy, that is, if and only if it is shown to be what it would be if it were maximally influenced by evidence and logic, meaning by "evidence" observational evidence and by "logic" inductive and deductive logic. And he tells us that by justification he means, roughly, that possible through inductive or deductive logic.[12] But, I suggest, neither his definitions nor his conception of justification correspond sufficiently to what is meant and sought in ethical inquiry, whether conducted by philosophers or by laymen. For example, it seems quite uncertain that selfishness, or benevolence, or both, or neither, are extinguishable under cognitive psychotherapy.[13] But we do not regard our usual appraisals of them to be at all uncertain. Brandt's unargued assertion that his definitions and procedure capture the only thing that could be clearly meant and rationally sought is in effect, I suggest, an espousal of skepticism. It expresses the belief that these definitions and procedure are the best we can do in ethics. I shall try to show in this book that we can do better.

Also motivated by the desire to be "scientific" are recent defenses, for example, by Nicholas L. Sturgeon,[14] of (at least the possibility of) moral realism based on the (possible) role that moral facts may serve in the explanation of actions and moral beliefs. As I have already indicated, I share neither their motive nor their highly dubious view that the test of reality is explanatory necessity, but consider such defenses nevertheless interesting and not in any obvious way incompatible with anything I shall say in this book. But at best they are highly programmatic and are open to difficulties, familiar in the philosophy of science, of specifying what would count as an explanation and particularly as a better explanation than the alternatives to it. (On this, much good sense can be found in Hilary Putnam's more recent works, especially those collected in the third volume of *Philosophical Papers*.) Moreover, again as I have remarked earlier, it is not enough just to talk of moral facts and to give one or two examples, such as that Hitler was a morally bad man, or that torturing an animal just for the fun of it is wrong. We need a theory of the moral facts we would appeal to in our explanations, and until such a theory is provided we cannot judge the adequacy of the explanations. It is not obvious that a theory such as Moore's or that to be defended in this book would not turn out to be explanatorily adequate. Indeed, it is not likely to be a physicalistic theory, though, as we shall see, even this is not obvious. In any case, if we allow only for physicalistic explanations, then the view we are considering becomes so programmatic as to be indistinguishable from mere speculation. On the other hand, if a nonphysicalistic theory does provide the only detailed and adequate explanations available, then this would be a major argument against physicalism. Whether it does or not should not be judged on the basis of global theses such as that of physicalism, but by looking at the details of the theory.

In *The View from Nowhere*,[15] Thomas Nagel defends what he calls "realism about values" (p. 139 *et passim*) but denies that this "would require crowding [the universe] with extra entities, qualities, or relations, things like Platonic Forms or Moore's nonnatural qualities" (p. 144). What are values, then? "Normative reasons" (p. 143). And what is that? Nagel writes: "The objective badness of pain, for example, is not some mysterious further property that all pains have, but just the fact that there is reason for anyone capable of viewing the world objectively to want it to stop" (p. 144). And again: "If I have a severe headache, the headache seems to me to be not merely unpleasant, but a bad thing. Not only do I dislike it, but I think I have a reason to try to get rid of it" (p. 145). It is curious that Nagel finds badness, if understood as a property that all pains have, mysterious (I doubt that any nonphilosopher does), but does not so find what from a logical standpoint is also a property, namely the property of every pain of being such that there is reason for anyone capable of viewing the world objectively to want it to stop. Surely, here the cart is put before the horse. That pains have the latter, extremely complex property is plausible, indeed comprehensible, only if the reality of the former property is taken for granted. The view that the latter is to be admitted but the former denied is hardly realism about values as these are ordinarily understood. I shall return to this (in my view obscurantist) use of the term "reason" at the end of chapter 2.

In his important work *The Theory of Morality*, Alan Donagan asserts that "the elementary deliverances of common morality are . . . true or false according to the realist, or correspondence, theory of truth," but we find him also claiming that these deliverances have the form "Practical reason itself—that is, anybody's practical reason, provided that no error is made—prescribes that actions of kind K may not (may) be done."[16] But until we are clear about what it is for practical reason to prescribe something, and especially about the epistemic significance of the fact that it does prescribe this or that (as distinguished from its disclosing to us this moral fact or that), and about what it is for it to make no error, we are left with the uncomfortable feeling that the truth of moral judgments is not understood by Donagan quite in the way implied by the correspondence theory of truth. Suffice it here to suggest that the Kantian belief that reason may make pronouncements from within itself, whether ethical or mathematical, whether with or without the aid of pure intuition, rested on the assumption that only thus could the possibility of synthetic a priori knowledge be explained. But there is the alternative that Platonism offers.

A very different approach is that of Alan Gewirth, who attempts to derive moral principles from an analysis of the concept of human action. I believe that his derivation is invalid.[17] But what is relevant to the present discussion is that his attempt aims at the right target. Unless we make the error of thinking that principles so derived are "mere tautologies" and not expressive of truths about their subject matter (we should think here of the analogy with mathematical principles), we would find their derivation as basing ethics on the most solid foundation possible, analogous to that of mathematics. (But only analogous, since, despite what he implies, Gewirth's "dialectically necessary method" is not purely deductive.) Even if the derivation is invalid, the attempt at it shows a clear awareness of the general goal a cognitivist ethical theory must have.

It should go without saying that the view expressed or implied in some recent writings[18] that we should use Wittgenstein's later philosophy of mathematics as the model for our understanding of the subject matter of ethics is at least as opposed to realism in ethics as Wittgenstein's philosophy of mathematics is opposed to realism in mathematics. It is an interesting view and very much merits extended discussion. But its interest and merit derive so directly from the interest and merit of Wittgenstein's general later philosophy that it is the latter that must be the subject of extended critical discussion—a task obviously not to be undertaken in this book. And it is characteristic of other, mostly earlier, defenses of cognitivism that seem to have been directly or indirectly influenced by Wittgenstein's later philosophy (I have in mind now Stephen Toulmin's *An Examination of the Place of Reason in Ethics*,[19] Kurt Baier's *The Moral Point of View*,[20] Joel J. Kupperman's *Ethical Knowledge*,[21] Renford Bambrough's *Moral Scepticism and Moral Knowledge*),[22] that they do not found, at least not in any clear way, ethical cognitivism on ethical realism—indeed, they sometimes explicitly deny such a foundation is possible or needed. For example, after a lengthy attempt to defend moral cognitivism by analyzing the concepts of reason and morality, Baier seems satisfied to say, "Our very purpose in 'playing the reasoning game' is to maximize satisfactions and minimize frustrations,"[23] without even seeming to be aware that this claim is controversial. Kupperman is explicit. He writes: "We . . . could do without the correspondence theory of truth in relation to ethics. Again the example of mathematics is useful . . . most philosophers would concede that some mathematical propositions are true, and virtually no one would apply the correspondence theory of truth to mathematics."[24] But mathematicians (and, *pace* Kupperman, many philosophers) are very much concerned with the question what, if anything, in reality corresponds to true mathematical propositions and, if convinced that the answer is Nothing, would find little consolation in the fact that this does not preclude them from continuing to *speak* of mathematical truth and knowledge. If cognitivism is to be severed from realism, I suggest, this would require not casual observations about language or about moral, mathematical, and scientific practice, but a revolutionary and detailed *unified* theory of reality and knowledge.

Nor can we take seriously as defenses of realism in ethics views, also inspired by Wittgenstein but perhaps by some recent continental philosophers as well, that rest on the claim that ethical judgments are no less realist than any other judgments since *all* judgments are founded in shared language-games, and "the world text" is at least partly written by ourselves. [25] The interest of such defenses reduces to that of the deep *global* irrealism on which they rest. And, obviously, to describe them as defenses of realism in *ethics* would be misleading. It would be like defending theistic knowledge by denying the general distinction between knowledge and belief. The global irrealism of the view, reminiscent of philosophies such as Hegel's and Bradley's, is of course an important position, but its adequacy cannot be discussed here.

It should also go without saying that the familiar appeal in recent works to so-called intuitions is hardly evidence of the espousal of a clearly cognitivist position. Sometimes it is an application of the ordinary language analysis practiced by Wittgenstein, Ryle, and Austin in earlier decades, an appeal to what we would or would not say in various, usually imaginary, situations. But more often the appeal to "intuitions" in recent ethics is merely the avowal of moral attitudes. In neither case does it attain the theoretical level on which the issue of cognitivism versus non-cognitivism arises. And the vagueness and inconsistencies of such intuitions were exposed long ago, in great detail, by Sidgwick. [26]

Doubtless, many readers will have remained dissatisfied by what I have said in this introductory chapter. For, generally, what I have tried to do is to distinguish my approach to the subject matter of this book from other contemporary approaches. But I have not attempted to argue in detail against any of them. And this may seem especially unsatisfactory to readers favoring varieties of what may be called the scientific approach and of the neo-Wittgensteinean approach. What justification can I offer for saying so little about them? The obvious, but also superficial, justification is that this book is not a critical survey of the contemporary scene in ethics; for that another book would be needed. But the deeper justification is that the *nonethical* bases of the two approaches mentioned are not arguments one can evaluate but rather attitudes.

The scientific approach in ethics is based, if not on straightforward physicalism, then on a general conviction that what there is and what we know about what there is can be determined only by the methods of the experimental sciences. I am unaware of anything even resembling a sustained, detailed argument for this conviction; that it may receive some support from the so-called causal theories of knowledge is not such an argument, for these theories are themselves rendered at all plausible only by that conviction. (That they avoid some Gettier-type counterexamples to the definition of knowledge as justified true belief is hardly what renders them plausible, for they themselves are open to such counterexamples.) [27] The neo-Wittgensteinean approach in ethics is based, of course, on the contention that thought, judgment, and knowledge are inherently linguistic in nature and that their linguistic nature is inherently social. But what is the argument for this contention?

Is it the so-called private language argument, an argument that even after thirty-five years of discussion remains so obscure and controversial as to be a most unlikely explanation of the popularity of the contention? The truth is that the Wittgenstein-ean contention expresses a deeply held attitude toward language on one hand and toward thought, knowledge, and the world on the other, and that so does the contention motivating the scientific approaches to ethics. Such attitudes are of course mainly intellectual and thus capable of being correct or incorrect. But I doubt that it can be *shown* by argument that they are incorrect.[28] One can only show that arguments supporting them are inadequate. And my point in this paragraph has been that either no arguments supporting them have been given, or that the arguments that have been given are not the basis of the attitudes, and even if the former are shown to be inadequate, this would not change the latter. I am certain, for example, that if I proved to a neo-Wittgensteinean that the private-language argument is inadequate, I would not have shaken his or her basic philosophical convictions at all.

I announced earlier that the purpose of this book is to explore the extent to which realism and cognitivism in ethics can be defended against the skeptic. To do so, I shall eventually offer (though not in full detail) an actual ethical theory that is reflective of ordinary ethical thought and is as realist and cognitivist as such a theory can possibly be. We shall find (though, unavoidably, much later in this book) that both its realism and its cognitivism must be qualified in important ways. Although in itself the ethical theory is thoroughly realist, its ultimate nonethical foundation may only be irrealist. And it must acknowledge severe limitations on our knowledge of ethical facts. But neither of these admissions should comfort the skeptic since neither is required by considerations peculiar to ethics. The element of irrealism in the theory, I shall argue, is present in any genuine cognitive activity, though not at all in the wholesale, indiscriminate manner supposed by recent Wittgensteinean writers, or for the reasons they offer; it is due to the special nature of the concept of identity, the failure to recognize which, I shall argue, explains the most common reason given for rejecting realism in ethics. That the reality of ethical properties and facts must be qualified in the manner I shall suggest is not a proposition even entertained in ordinary ethical thought, but this is so because of the highly technical nature of this proposition and especially of the reasons for accepting it. Yet the qualification of the realism of the theory would be entirely consonant with ordinary ethical thought, since it must be made regarding realism with respect to, for example, colors and shapes as well. Ordinary ethical thought would be satisfied with the conclusion that ethical properties are as real as colors and shapes, especially when assured that the implied reservations regarding both have nothing to do with Humean or global Wittgensteinean considerations. And the element of noncognitivism in the theory that I shall acknowledge is required by what I believe are *general* limitations on human knowledge. These limitations are familiar and usually acknowledged in ordinary ethical thought, and they are indeed implied by the ordinary conception of knowledge.

I shall begin with an account of the conceptual scheme our theory will employ.

# CHAPTER TWO

# A Conceptual Scheme for Ethics

## *1. The Method*

In my outline of what I consider to be the basic concepts of ethics I shall be guided by the ordinary uses of the corresponding ethical terms, but only because otherwise the concepts outlined might be irrelevant to the issues that led to the emergence of such a branch of philosophy as ethics. This is why the outline, though guided by the ordinary uses of certain ethical terms, is not at all intended to capture these uses; it is not at all a set of definitions subject to appraisal by appeals to actual or imaginary examples of what we would or would not be ordinarily inclined to say. Even if such definitions were possible, it is not clear what philosophical value they would have. But they are not possible. The idea that the ordinary use of a term such as "duty" (or, for that matter, "knowledge") can be captured in a definition can only issue from a misunderstanding of the nature of ordinary language. The definitions I shall offer (all of them quite informal) are motivated by a mild criticism of the relevant part of our ordinary conceptual scheme and constitute a no less mild regimentation of it. (Such a regimentation is absolutely essential in any inquiry, whether in philosophy or in science.) Therefore, neither will they be intended to constitute an "analysis" of concepts, whatever this might be, and so would not be subject to the Moorean accusation of confusing one property with another.[1]

Nor shall I engage in a detailed account of the ordinary uses of ethical terms, one that does not attempt to capture these uses in definitions. At its best, such an account deserves to be called linguistic phenomenology, which J. L. Austin described as follows: "When we examine what we should say when, what words we should use in what situations, we are looking . . . not *merely* at words (or 'meanings,' whatever they may be) but also at the realities we use the words to talk about: we are using a sharpened awareness of words to sharpen our perception of, though not as the final arbiter of, the phenomena."[2] Linguistic phenomenology can be of considerable value, but also it can easily be carried to extremes, and in any case I am doubtful that it is necessary for an inquiry such as ours, even though occasionally I shall employ it. It is needed more in the *account* of an adequate ethical theory than, as in this book, in the *defense* of that theory against philosophers' objections.[3] This is why what I shall say about crucial notions such as goodness, right, or virtue, will simply ignore some of the uses of the corresponding words. To take an extreme example, I shall say nothing relevant to the use of "ought" in

"I've checked the ignition system, the gas, the battery, and the car ought to start with no trouble."[4]

Moreover, it is at most a conceptual scheme for *ethics*, not for a general *theory of value*, that I shall offer. I shall say nothing about the concepts of aesthetics or about some familiar value-concepts that resist easy classification, though in chapter 3 I shall have occasion to mention what some others have said about a few of them. For example, the conceptual scheme to be proposed will not include the concepts of the beautiful and the ugly, the noble and the contemptible, the charming and the disgusting, the funny and the boring, the cute and the homely, the stately and the flimsy, the poignant and the dull, the important and the trivial, the striking and the ordinary. The reason is not any conviction that ethics can be sharply distinguished from the other branches of the theory of value (for example, both Plato and Moore, and more recently Iris Murdoch,[5] insist on the connection between goodness and beauty), but the limitations on what can be undertaken in a book the task of which is not even the provision of a complete ethical theory but rather the provision of the phenomenological, metaphysical, and epistemological foundations of an ethical theory that can withstand (within certain limits) the challenge of skepticism.

## 2. Concrete Goods and Abstract Goods

I shall assume that realism and cognitivism in ethics are, fundamentally, realism and cognitivism with respect to the *properties* goodness, rightness, and morality, and their contraries, in the ethically relevant senses of "goodness," "rightness," and "morality." I begin by taking the (ethically relevant) *notions* of goodness, evil (or badness), degree of goodness or of evil, and quantity of goodness or of evil as primitive, but will focus my discussion here on the first. To take a notion as primitive, however, is one thing; to fail to elucidate it is quite another. This whole book may be regarded as devoted to the elucidation, phenomenological, metaphysical, and epistemological, of the notion of goodness. A great deal can be said about a notion that cannot be usefully defined. Elucidation is not definition. Indeed, ordinarily, it is far preferable, even when a definition is possible. This much we should have learned both from Husserl, Heidegger, and Sartre, and from Wittgenstein, Ryle, and Austin.

About the other primitive concepts it should suffice here to make the following remarks. Evil is usually understood to be the contrary, not the mere absence or at least privation, of goodness, but whether this is so cannot be decided in advance of a detailed account of goodness. If it is the absence or privation of goodness, then of course it can be defined in terms of goodness and would no longer be primitive. (For example, Thomas Aquinas held that "no being is said to be evil, considered as being, but only so far as it lacks being,"[6] that evil, though not the mere absence of good, is the privation of good.) Degree of goodness would be exemplified in the fact (if it is a fact) that happiness is better than gustatory pleasure. Quantity of goodness would be exemplified in the fact (if it is a fact) that, everything else being equal, a marriage in which both persons enjoy a certain degree of happiness contains more goodness than a marriage in which only one enjoys that degree of happiness, and therefore is better than the latter, though in a sense of "better" different from that in which happiness may be said to be better than gustatory pleasure. Another example would be the fact (if it is a fact) that, everything else being equal, ten years of happiness is better than just two years.

We will need yet another sense of "better," namely, that in which we may say that a certain situation is better than a certain other situation when we take into account both the degrees and the quantities of goodness involved. It is not primitive; it is to be understood in terms of the concepts of degree and quantity of goodness. Its application would be exemplified by the statement (whether true or false) that, everything else being equal, the happiness of one person constitutes more total goodness, is better than, the gustatory pleasures of two persons. Obviously, in many actual cases it would be extraordinarily difficult to decide that one situation is better than some other situation, in this sense of "better," a fact familiar to students of utilitarianism. But it does not follow that we do not have or do not need the concept it expresses. We must not, however, assume that the totalities of goodness compared in this third sense are numerically measurable, that it makes sense to say, for example, that one is twice better than another. For we must not assume that *degrees* of goodness are arithmetically additive, even though we may assume this in the case of *quantities* of goodness. Happiness may be better than gustatory pleasure, but it is probably absurd to say that it is twice, or three times, etc., better. Degrees of goodness are not unique in this respect. The same is true of degrees of likeness. A shade of color may be more like another shade than it is like a third, but perhaps we cannot sensibly say that it is twice or three times more like the second than like the third. But while we may not be able to say of a certain case of goodness A *how much* better it is than another case of goodness B, in the third (as well as the first) sense of "better," this is not a reason for affirming that A is *not* better than B, or for denying that, in general, either A is better than B, or B is better than A, or neither is better than the other. In the rest of this book I shall use "better," and related expressions such as "more goodness," in the third sense, except when the context makes clear that it is used in one of the other two senses. I shall return to some of the issues mentioned in the present paragraph in chapters 6 and 8, to which alone they are relevant.

I shall assume that the metaphysical distinction between concrete entities and properties ("abstract entities," "universals") is legitimate and that goodness is a property, if it is anything at all. (In what follows in this chapter I shall often omit this or other similar qualifications, in order to avoid complexity of exposition. But it must be understood that I shall only be describing a conceptual scheme, without presupposing that it has application). If to say of a certain thing that it is good is to describe it, to say something true or false about it, then it is to attribute to it a certain property. It follows that we must distinguish sharply between goodness itself and the things that are good, just as we must distinguish sharply between the geometrical figure triangularity and the concrete entities (if there are any) that are triangular.

For our purposes, we can regard as concrete entities not only what would ordinarily be called individual things, but also actions, as well as such things as a certain person's life, on grounds similar to those that would allow us to call a flash of lightning or yesterday's weather concrete entities. It may, of course, be asked whether events, for example, a flash of lightning or a certain action, are not states of affairs and therefore not concrete. A detailed answer to this question cannot be attempted here. It is worth noting, however, that the main metaphysical reason for an affirmative answer, namely, that events are complex entities, would also be a reason for regarding individual things such as color spots and even persons as states of affairs.[7] That it is not a good reason for either view can be seen from the fact that although an action, or a flash of lightning, or a color spot can be said to have spatial and temporal properties, and to be perceived, none of these can intelligibly be said of a state of affairs. (I may see that the spot is blue, but not in the sense in which I may see the blue spot. *Perhaps* the former entails the latter, but not vice versa. Seeing-that is an epistemic state, seeing is not.) It is worth noting also that the typical referring expressions for actions are genitives with gerunds, and these are not expressions referring to states of affairs. "John's flipping the switch" refers to a flipping, not to the state of affairs that John flipped the switch, just as "John's daughter" refers to a certain female person, not to the state of affairs that John has a daughter. And we must not suppose that the needed referring expressions are what Fowler called fused participles, for example, "John flipping the switch." Such expressions, as Fowler pointed out, are grammatically corrupt, like "I flipping the switch."[8]

Goodness is usually attributed to concrete entities. But sometimes it is attributed to certain properties, to abstract entities.[9] We may say that a certain person's life is good, but we may also say that happiness as such, that is, the property a life may have of being happy, is good. Now, I suggest, a person's life can be said to be good on the grounds that it is happy only if happiness itself can be said to be good, and in general a concrete entity can be said to be good only on the grounds that it has some other property or properties that themselves have the property of being good. (A number of distinctions are needed here, which I shall make shortly.) This is the point and, I suggest, the only clear sense of describing the goodness of concrete things as a consequential or supervenient property, not an intrinsic property. I shall return to this point.

It may be argued, as W. D. Ross did, that happiness is good only in the sense that it is good to be happy, that what is good is the fact that something (someone) is happy.[10] But, I suggest, Ross's argument seems to be merely a misguided and anyhow unsuccessful attempt to avoid commitment to universals. It is misguided because the category of facts or states of affairs seems much more questionable than that of universals.[11] It is unsuccessful because the facts that supposedly are good fall into classes defined by certain lower-ranking properties, and these properties could themselves be described as good. For example, let us say that facts of the form expressed by "$x$ is happy" have in common the property of involving happiness in a certain specific way. Surely they are good only because they have that property. And why then would we want to deny that that property itself is good? Moreover, it may well be the case that the fact that a certain person's life is happy is not good (is not "a good thing"), because it has some other, very bad characteristics or very bad consequences. If we say, as Ross did, that the fact is good in itself, taken abstractly, whatever its other characteristics or its effects, would we be saying anything more than that that life's being a happy life entails its being at least in one respect a good life? And if asked why and how this entailment holds, would we not reply, because happiness is good? We should think here of the parallel with the entailment of being colored by being blue. It would be sheer mystery if this entailment were not grounded simply in the fact that blue is a color. It would be equally mysterious that being a happy life should entail being at least partially a good life if happiness were not itself good. As to the straightforwardly nominalist claim that to say that happiness is good is to say that all happy lives are good lives, let me point out again that, if some happy lives are not good, say, because their being happy has very bad consequences, then this universal statement is not true, even if it is true that happiness is good. (If Wittgenstein had been a happy man, he might not have written his philosophical works.) And even if it is true that pleasure is good, whole classes of concrete pleasures are presumably bad, for example, those of sadism. It would be better if they did not occur, because they involve great pain in another person. The universal statements that would be true are, respectively, "All happy lives are at least partially good" and "All pleasures are at least partially good." But why are they true? Because all happy lives are good *qua* happy and all pleasures are good *qua* pleasures. I suggest that these last two assertions can be understood only as derivations from the assertions, respectively, that happiness is good and that pleasure is good.

But the metaphysical assumption that there are properties in the sense of universals will not be defended here. The defense of our ethical theory would be successful if it could be questioned only by denying this assumption. We may note that the alternatives to the theory of universals provided by strict nominalism and by the various resemblance theories are seldom adopted today by writers on the problem of universals.[12]

But, despite my misgivings regarding the category of states of affairs, it is not part of my thesis that if there were such entities the property goodness could not be exemplified by them. Indeed, any property that can be exemplified by both properties and states of affairs would have a special ontological status. I shall return to this point in chapter 5. Suffice it here to observe that there are other predicates that have such an apparently heterogeneous application—for example, "exists," "is being considered," "is beautiful," perhaps "is one"—and to recall the special status Plato assigned to the Form of the Good and the fact that the medievals regarded goodness as a transcendental, not as a genus, some of the other transcendentals being being, truth, beauty, and one.

In addition to happiness and pleasure, a number of other properties, or abstract entities, may be, and ordinarily would be, called good, for example, life, health, knowledge, justice, friendship, certain kinds of action such as promise keeping, irreducibly societal properties such as the flourishing of the arts and sciences.[13] Although this fact will occupy us in detail throughout our inquiry, it is worth noting here that there is nothing mysterious, or queer, or nonnatural about these properties. Nor is there any ordinary reason for denying that there are such properties, that they are real, or that they are knowable. Nor is the description of them as good a matter of widespread disagreement, except through ignorance or easily eliminable misunderstanding. The history of ethics, especially in modern times, has consisted largely in attempts (in my view unsuccessful) to reduce the goodness of some of them to that of others, not in disagreements about their being good. What has seemed *philosophically* questionable is that they should be described as having a common property, namely, goodness, and this question will be a central topic of this book. I shall therefore postpone discussion of it. I am assuming here that the goodness predicated in such statements is a monadic property (if there is such a property at all). The view that it is a relational property will be considered in the final section of this chapter.

Continuing with the point with which we have been concerned so far, we may say that goodness is, strictly speaking, a property of properties, and that good concrete entities, which we may call concrete goods, exemplify it only, so to speak, indirectly, by exemplifying some other properties that themselves exemplify goodness directly, and which we may call abstract goods.[14] (Using Platonic terminology, we may say that the Form of the Good is a form of forms, in which concrete things can participate only indirectly.) It follows that the sense in which a concrete entity may be said to be good is not the same as, but is derivable from and explainable through, the sense in which an abstract entity may be said to be good. The term "good" is not used univocally with respect to concrete entities and abstract entities.

Indeed, the difference between its two senses is even greater than it appears to be at first glance. A concrete entity that has a good monadic property is to that extent good, "intrinsically good," "good in itself," just in the sense that it has a property that is itself good in the primary sense. Usually it is on the basis of such facts that we make our ethical decisions, however unjustifiably, and it is in relation to such facts, which of course are of great variety and richness, that moral life emerges. But a concrete entity may have any number of relevant properties, some good, some bad—somewhat as the waters in the Bahamas are, though mostly turquoise, at some places blue, at others brown, and at still others white. Also a concrete entity may contribute to certain other things' being good; it can be "good as a means," in virtue of its relational properties, whether causally or by being an element of what Moore called an "organic unity."[15] To describe it as good without qualification, that is, without adding after the adjective "good" some term F or a phrase such as "*qua* an F" or "insofar as it F's" or "to the extent it is F," can only be, I now suggest, to make a claim about the balance of goodness over badness in the sum total of all its own relevant monadic and relational properties, and of the relevant properties of what it is a means to. It would be analogous to saying that the waters in the Bahamas are turquoise. The conceptual justification of the general utilitarian account of right action is provided by this fact about the unqualified use of "good" with respect to concrete entities. The unqualified goodness of a concrete entity such as an action can only be its contributing at least as much total goodness, or as little total badness, as any of its alternatives would contribute. There is no conceptual room for any other content of the idea of the unqualified goodness of an action, and it is the unqualified, not any qualified, goodness of an action that is of central concern in ethics. I shall, of course, repeatedly return to this crucial point.

Yet, ordinarily (but by no means always), the unqualified application of the term "good" to a concrete entity seems to have no determinate sense, a fact emphasized by P. T. Geach in his claim that "good" is an attributive rather than a predicative adjective, that a statement of the form "$x$ is good" requires completion into a statement of the form "$x$ is a good $F$."[16] (Nevertheless, millions have thought they understood Genesis 1:31: "And God saw every thing he had made, and behold, it was very good.") But a determinate sense *can* be specified in the way I have suggested, namely, by saying that a concrete entity is unqualifiedly good if and only if it contributes, through its intrinsic (monadic) properties or through its causal or noncausal relations to other things, more goodness or less badness than there would have been if the thing had not existed. In the special case of human actions, where the unqualified use of "good" is common, this would mean that the action contributes at least as much goodness (or as little badness) as any of its alternatives open to the agent would contribute, in the wide sense of the term "contribute" just specified. We may express all this more succinctly by saying that a concrete entity is unqualifiedly good in the sense that it is optimizing. (But it can be optimizing even if not optimific.[17] It may contribute most goodness not in virtue of its consequences but in virtue of its monadic properties.) My point is not that the term "good" in fact has such a sense, though I believe that it does, but that it can be given such a sense and that this sense is logically impeccable, though admittedly vague as long as the concepts of goodness, badness, and degree and quantity of goodness or badness have not been adequately elucidated.[18] Moreover, as I have pointed out, and will argue later in detail, this is the sense that is ethically central, indeed indispensable, for it is the sense in which *actions* are to be described as good.

Geach seems aware that his view is less plausible regarding statements such as "Pleasure is good" and "Preferring inclination to duty is bad," in which "good" is predicated of abstract, not concrete, entities, but dismisses them on the grounds that they involve peculiarly philosophical uses of words that require explanation. But, of course, there is nothing peculiarly philosophical about these statements. And even if an explanation of them cannot be given, if this means the provision of definitions of "good" and "bad," an explanation in the sense of a theory of good and bad may still be available. Another author, Paul Ziff, avows that "Pleasure is good" sounds to him remarkably odd.[19] It does not sound so to me. One reason for my skepticism regarding great concern with the ordinary uses of words is that discussions of them consist chiefly in exchanges of avowals about what sounds "odd" to one and what does not.

If such statements strike some of us as odd, the obvious reason is that they are seldom made in ordinary discourse, since we seldom have a reason for making them. "If something is blue then it is colored" also may strike us as odd, since we seldom need to contrast colored entities with colorless ones. In English it may be better to say, "Pleasure is *a* good," and there would be philosophical reasons for preferring this if the relation of pleasure to goodness is that of a species to its genus. Then the statement would be analogous to "Blue is a color," again a statement we seldom have reason for making in ordinary discourse yet one that is logically impeccable. Or, we may express ourselves informally with sentences such as "Pleasure is a good thing," "thing" being, of course, not a sortal word at all in such a context.

But except to human actions, we would seldom apply the word "good" to concrete entities in the sense of optimizing. The reasons are several and closely related. First, the existence of the concrete entity is ordinarily already a fact, not something we must decide whether to bring about or not (and when it is the latter, the action of bringing it about is what we may judge to be unqualifiedly good). Whether it is on the whole better that it exists or not is often of no clear practical importance. But what often *is* important is some property or relation of the entity, and so we qualify the description of it as good by saying that it is good for such-and-such a purpose, or a good so-and-so, or good in such-and-such a respect. The second reason is that the totality of respects in which a concrete entity may be described as good is intellectually and epistemologically overwhelming; we can hardly comprehend it and can know, at most, a very small part of it. Indeed, as we shall see, this is true also of actions. But there, overwhelmed or not, we must make a judgment, for we must make a decision about how to act. And the intrinsic nature, the monadic properties, of the action (for example, its being the keeping of a promise) or its immediate consequences (for example, another person's being pleased) are ordinarily quite easy to comprehend and therefore form a convenient basis for judgment. The third reason is that with respect to most concrete entities we have no clear idea, perhaps no idea at all, of what would, or even could, have existed in their place if they did not exist. Is Germany good in the sense of optimizing? We have no clear idea what the specific long-range alternatives to the existence of Germany might have been, even though we have some idea of what is meant by the existence of Germany and of what would be relevant to the judgment that it has contributed more goodness or less badness than there would have been if it had not existed. The case with actions is obviously and dramatically different. The idea of the alternatives *open to an agent* is reasonably clear, especially when we stipulate, as we shall, that only actions the agent contemplates, of the possibility of which he or she is aware, are open to the agent. It is not surprising, therefore, that the question "Is Germany good?" strikes us as nonsensical, though the question "Was appeasing Germany in 1938 good?" does not.

## *3. Right Action*

I shall use the adjective "right" to express the sense of "good" when this latter adjective is applied to actions without qualification, but subject to the stipulation that they be open to the agent in the sense explained. (I shall count omissions as actions, subject to the same stipulation. Often the alternatives genuinely open to an agent, those the agent has considered, are only two: to do a certain action or to refrain from doing it.) A right action is one that is (or was, or will be, or would be, or would have been) optimizing, even if not optimific.[20] By an action that *ought* to be performed, I shall mean an action that is optimizing and is also such that none of its alternatives is optimizing. In a given situation several actions might be optimizing, and therefore none would be one the agent ought to perform but all would be right. A wrong action is one such that it is not optimizing but at least one of its alternatives is optimizing. The reason for the qualification, that is, for not defining a wrong action simply as one that is not right, is to allow for the logical possibility of cases in which no action open to the agent would be optimizing.[21] Throughout this book, when I speak of actions I mean particular, concrete actions, not kinds or sorts of actions; when I need to speak of the latter, I shall do so explicitly.

I have emphasized that a right action must be one that is "open to the agent" partly in order to reflect a familiar restriction in ordinary thought on the notions of "right action" and "action one ought to do," namely, to actions the agent *can* perform, at least in Moore's sense that the agent would perform them if he or she chose to do so,[22] but partly to draw attention to an important respect in which the unqualified application of "good" to actions is quite unlike its unqualified application to other concrete things. If by "action" we meant any physically possible movement of the agent, the question whether a certain action is optimizing might have no clearer sense than the question whether Germany is optimizing. Of course, the ordinary use of "action" is far more limited than that of "movement," but it is still too broad for our purposes. Hence I have also restricted the set of alternatives relevant to any judgment that a certain action would be optimizing to the set of actions the agent actually contemplates when making the judgment. Indeed there is an obvious sense in which an agent cannot perform an action of which (of the possibility of performing which) he is unaware, because he cannot choose to perform it.

No analogous restriction with respect to concrete entities other than actions seems possible, and even if one were possible it would probably have no importance. In the case of actions it is not only possible but needed. For actions open to the agent in the sense I have explained have a special, obvious, central ethical significance. They are the ones from which the agent must choose. Moreover, at any one time their number is quite limited, and therefore a clearer sense can be attached to the idea that at least one would be optimizing, since a genuine comparison at least seems possible. Without the restriction the set of relevant alternatives the agent faces seems to become logically unmanageable.[23] Indeed, a consequence of it is that the right action for an agent to perform at a given time may well not be the optimizing physically or psychologically possible action. But this consequence (which is the reason Lars Bergström rejects the restriction) is inevitable if we take seriously the fact that an agent faces no ethical decision regarding actions of the possibility of which he or she is unaware, and if we are not to treat actions merely as ordinary concrete entities, with all the difficulties we have noted regarding the determination of whether a certain concrete entity is optimizing. It is worth repeating that many, if not most, of the moral choices we actually face concern only two alternatives, for example, the breaking or the keeping of a promise, lying or telling the truth, helping another person who is in distress or doing nothing.

Our restriction on the applicability of the notion of right action is much more severe than the usual restrictions. For example, although Moore insisted that by duty we understand "that action, which will cause more good to exist in the Universe than any possible alternative," that is, "the best of all possible alternative actions" for an agent at a given time, he allowed "for Practical Ethics" the "humbler task" of "shewing which among the alternatives *likely to occur to any one*, will produce the greatest good."[24] But for the purposes of relating the theory of the good to conduct, that is, the purposes of practical ethics, Moore's restriction is insufficient. Of course, we may say that in contemplating an action the agent ought to consider in detail what alternatives to that action are possible. And we (and the agent), in retrospect, can regret his not having performed a certain action that he could (and perhaps would) have performed had he considered it. If he had been aware of the possibility of considering what alternatives to his action there were and yet did not engage in such a consideration, then he would be culpable for failing to perform the second-order act of *considering* what alternatives were open to him. But if he had not been aware of the possibility of such consideration, he would be morally (though perhaps not legally) culpable for nothing; it would only be regrettable that he was that sort of person. Nor would he be culpable for not performing the action that he would have performed had he been aware of it, even if he had engaged in the second-order act of considering what alternatives were open to him. For however conscientious he might have been in his activity of considering, he might have just failed, through weakness of intellect, insufficient information, or pure accident, to think of that action. These are not remarks about what we ordinarily regard as culpable ignorance. They are suggestions about how the notion of culpable ignorance is to be regimented in a philosophically acceptable way. Our actual employment of this notion is too disorderly and murky to be used as an arbiter.[25] But even if my suggestions are inadequate, this would not affect the issue before us. That issue is, Which is the class of possible actions to which the agent can apply his or her ethical principles? And the answer surely is: the class of possible actions of which he or she is actually aware.[26] Here, as in epistemology, I suggest, we must take as central first-person, present-tense judgments. Just as the primary epistemological question, What am I to believe? cannot be answered by appeal to considerations of which one is unaware (this fact should give pause to causal or reliabilist theories of knowledge), so the primary question of ethics, What am I to do? cannot be answered by such an appeal. I shall return to this point in chapters 7 and 8.

In my definition of right action I have allowed that an action may be optimizing even if not optimific. I have done so, of course, in order to leave conceptual room for the thesis that actions may have intrinsic goodness (one due neither to motive nor to consequences), a thesis the independent merits of which we shall consider in the next section. Here we need only note two facts about it. First, this thesis makes it possible to avoid some, though not all, of the standard objections to act-utilitarianism (for example, that it allows for the rightness of some cases of injustice), and thus may make less appealing any attempts, in my opinion bound to be futile, to answer these objections by proposing the sort of definitions of rightness that rule-utilitarianism and utilitarian generalization suggest. I shall return to this topic in chapter 8. But what is more important for our present purposes is that, second, this thesis allows us to avoid the need to acknowledge an additional *primitive* ethical notion, a notion of rightness other than that which I have defined and also other than a species of the primitive notion of goodness, the sort of notion of rightness that, for example, Prichard and Ross defended. This is desirable not because of any commitment to theoretical parsimony but because of what I believe is the evident conceptual primacy of the concept of goodness. And this primacy is itself due, I suggest, to the phenomenological fact that while we can find in the world such a property as goodness, even in actions, we cannot find a *distinct*, primitive property of rightness. The belief that we can probably rests on failing to see the intrinsic goodness of certain kinds of action as a kind of goodness. I shall have more to say about this shortly.

As to our defined notion of right action, it is much more common, of course, to object to it not on phenomenological grounds but by appealing to our moral "intuitions," or to "the meaning" of the word "right," or to "the content of our concept of right action." I have already given my reasons for not taking such appeals seriously. At best they are appeals to facts about ordinary usage, but in reality usually only to one's moral attitudes, even if they happen to be widely shared. I see no reason for regarding facts about ordinary usage as decisive in constructing a conceptual system for ethics. As presumably we all agree, the facts about ordinary usage are not decisive at all, for example, in the taxonomist's constructing a conceptual (classificatory) system for zoology. Indeed, as Moore might have said, to ask, "Is an optimizing action right?" is not to ask, "Is an optimizing action optimizing?" But then neither is asking, "Is a circle a closed plane figure all points on which are equidistant from a given point in the same plane?" the same as asking, "Is a circle a circle?" But I should note that for my purposes in this book it is unimportant whether the sentence "An action is right if and only if it is optimizing" is taken to be true by (a more or less revisionary) definition or because of a "synthetic a priori" necessary coextensiveness of a primitive property rightness and the property of being an optimizing action, as Moore thought in *Ethics*. I don't believe that there is such a primitive property, but my concern is only that the sentence be accepted as true.

As to our moral attitudes, let us remember that one of our goals in ethics is to determine which of them are justified and which are not, and even which of them are at all intelligible and which are not. Even as committed an opponent of consequentialism as Philippa Foot feels constrained to admit the power of the conviction (which she does not share) that "utilitarian morality is the only *rational* morality." For, "how can it be right, we ask ourselves, to choose to produce a state of affairs less good or worse than another that is equally within our reach?"[27] On the other hand, as I have already observed, our allowing for the possibility that actions (and of course any other concrete entities) may exemplify a great variety of intrinsic goods explains the feeling many share that a utilitarian definition of right action ignores the richness of moral life. The conceptual scheme I am proposing is in part intended to do justice precisely to that richness. But this does not justify dispensing with the notion of what we should do on a particular occasion when everything has been considered. That notion is central to ethics and naturally expressible by the words "ought" and "right." The fact that we seldom can apply it with any degree of confidence does not detract from its centrality. We seldom (if ever) can apply with confidence the geometrical notion of the circle to any particular surface, yet that notion remains central to our judgments of the (approximate) shape of a great variety of objects. Indeed, the notion of an optimizing action is relatively complex and not likely to be explicitly entertained in everyday ethical thought. But the notion of an action that has good results is quite familiar and does represent *one* of the standard notions we express by the word "right." Its regimentation into the notion of an optimizing action can readily be understood and accepted, since it is obvious on even elementary reflection that an action that has merely *some* good results might well not be right. Thus our definition of right action has firm roots in everyday ethical thought. But it must be admitted that there are other notions of right action, some of which we shall try to accommodate shortly. And I shall have much more to say about this topic in the last section of this chapter and especially in chapter 8.

It should be noted that our definition of right action fully allows for the *possibility* that only optimific actions are optimizing, that if we take seriously the idea of the totality of the consequences of an action, however remote they may be, we may recognize that the goodness or badness of that totality is so much greater than that, if any, of the action itself as to render the latter insignificant. To be sure, in everyday life we restrict our attention to the causal contribution the action would make in a rather narrow sphere—to the more or less immediate environment, to the near future, to the persons we know. The reason is that it is with respect to these only that the consequences of our actions are likely to be visible. But this does not mean that when we do so we use "right" in a different sense. This becomes evident when we learn, usually to our surprise, of the possibility of certain remote consequences or ramifications that might affect our decisions. That something one does now might affect adversely one's yet unborn grandchildren, or even certain complete strangers in another country, is often an important consideration. And, of course, statesmen are (or ought to be) *ex officio* concerned with questions about the total goodness or badness their actions may produce, and one of their qualifications (seldom genuine) for office is that they have much greater than ordinary knowledge of the remote consequences of actions. The fact that even when aware of the wider implications of our actions we may ignore them and remain within the restricted viewpoint is merely a consequence of the much greater power of our inclination to be concerned with our own good, or that of those close to us, and that realizable in the near future, not a consequence of our employing a different concept of right action. The restriction of the concept of right action to actions of the possibility of which the agent is aware has an obvious rationale. Insofar as ethics provides us with guidance with respect to conduct, it must be concerned with those and only those actions. But to restrict the concept to, say, those actions that would produce the most good within the next two hours and within a radius of one hundred yards would be at best humorous.

A familiar objection to a definition of right action such as ours is that it places an enormous moral burden on the agent. It implies that the agent should constantly think about what he or she could do that would be optimizing, that there is no room for the notion of supererogation, that, in J. O. Urmson's terms, we all are expected to be saints and heroes.[28] To some extent this is a caricature of what such a definition implies. Constantly or even frequently thinking about what would be optimizing may well be itself not optimizing. Kurt Baier writes: "The view that we always ought to do the optimific act, or whenever we have no more stringent duty to perform, would have the absurd result that we are doing wrong whenever we are relaxing, since on those occasions there will always be opportunities to produce greater good than we can by relaxing."[29] Baier would have done well to consider what these opportunities might be in ordinary cases of relaxation. The truth is that in such cases there usually isn't any greater good for one to produce, or at least one is not aware of any greater good that one might produce. In any case, as a result of our discussion in chapter 8, the objection will be seen to have very little force.

But here I must emphasize that it is no part of the task of an ethical enquiry to lessen moral burdens or even to make them bearable, let alone to provide for the application of the notion of a supererogatory act (but see below, p. 28). Its task is to provide an ethical theory for each thesis of which there is a clear rationale. The rationale for requiring the agent to do the optimizing act is that this is the kind of act with a clear and central connection with goodness. It is significant that, as Urmson himself admits, the saint or the hero regards himself as *obliged* to perform the saintly or heroic action, even though, unsurprisingly, *we* would not call the action a duty.[30] (As I have already remarked, our everyday ethical decisions are largely based, however unjustifiably, on the perception of the goodness or badness of some of the intrinsic qualities or more or less immediate consequences of concrete entities, especially actions, including those I shall shortly label duties.) What would be the rationale for requiring the agent to do something less than the optimizing act? Just so that he or she feel morally unburdened? But even if we regard this as intrinsically desirable, how much weight is it to be given? And what is the rationale for (the relative) unburdening of the agent in the most obvious way, namely, by allowing for preferential treatment of oneself and of one's friends and relatives, by assigning a special value to one's personal projects and attitudes, what is misleadingly called one's "personal integrity,"[31] or by acknowledging an "agent-centered prerogative"?[32] If it is a watered-down form of egoism, we shall discuss it in detail in chapter 6. If it is a mere appeal to our "intuitions," I have already said enough about it.

Indeed, the aim of ethics is ultimately to provide guidance for action. But it is not its business to provide guidance if such guidance is not worth having, if its only or at least chief rationale is that it can be followed easily. Moreover, it would be well to remember Mill's observation, made in defense of his universalistic hedonism, that: "It is the business of ethics to tell us what are our duties . . . no system of ethics requires that the sole motive of all we do shall be a feeling of duty."[33] We may add the observation, rather obvious but apparently unacceptable to many philosophers, that one of the theses of the true ethical theory may well be that it would be (instrumentally) better that agents be motivated by false ethical beliefs, that is, by beliefs that contradict the theses of the theory. (Thus we need not disagree with Urmson's thesis, in the article cited earlier, that a far less stringent "moral code" would be more effective, indeed perhaps alone possible.) A familiar example is that an egoist theory may hold that a person is more likely to achieve his own good if he does not aim at it, if he is not an egoist. It may be plausible to suggest also that a theory such as ours would allow that it would be better if some, most, perhaps even all, agents were motivated by some other theory.[34]

I shall continue my defense of our definition of right action in the final chapter of this book, where it will be necessary to consider specific alternative definitions.

## 4. Virtue and Duty

However, according to Kant, the only thing that is unconditionally good is a good will. Our conceptual scheme should capture what seems to be true in this assertion without including also what seems to be false. Let us call *virtuous* an action that is motivated solely or at least sufficiently by the agent's belief that the action is right or at least likely to be right. We may then proceed to define a virtuous person as one who is generally, or on the whole, disposed to perform virtuous actions, and mean by "virtue" the disposition itself. This notion of virtuous action (and the notions, derived from it, of a virtuous person and of virtue) corresponds to a third sense of the word "good" (the first being that in which abstract entities are said to be good, and the second, that in which concrete entities, especially actions, are said to be [unqualifiedly] good or, in the case of actions, to be right or such that they ought to be done). Indeed, it is the word's characteristically moral sense, but, like the second, wholly explainable in terms of the first, primitive sense. It follows from our account of it that an action can be good in the sense that it is virtuous even though it is bad in the sense that it ought not to be performed (for example, if its consequences would be very bad), and that an action may be one that ought to be performed even if it would not be virtuous, even if it would not issue from a good will. Of course, the action would be virtuous only if the agent believed that it was right or likely to be right. And it would still be virtuous if the agent believed that it would lead only to something good for him, as long as his motive was not (or was not mainly) his desire for that good, but rather his belief that it was good and that none of the alternatives open to him would contribute more goodness in general. But we do not want to say that an action is *vicious* if and only if it is motivated by the agent's belief that it is wrong; such a notion of vice would be too narrow, perhaps applicable, as W. D. Ross suggests, only to a devil's actions.[35] Let us say, instead, that an action is vicious if and only if the agent believes that it is wrong, whether or not he performs it because of that belief. A vicious person would be one who is disposed to perform vicious actions, and vice would be that disposition.

Indeed, there are two other, broader senses of "virtuous action" (and thus of "virtuous person" and "virtue"), namely: (1) a virtuous action is one done from a good motive (perhaps the belief that it is right, and then the action would be virtuous in our sense, but perhaps also a feeling of love, or benevolence, etc.); and (2) a virtuous action is one that manifests a good disposition or habit of the agent. (1) expresses, though very roughly, a characteristically Christian notion, and (2) expresses, also roughly, the Aristotelian notion. The crucial idea in both is that of a certain kind of psychological state or event. But such *kinds* of state or event are likely to be among the most plausible examples of what I have called abstract goods. (For example, although I defined virtue as the disposition to perform right actions because of the belief that they are right, this does not preclude us from regarding it as itself being an abstract good, though perhaps not the only unconditional good as Kant thought.) Thus no special provision is needed in our conceptual scheme for the Christian and the Aristotelian virtues, insofar as they are goods at all. Our conceptual scheme is compatible with what is plausible in so-called virtue ethics. As to the notion of an action that proceeds from such a virtue, it can be easily accommodated in our conceptual scheme simply by describing it in the way I have just done, namely, as an action that proceeds from such a virtue. It is unclear that anything more needs to be said, and it may be that nothing more can be said. For such actions may have no independent characterizations. Perhaps, as Aristotle argued, we may recognize a certain action as virtuous only if we recognize it as the sort of action a virtuous person would perform in the particular circumstances in which it takes place.

We need yet another addition to our conceptual scheme, to which I referred in the previous section. H. A. Prichard argued that it is simply false that "our sense that we ought to pay our debts or to tell the truth arises from our recognition that in doing so we should be originating something good."[36] Our conceptual scheme should capture what is certainly true in this view, without including what in the previous section I suggested is false, namely, that there is a primitive property of rightness or obligatoriness, one not reducible to goodness. Let us define a duty, not as Moore initially did, that is, as an action that ought to be done, one that would contribute more goodness than any of its alternatives would, but rather as an action that is good in itself, even if not optimizing. Let us, in other words, acknowledge, as we have already repeatedly done, that among the abstract goods there may be those we should call *kinds* of action. Plausible examples would indeed be paying our debts and telling the truth. If understood broadly, they would also include many of the actions we perform in virtue of our occupying certain offices and stations, for example, those of the judge and the teacher, but also those of the parent and the older child, and of the mature citizen of a state. Such a notion of duty would accord well with much of the ordinary use of the term. We do consider certain actions to be good in themselves, appropriate or fitting, regardless of motivation or consequences, and our performance of them is sometimes due solely to our belief that they are such. Many of these actions are part of our mores, and, as I have noted, many are defined by the requirements of the offices and stations we occupy. And we also attach a clear sense to the idea that sometimes one ought not to do one's duty (perhaps because the consequences would be very bad) and that sometimes one ought to do what is contrary to one's duty (perhaps because the consequences would be very good). This idea is accommodated by our definitions of "ought" and "duty."

To some extent, so are, I believe, the important notions of the imperativeness of duty and of a sense of obligation; after all, the abstract goods in question are kinds of *action*. But only to some extent. As Sidgwick observed, these notions are among "the quasi-jural notions of modern ethics," their quasi-jural character being perhaps religious in origin.[37] And there are other, no less plausible, explanations of the idea of constraint that is doubtless present in the ordinary idea of duty. Hastings Rashdall observed that "if the sense of duty be really the sense of the relative value of ends, it is obvious that some sense of constraint or 'obligation' must always be connected with the idea of duty, so long as any of the ends which we rationally desire are incompatible with the attainment of any other such ends which we either desire or feel that we ought to desire."[38] This fact also explains the occurrence of moral dilemmas and conflicts, a topic to which I shall return. Nevertheless, it must be admitted that our definition of "duty" is another case of the conceptual regimentation I have practiced in this chapter. But this regimentation does not leave out any concept essential to ethical thought. Indeed, in particular circumstances, often we are guided by our perception of what I have called our duties and describe the latter as what we *ought* to do. But the distinction I have made between what we ought to do and what is our duty must be made. It does not disguise, or leave insufficiently acknowledged, the fact that in everyday life we are more often governed by what we take to be our duties, in my sense of "duty," than by what we think we ought to do, in my sense of "ought." This fact may be morally deplorable, but it is a fact we have conceptually provided for fully.

If there are intrinsically good kinds of actions, there are also, presumably, intrinsically bad kinds of actions. Lying and stealing would be common examples. We may call such kinds of actions *offenses*, even if in some concrete cases they ought to be performed because they would be optimizing.

Indeed, Prichard argued explicitly against a definition of duty such as ours, but his argument rested on the claim that an action can be described as intrinsically good only in the sense that it is done because of the belief that it ought to be done (our sense of "virtuous action") or because of some other good motive.[39] But this claim is just false. We may describe the keeping of a promise as a duty but we may even more naturally describe it as an action that is good in itself, quite independently of motive. We certainly would describe a society in which debts are often not paid (when they could have been) and lying is common as rather bad to that extent, regardless of the motives for such actions (and, I should add, regardless of their consequences). Indeed, we often describe certain actions as *bad* even when we know that the motives behind them are not bad or even perhaps are good. W. D. Ross, who agrees with Prichard, discusses theft that is motivated by the desire for personal pleasure,[40] which is *not* a bad motive, and an unjust act involving nepotism that is motivated by interest in the good of another person,[41] which is a *good* motive. But he defends Prichard's view even with respect to such cases, on the implausible grounds that the action is bad, in the case of theft, "because it lacks a good motive" and "because of a moral insensitivity . . . to the rights of others," and, in the case of nepotism, because the agent "is not being deterred as an ideally good man would be by the thought of the injustice." Surely, when we call such actions bad we don't mean this.

Are there actions good in themselves that would not be naturally described as duties? Some actions are said to be good on the grounds that they are pleasant or enjoyable. But even if the pleasure or enjoyment is not an *event* distinguishable from the action and thus describable as its effect, it is still distinguishable from the action as an accidental characteristic of it (in the Aristotelian sense), while the kind of the action constitutes *what* the action is. And to say that an action is good in itself is to say that its kind is an abstract good, not that it has a characteristic that is good in itself. In the latter case we would better say that the action is good as a necessary, though perhaps noncausal, condition for something else that is good in itself.

An example of an action that would be a duty according to our definition but would not ordinarily be called a duty is telling someone who asks you the time of the day, in ordinary circumstances and quite independently of considerations of consequences or of the virtue (if any) such an action characteristically exemplifies.[42] It would not ordinarily be called a duty but calling it such would not be unintelligible.

It should be noted that while our notion of duty does connect with the notion of mores (that is, customary actions regarded as duties), it bears no direct connection to our notion of morality. And this is as it should be. We do want to say that sometimes morality requires us to refrain from doing our duty, and sometimes to do what is not our duty. It is our Kantian notions of virtuous action, of a virtuous person, and of virtue that come closest to reflecting the rather vague ordinary notion of morality.

We may even follow W. D. Ross[43] and say that an action that is right, in our sense of being optimizing, is also a duty in the sense of "duty" I have defined, that it is intrinsically good, that it is good in the primary sense of "good," in which, say, pleasure and knowledge may be said to be good. Its goodness in this sense must not be confused with its goodness in the derivative sense expressed, by definition, in saying that it is right. A way of seeing the point of the distinction is to note that the total goodness in the universe may be greater if it resulted from an *action*, rather than from, say, a cosmic accident. Should we then say that right action is the highest duty, that it is the kind of action that has greatest intrinsic value (and not only greatest extrinsic value, as it does by definition)? I shall assume that we should. Acknowledging this, together with our previous acknowledgment that virtue, in the sense I have defined, is itself an abstract good, is important for our understanding of moral motivation. For the agent can now regard his virtue and his right actions not merely as good as means but as good in themselves, moreover as goods that are *his*. Hastings Rashdall argued persuasively that the apparent conflict between egoistic and universalistic hedonism, which Sidgwick thought could be resolved only if we make theological assumptions, can be resolved far more plausibly if we acknowledge that virtue, which for the universalistic hedonist would consist chiefly in the commitment to promoting the happiness of others, is itself an intrinsic good of the agent; Rashdall concluded that to acknowledge this would be to abandon hedonism, since virtue would now be an intrinsic good additional to happiness or pleasure. On the other hand, his view is hardly a concession to egoism. One's aiming at one's own virtue, so understood, is hardly describable as egoistic.[44]

We are able now to provide some room in our conceptual framework for the notion of a supererogatory action. I argued earlier that it has no application to right actions, since by definition a right action is one that is optimizing and, again by definition, one that ought to be done if no alternative action would also be optimizing. Even if we follow the suggestion made in the previous paragraph and regard an optimizing action as a duty, in the sense of having intrinsic goodness distinguishable from, though of course included in, the total intrinsic goodness it contributes, we must say that such an action cannot be supererogatory, "beyond the call of duty," because it is the highest duty, meaning by this that it is the kind of action that has greatest intrinsic goodness; nor (obviously) can any other action be supererogatory in relation to it by being "more optimizing." But in relation to other duties there are many actions that can be described as supererogatory, as going beyond what the respective duty requires. For example, a teacher has a duty to be available to his students during his office hours, but he may make himself available also at other times. If he does, his action would be of special value, as exceeding what that duty requires. But what justifies the ascription to it of such special value? The answer is that it is another *kind* of action that has greater value, that it is a different and higher duty, whether the duty to promote one's students' education or the ultimate, highest duty to do the optimizing action. So there can be no absolutely supererogatory actions; there can be no such thing as doing more good than duty requires, even in our sense of "duty." But there can be, indeed usually there are, actions that are relatively supererogatory, that is, supererogatory with respect to some particular duty. Only with respect to the duty to do what is optimizing could there be no supererogatory actions in this relative sense.

The concept of duty that I have introduced allows us also to understand better what is involved in a case described by Michael Stocker.[45] "Imagine that Joe is taking a walk on a hot day and that, while not suffering from heat, he would enjoy some ice cream; and further imagine that of all the acts then open to him, eating ice cream would produce the most pleasure, or more generally the most good." Stocker argues convincingly that it would be absurd to say that it is obligatory for Joe to eat the ice cream. Indeed, we may agree, it would be absurd to say that he has a duty to do so, if we mean a duty other than that of doing the optimizing action. But (especially if we add, as we must, that he wants to eat the ice cream) it is not absurd to say that he ought to eat the ice cream. On the contrary, if he hesitated we might say to him, "You ought to eat it, why miss the chance, the opportunity!"

## 5. The Three Senses of "Good" and the Three Parts of Ethics

I have distinguished three senses of "good": first, that in which it is attributed to abstract entities, including some kinds of action, those I called duties; second, what I have called the rightness of actions, but more generally the unqualified goodness of concrete entities; and third, what I have called virtue. The first is primitive. The other two are senses in which "good" is applicable to concrete entities, in particular to the special class of concrete entities we call actions and to dispositions to perform certain actions and persons who have such dispositions. Both are definable in terms of the primitive sense, though in different ways. I should note that the third sense is really a set of three senses, those in which an action, a disposition, and a person may be said to be virtuous. And, of course, the word "good" has also a sense that corresponds to what I have called its qualified uses with respect to concrete entities, e.g., in calling something good *qua* an F. I shall ignore these further distinctions here, since they are not central to my concerns in this book.

The relationship between the three senses I have identified is of the same general sort as the relationship, noted by Aristotle, between the senses of "healthy" as applied to organisms, to a medicine, and to urine. "Good" is not univocal but neither is it simply equivocal. The crucial distinction is that between the goodness of abstract entities and the goodness of concrete entities. The attribution of goodness to an abstract entity is a case of essential predication, in the Aristotelian sense in which the statement "Socrates is a man" or "Man is an animal" is such a case, or, more nearly, the sense in which "Blue is a color" is such a case. The attribution of goodness to a concrete entity, on the other hand, is a case of accidental predication, in the Aristotelian sense exemplified in the statement "Socrates is white." The latter means that Socrates has a certain particular quality, that is, a color, and it is that quality, not Socrates, which strictly speaking is white.

Our distinction of three senses of "good" suggests a natural division of ethics into three parts. The first is the theory of good and evil. It is primarily concerned with the nature of the property goodness and with what I have called the abstract goods, including their systematization and their degrees of goodness. Clearly, this part is most closely connected with metaphysics. The second part of ethics is the theory of right and wrong. It is the part directly concerned with conduct, with actions, and, in view of what I have said about the complexity of what is judged when we judge that an action is right or wrong, it should be evident that the theory of right and wrong is most closely associated with epistemology. The third part of ethics is what may be called the theory of virtue and vice. It is the part concerned with the conditions of praise and blame, and since the relevant praise and blame would naturally be described as moral we may also call this part of ethics the theory of morality. It is directly concerned with the motives of our actions and indirectly with important phenomena such as pride, guilt, remorse, and shame. It includes what may be called the theory of moral education and the theory of punishment, as well as certain aspects of the theory of distributive justice. Its connection with the science of psychology is obvious, but so is its connection with the metaphysical topic of the freedom of the will. It is worth noting that this latter topic is quite irrelevant to the other two parts of ethics, the theory of good and evil and the theory of right and wrong. (I have said that an action is open to an agent in the sense that he would do it if he chose; I have not made and need not make any assumptions about the conditions of choice.) We must not say, however, that the theory of virtue and vice is concerned, even in part, with the conditions under which one *ought* to be praised or blamed. This concern belongs in the theory of right and wrong, and we must be satisfied with saying that one ought to be praised or blamed for something one is or has done if and only if such praise or blame would be optimizing.

In this book I shall be concerned almost exclusively with the first two parts of ethics. Skepticism is a position within those, and only derivatively within the third, the theory of virtue and vice, of morality. The familiar phrase "the moral point of view" may be useful, but it is central or at least indispensable chiefly in ethical theories that are nonrealist or noncognitivist or both. According to the position defended in this book, it belongs, if at all, at the end of the exposition of an ethical theory, not at the beginning.

## 6. Remarks and Explanations

There are several remarks to be made about the conceptual framework I have outlined. First, it involves no assumptions regarding the topic of the freedom of the will, except the innocuous Moorean assumption that some actions are such that an agent would perform them if he or she chose to do so. No assumption is made about the genesis or causal determination of the act of choosing itself. One reason for this is that I neither have nor am aware that anyone else has a satisfactory theory of causality on which a responsible assumption of this sort could be made. A second reason is that my topic in this book is the possibility of knowing good from evil, and ultimately right from wrong, in the senses of "right" and "wrong" defined. My topic is not the conditions of moral praise or blame. I want to know how to act, not whether I would deserve to be praised or blamed for so acting.

Second, the definition of right action I have proposed raises a number of difficult questions about the nature and individuation of actions, about the notion of alternative action, about the notion of the consequences of an action, and about the sort of deontic logic that would be compatible with the definition.[46] As with the topic of the freedom of the will, I cannot deal with these questions here, and perhaps I cannot deal with them adequately at all. But I hope that in the final chapter, to which alone these questions might be relevant, it will be evident to the reader that it is not necessary for the argument of this book that I do so. In any case, as R. M. Hare points out, they are questions facing any theory of rational choice, not merely utilitarianism or the ethical theory sketched here.[47]

Third, our definitions of right action and of an action that ought to be done seem to entail that egoism is false. Should we thus reject by definition one of the standard ethical positions? Certainly not, if in the course of the complete argument of this book no reason is provided for such a rejection. But a reason will be provided.

Fourth, it is the richness of the dimension of appraisal of concrete goods, including actions, that explains some of the phenomena of moral conflict to which Bernard Williams has drawn attention,[48] and generates the illusion of pervasive and intellectually unresolvable ethical dilemmas, which motivates so many, wholly or partly, irrealist views, including Williams's.[49] If I must choose between a and b, I may choose a, even though continuing to recognize the merits of b, which just happen to be lesser than those of a; and my recognition of the merits of b may lead to a perfectly understandable feeling of regret, remorse, perhaps even guilt. If a and b are of equal merit, then the conflict would be intellectually unresolvable, but tautologically so. (Choice, of course, would remain possible, for example, by flipping a coin.) Nothing follows from this regarding the truth or falsehood of ethical realism. On the definitions of "right" and "ought" that I have offered, two incompatible actions can both be right (though it may be deeply regrettable that they are incompatible), but it cannot be the case that both ought to be performed.

Fifth, what I have just said provides also a sufficient explanation of the fact, insisted on by A. I. Melden, that even when "reason requires that it is better to break [a] promise and act on the basis of a competing circumstance," this "in no way shows that there is no infringement of a right. The lesser of two evils remains an evil however reasonable it is to choose it; and the denial of a right remains a transgression against another person, unavoidable as it may be."[50] To understand this fact we need not include in our conceptual framework a distinct notion of rights, as Melden does, or of obligation to a person as distinct from obligation to do something for a person.[51] (What could the difference between the two obligations be? Can one have an obligation to a person but not an obligation to engage in some action, if one is possible, however vaguely the action may be characterized?) The "lesser of two evils" in the case described strikes us as still being very much an evil because it constitutes the failure to do our duty, to keep a promise, an action of intrinsic worth, and we attach special importance to such actions, but this motive for talking about rights is not a sufficient justification for doing so.

As a distinct, irreducible, ethical notion, the concept of a right is hopelessly obscure. Mary Midgley writes: "In its moral sense, [the word 'right'] oscillates uncontrollably between applications which are too wide to resolve conflicts ('the right to life, liberty and the pursuit of happiness') and ones which are too narrow to be plausible ('the basic human right to stay at home on Bank Holiday'). As many people have already suggested, its various uses have diverged too far to be usefully reunited. If this is true, however, it seems very important to stop relying on it."[52] I tend to agree with Midgley, but a reasonably clear notion of a right can be defined. In defending his "rights-based" philosophy of law, Ronald Dworkin opposes any "reification" of rights and merely says that "if someone has a right, then it is wrong for others to treat him otherwise than as specified, at least unless some strong countervailing reason for doing so is available."[53] The essential idea behind the notion of a right is that of a good that it is always (except perhaps in very special circumstances) impermissible to deny to, or deprive of, the holder of the right. Our conceptual scheme obviously is incompatible with this idea, as might be expected from any scheme that is even roughly utilitarian. But there is more to a sophisticated notion of a right, as is made evident in Melden's book and especially in the works of Alan Gewirth.

In a recent article,[54] Alan Gewirth has argued that while it is not the case that "all other moral values and precepts are derivative from rights," nevertheless "human rights . . . are basic to morality in that they are the necessary even if not the sufficient condition of all moral values" (pp. 342–43). The latter part of the argument is essentially that of his book *Reason and Morality*, and I have already indicated my reasons for questioning it. But here it is appropriate to note that Gewirth's approach would be an important alternative to mine, should mine fail. One test of whether it fails would be whether it can do justice to "the individual's personal dignity as an agent," to the conception of the person as an entity of moral standing, which Gewirth plausibly claims his theory succeeds in doing (p. 343). I shall assume that our theory will also succeed in doing this, and for the present simply accept Ramon M. Lemos's definition: "To say that someone, $a$, has a natural right to something, $x$, is to say (1) that if $a$ attempts to acquire or retain $x$ his act is at least *prima facie* right and (2) that if any moral agent, $b$, is capable of affecting $a$'s acquisition or retention of $x$, then $b$ has at least a *prima facie* obligation to act compatibly with $a$'s acquiring or retaining $x$."[55] Clause (1) captures the idea that only moral agents have rights, though Lemos argues that we have obligations also to subhuman animals, plants, and even inanimate objects; the definition as a whole renders the notion of a right no longer primitive, but rather reducible to that of obligation. I shall return to this topic in chapter 5.

Sixth, the richness of the dimension of appraisal of concrete goods, including actions, also explains the plausibility of what Sidgwick called perceptional intuitionism,[56] which has been revived in recent years, though under the influence of Wittgenstein's later philosophy.[57] By perceptional intuitionism, Sidgwick meant the view that one can make an "immediate judgment as to what ought to be done or aimed at," without inference from past experience or general rules. Renford Bambrough gives as an example one's judgment that a child about to undergo an operation ought to be given an anesthetic. The truth in this view is that often the goodness (badness) of one or more good (bad) qualities of a concrete entity, especially of an action, is striking and can be acknowledged without inference. But, of course, it would be a mistake to conclude that the concrete entity can be judged also to be unqualifiedly good (bad) in such an immediate way. A physician, I hope, would consider carefully the possible harmful effects of anesthesia on the child before deciding to use it.

Seventh, the richness of the dimension of appraisal of concrete goods explains much of the plausibility of some familiar criticisms of utilitarianism, such as

F. H. Bradley's and, more recently, Bernard Williams's. I have in mind especially the claim that there is far more to the moral life than is captured by the single-minded utilitarian principle that one ought to act so as to produce the maximum amount of goodness possible. Indeed, the claim is true. The details of our everyday lives, including the social structures of which we are members and the particular duties this membership involves, exhibit a great variety of good and bad properties, each of which may be the object of ethical concern independently of overarching considerations about what the optimizing action on the particular occasion might be. But this does not mean that such overarching considerations would be out of place or not genuinely overarching. However valuable attention to, and faithful description of, our actual moral life may be, it must not be confused with the ultimate critique of it that constitutes the *raison d'être* of ethics as a branch of philosophy. If the difference between the two is not respected, ethics is likely to degenerate into a mere pandering to whatever happens to be the current moral opinion.

Eighth, our sharp distinction between abstract and concrete goods allows us to see our way clear through some familiar puzzles. For example, Philippa Foot asks whether, granted that courage is a virtue, an inveterate criminal may be said to possess it and exemplify it in his bad actions.[58] What Foot calls the virtues are (as we shall see) prime examples of abstract goods, but, as I observed earlier in this chapter, it does not follow that all their concrete exemplifications are unqualifiedly good. We shall return to this point on several occasions in the course of our inquiry.

Ninth, it should be evident that the conceptual scheme I have proposed is not that of classical utilitarianism or indeed of any pure consequentialism, and thus it is not so obviously open to the familiar objections to the latter from the requirements of justice.[59] For example, Rawls's rejection of utilitarianism on the grounds that it is compatible with the acceptance of injustices is in part due to his decision to understand by that view classical, hedonistic utilitarianism.[60] If he had considered a view such as Moore's or Rashdall's or the one outlined here, its incompatibility with the requirements of justice would not have been obvious. We might assign to justice a very high degree of goodness as an abstract good, whether or not it is to be understood as Rawls understands it. (It may be a certain set of intrinsically good actions, that is, duties, or an intrinsically good social state to be produced by actions.) To allow for this possibility is to defuse the simplistic dispute between "teleologists" and "deontologists." Indeed, the basis of my defense of our definition of "right action" is summed up in Thomas Aquinas's assertion that the first principle of natural law is "Good is to be done and promoted, and evil is to be avoided."[61] He held, in my view correctly, that this principle is self-evident, knowable by unaided reason.

But although a view such as ours can consistently allow for a very high degree of the goodness of justice, it is not likely to ascribe to it absolute priority. Any theory that regards the rightness of an action as even in part determined by the goodness of the totality of its consequences must allow for the possibility of cases in which an action of a kind we would ordinarily regard as most unjust would nevertheless be right. Perhaps such cases are very rare. And with respect to any of them we should have grave doubts that our estimate of their consequences is reliable. (This is the well-known weakness of hypothetical, usually science-fiction examples of such cases.) But from a purely theoretical point of view, we must allow for their possibility and regard them simply as cases in which doing what is right conflicts with the preservation or promotion of a lesser good. On all this, much good sense may be found in R. M. Hare's recent book *Moral Thinking*.[62]

Tenth, it should be evident that my choice of primitive notions is hardly idiosyncratic. As W. K. Frankena has avowed, "I find it hard to believe that any action or rule can be right, wrong, or obligatory in the moral sense, if there is no good or evil connected with it in any way, directly or indirectly."[63] The notion of goodness is at least as crucial in recent writings in ethics as it was in traditional ethics. Indeed, John Rawls argues for "the priority of right over good," but, as implied by what he says a few lines earlier, he must mean by this normative, not conceptual, priority.[64] His derivation of the principles of justice presupposes what he calls "the thin theory of good" and thus indirectly the notion of good employed in the full theory; the original contractors do not know their particular plans of life but do know that they have, or may have, such plans, the realization of which would require the possession of the primary goods of "the thin theory," and constitute their ultimate good.[65] Alan Donagan has described (and so has Rawls) self-respect as a fundamental human good, even though for him respect for something rests on the recognition of it as intrinsically worthy of respect and the foundation of morality is the respect for rational nature as such.[66] Richard B. Brandt has developed in detail a certain notion of what is the rational thing for one to do (namely, it is what one would do if one's "decision procedures had been subject to criticism by facts and reason to a maximal extent"), presumably because of his belief that it is the clearest notion with which to identify the notion of good employed in the question "What is the best thing to do?"[67] And Alan Gewirth identifies as "the substantive question" of moral philosophy, "of which interests should favorable account be taken? Which interests are good ones or constitute the most important goods?"[68]

Eleventh, it should be equally evident that my definitions of the ethical terms that I do not regard as primitive are also not idiosyncratic, though of course they are revisionary. The definition of virtue surely expresses a sense familiar to all of us. The definition of duty reflects an important part of the ordinary notion, and the part it leaves out is intended to be expressed by the definitions of "ought" and "right." It is to these latter definitions that objections are most likely to be raised. I have said something in defense of them already, and much of the final chapter will be devoted to further defense. But it may be worth repeating here that, especially when we keep in mind that the good in terms of which they are defined is not at all limited to pleasure or desire-satisfaction, and that actions and institutions are explicitly allowed to have intrinsic goodness, these definitions, though not wholly capturing the ordinary notions of "ought" and "right" (I am unaware of any definitions that do this), would generally seem acceptable to common sense, certainly more so than any proposed alternatives. The general appeal of utilitarianism is surely no accident. And the usual obstacles to accepting it are precisely those I have explicitly removed. What could be more in consonance with everyday ethical thought than that good is to be promoted as much as possible, and evil shunned as much as possible?

## 7. Definitions of "Good"

My choice of primitive notions and my definitions of those I do not take as primitive may not be idiosyncratic, yet my regarding the notion of goodness as primitive and indeed as standing for a monadic property (if it stands for anything at all) sets the conceptual scheme I have outlined sharply apart from most ethical theories. I shall not argue in detail against these theories. The plausibility of all derives largely from the belief that the chief alternative to them, namely a theory like Moore's or ours, is unacceptable, for phenomenological, or metaphysical, or epistemological reasons. If I am successful in this book, I shall have shown that these reasons are spurious. But an outline here of the theories in question and of some direct reasons for rejecting them may be useful. They are all theories according to which the notion of goodness is definable.

The simplest such theories merely identify goodness with some property such as pleasure or desire-satisfaction. Their plausibility derives from the fact that the property in question indeed is *a* good, a species or subgenus of goodness, if goodness is a generic property. They are implausible for reasons too familiar from the literature to need recounting here. The chief is that *obviously* there are many other goods. If this is not obvious to the reader now, I hope to make it obvious in chapter 5. Our account of goodness has the virtue of explaining both why such theories have appeared plausible to some and why they have appeared implausible to others.

The more sophisticated of the theories with which ours is to be contrasted define goodness as a *relational* property. Some are "nonnaturalistic," insofar as the definiens proposed includes an ethical, usually deontological, term. For example, Brentano held that "the good is that which is worthy of love, that which can be loved with a love that is correct."[69] C. D. Broad wrote: "I am almost certain that 'right' and 'ought' cannot be defined in terms of 'good.' But I am not sure that 'X is good' could not be defined as meaning that X is such that it would be a fitting object of desire to any mind which had an adequate idea of its non-ethical characteristics."[70] A. C. Ewing defined "good" as "what ought to be the object of a pro attitude."[71] And more recently Roderick M. Chisholm has defined the notion of intrinsic value in terms of the notion of intrinsic preferability, and the latter in terms of the notion of what one is required to prefer.[72] It is fair to say, I believe, that such deontological definitions are motivated by the desire to acknowledge the nonnaturalistic status of ethical terms but avoid accepting a view such as Moore's. And they have been unwilling to accept a Moorean view for the familiar reason that it is believed to face insuperable phenomenological, metaphysical, or episte-mological difficulties. I shall try to show in this book that this is not so. For now it should suffice to observe that (1) the deontic properties such theories appeal to are hardly free from similar difficulties, and (2) that they offer nothing deserving to be called a phenomenological examination of the psychological attitude, whether desire, love, approval, or preference, to which they appeal. In chapters 3 and 5 I shall argue that such attitudes involve the awareness of the real or apparent goodness of their objects and therefore cannot be appealed to in a definition of goodness.

Simple *naturalistic* relational definitions of goodness hold that it is the same as being the object of desire (Mill), or of interest (Ralph Barton Perry), or of some other psychological attitude, whether one's own, or someone's, or everyone's. G. E. Moore argued against such definitions (in *Principia Ethica*) on the grounds that they commit the naturalistic fallacy and (in *Ethics*) on the grounds that they either lead to contradiction or make ethical disagreement incomprehensible. (Stevenson, in his contribution to *The Philosophy of G. E. Moore*, tried to meet the latter objections, but only by adopting a noncognitivist account of ethical statements, which we shall consider in the next chapter.) I have little to add to Moore's arguments except to note (1) that whether the definitions commit the naturalistic fallacy or not, they obviously do not do justice to the complexity of ordinary ethical thought about goodness, and (2) that they too fail to offer a phenomenology of the psychological attitudes in question, which at least seem to involve awareness of actual or apparent goodness.

Far more common today are naturalistic relational definitions (or at least explications) of goodness that appeal to what persons who are suitably qualified with respect to knowledge, motivation, and intellectual capacity would desire or choose in again suitably qualified circumstances. It is characteristic of such theories that they rest in part on dogmatic epistemological and metaphysical assumptions, dogmatic not only because generally they are unargued but also because they preclude our taking seriously and examining other perfectly reasonable alternatives. For example, Brandt rests his theory of the good on certain beliefs (derived in part from cognitive psychology) about what a fully rational person would want and do. For him a fully rational person is one whose desires would survive confrontation with all available relevant information and whose actions accord with that information. But by such information Brandt explicitly means "a part of the 'scientific knowledge' of the day, or [beliefs] which are justified on the basis of publicly available evidence in accordance with the canons of inductive or deductive logic, or justified on the basis of evidence which could now be obtained by procedures known to science."[73] But suppose that there is also knowledge, available and certainly relevant, of ethical facts of the sort G. E. Moore or Nicolai Hartmann believed there were, quite outside the scope of scientific investigation. Clearly, what a fully rational person possessing such knowledge would want and do could be quite different from what Brandt supposes. Brandt ignores this possibility and, startlingly, dismisses the view that some things, for example, knowledge and virtue, are worthwhile in themselves, whether or not we desire them, on the grounds that this view is "obsolescent."[74] And though he mentions the view that there are simple ethical properties such as goodness and rightness, he decides to ignore it by just characterizing it as the "older view."[75] This sort of argument belongs in Detroit, not in philosophy.

John Rawls derives substantive principles of justice from what rational persons with knowledge of general facts but not of their particular situation would agree to regarding the basic structure of their society. But he restricts his conception of rationality to means-ends calculation.[76] The restriction is present even in Rawls's development of what he calls the full theory of good. The choice of ultimate ends (plans of life) is said to be subject to rational appraisal, and the rational plan for a person is said to be the one "he would choose with deliberative rationality. It is the plan that would be decided upon as the outcome of careful reflection [regarding] the course of action that would best realize his more fundamental desires."[77] Rawls agrees that desires themselves can be appraised from a rational standpoint, but only in Brandt's sense I mentioned earlier.[78] To meet the obvious criticism that so understood one's rational plan might not include the pursuit of goods such as "personal affection and friendship, meaningful work and social cooperation, the pursuit of knowledge and the fashioning and contemplation of beautiful objects,"[79] Rawls postulates the so-called Aristotelian principle: "other things equal, human beings enjoy the exercise of their realized capacities (their innate or trained abilities), and this enjoyment increases the more the capacity is realized, or the greater its complexity."[80]

Such speculation about our desires and enjoyments, even if true, is hardly an argued answer to the question, What ends is it rational to pursue? Like Brandt, Rawls ignores another, far more fundamental notion of rationality in ethics, namely, that of the capacity to perceive intellectually, to understand, to grasp the intrinsic values of certain ends and to compare them. If there is such a kind of rationality, ignoring it would be like regarding as a manifestation of rationality in deductive logic only the mastery of deductive techniques, and not also the grasp, understanding, and rational acceptance of the truths of logic, of the *principles* of valid deductive inference. For example, the persons in Rawls's original position are supposed to have no opinion about the intrinsic value of cultural institutions and scientific achievement. (Indeed, Rawls seems to deny that these have intrinsic value.)[81] Since they are supposed to be "ignorant of their final ends and of much else, they must try to work out which conception of justice is most likely to secure the social conditions and all-purpose means necessary to realize their highest-order interests and determinate but unknown conception of the good."[82] But it should be evident that, for example, if one's final end, or highest-order interest, or conception of the good, were roughly like Plato's in the *Republic*, one would not want to be a party to any agreement on the principles of justice Rawls advocates. And if one's final end, etc., is known by *reason* to be such, then the Rawlsian procedure and its outcome would be profoundly irrational.

In "Fairness to Goodness"[83] Rawls considers the objection that "by excluding information about people's conceptions of the good the original position rules out morally relevant information"[84] and admits that "the original position as a whole is not neutral between conceptions of the good in the sense that the principles of justice adopted permit them all equally. Any definite agreement is bound to favor some conceptions over others."[85] For example, conceptions that are in direct conflict with the principles of justice (that is, those agreed upon in the original position) will be excluded.[86] My point, however, has been not so much that the original position leaves out information about people's conceptions of the good (about what in *Freedom and Reason* and elsewhere R. M. Hare calls ideals, whose moral importance as well as likely conflict with one's own or others' "interests" Rawls acknowledges), but that it leaves out the possibility (traditionally regarded as actuality) of persons' possessing and using a capacity for a certain kind of knowledge. Such an impoverished notion of rationality can hardly promote confidence in Rawls's fundamental premise that good is what it is rational for a person to want.[87] It is of some interest that this notion of rationality is challenged by Hilary Putnam in his most recent work. He writes: "interpretation, in a very wide sense of the term, *and value* are involved in our notions of rationality in every area" (my italics).[88]

The appeal in recent ethics to such a notion of rationality is evident also in (at least one stage in the development of) the work of Philippa Foot, with much of which otherwise I am sympathetic. She writes, for example, that "Irrational actions are those in which a man in some way defeats his own purposes, doing what is calculated to be disadvantageous or to frustrate his ends. Immorality does not *necessarily* involve any such thing."[89] Such views about rationality are often presented in connection with certain views about motivation. I shall consider these latter views in the following chapter. But here it would be worth recalling Sidgwick's assertion, "By 'Reasonable' conduct—whether morally or prudentially reasonable—we mean that of which we judge that it 'ought' to be done."[90] In effect he suggests that we should understand the notion of reasonable (rational) action in terms of the notion of an action that ought to be done—the exact opposite of current fashion. Sidgwick did not deny that reason discovers what ought to be done or what ends are to be pursued; on the contrary, he affirmed it. The significance of his suggestion (how aware of it he in fact was is unclear; he could hardly have foreseen the almost lawless current use of the word "rational") is that while the notion of an action that ought to be done has a rich and clear intuitive content and at least appears to be primitive, the notion of an action that is reasonable (or rational) does not. The latter notion is highly general and of course definable: it is the notion of an action that accords with reason. It certainly involves no reference to human purposes and their possible frustrations. And to "explicate" it so that it would involve such reference would be an act of stipulation, not explication. If we want to provide it with more specific, yet neutral, content, we could say, with Sidgwick, that it is the notion of an action that ought to be done. Compare, in this respect, our unwillingness to just say that a valid deductive inference is one that accords with reason, though saying this would be true. Rather, we provide the notion of such an inference with intuitively clear and specific content by saying that it is an inference such that it would be self-contradictory to assert its premises but deny its conclusion.

Indeed, Sidgwick argued that even in the case of hypothetical imperatives, in which reference to human purposes and the means of their satisfaction or frustration is made, the notion of "ought," and thus, in *his* sense, of what it is rational to do, is ineliminable; it cannot be understood solely in terms of purposes and means-ends relationships. We may know that "Early rising is an indispensable condition of the attainment of health" is true, but this assertion is not to be confused with the assertion "If you wish to be healthy you ought to rise early."[91] Our knowledge of the truth of the latter presupposes, but is not reducible to, indeed is *categorially* different from, our knowledge of the truth of the former. The one assertion is purely empirical. The other, that involving the notion of "ought," is not; it is irreducibly normative and its truth can properly be described as disclosed by reason, though in part on the basis of the empirical knowledge we have of the truth of the first assertion. If all this is true of such hypothetical imperatives, what reason is left for denying that it may also be true of categorical imperatives, that reason may disclose, even if partly on the basis of empirical knowledge, what we ought to do, regardless of our purposes and desires?

Of course the word "reason" also has senses other than that of a capacity for a certain kind of knowledge, which we may but need not call intellectual intuition. Closely related to this sense is the sense of *evidence* for the truth of a belief, and thus for the rightness of an action if the belief has as its content the proposition that a certain action is right. A third sense (actually a family of senses) is that of an agent's intention or purpose in performing an action. A fourth sense is that of a motive, a certain state or condition of the agent that causes or at least serves to explain the action, which of course may also be a reason in the second and third sense. Much of recent ethics has rested on confusing the second with the third and fourth senses, on not distinguishing "justifying reasons" from "exciting reasons," a distinction Hutcheson made clearly about two and one-half centuries ago.[92]

Needless to say, the suggestion, implicit in my criticism of Foot, Brandt, and Rawls, that certain desires and actions may be *rational* solely in the sense that they aim at ends that reason discloses as intrinsically good, is controversial. This whole book may be thought of as constituting an argument for it. But much less controversial is the view that certain desires and actions are *irrational* in the sense that reason discloses the intrinsic badness of the ends at which they aim. Examples would be someone's desire to die or to be mutilated or to be in pain, and the action it may prompt, not as a means to some other end, or because of religious conviction, etc., but for its own sake; or someone's preferring the destruction of the whole world to the scratching of his finger, a preference Hume claimed to be "not contrary to reason." Such desires or preferences need not be based on false belief or early conditioning; it would be merely a matter of faith to believe that they would not survive "cognitive psychotherapy." But whether they would or would not, the natural characterization of them, and of the actions they prompt, is as *crazy*.[93]

My remarks in the previous several paragraphs are intended not as an explication of the notion of practical rationality, but only as an insistent attempt to preserve the *notion* of ethical truths that are disclosed by reason. I am skeptical about the value of the former notion. As Ramon M. Lemos has argued recently,

> there is no single antecedent, impartial, nonquestion-begging concept of practical rationality to which in moral philosophy an appeal can be made to establish that people ought to act in one way rather than another. . . . Rather than attempting the impossible

task of establishing the criteria of rightness and wrongness of acts of various sorts by appealing to a nonexistent concept of practical rationality, we can instead give content to the concept of practical rationality only by considering what sorts of things are good and what sorts of acts are right and obligatory.[94]

The popularity in ethics of defining goodness in terms of what a certain sort of person would want or do or prefer if he or she were in appropriate circumstances is not difficult to explain. Indeed, if we have in mind a person who is in possession of *all* relevant knowledge (including knowledge of irreducibly ethical facts, if there are any), capable of reasoning faultlessly, and acting (choosing, preferring) *solely* on the basis of such knowledge and reasoning, then it follows trivially that what such a person would do (or choose) if he or she were in appropriate circumstances would be the best (if there is such a thing as being best or good at all). It would be very much like defining truth as the set of propositions that God accepts. Such a definition of good (or best) would not admit of counterexamples. And it may seem attractive because of the illusion that the definiens is clearer and closer to familiar notions than is the definiendum. (This is an illusion at least because of the heavy reliance in the definiens on a subjunctive conditional—probably the least understood kind of statement.) But it would not admit of counterexamples only if the notions of knowledge and reason are not restricted, only if knowledge by reason of irreducibly ethical facts, if there are any, is also included. Yet they are restricted by philosophers such as Rawls and Brandt. And once the restrictions are imposed, possible counterexamples, such as those I have mentioned, abound. Moreover, no reason is provided for believing that the so-restricted hypothetical chooser would not at one time choose one thing and at another time the exact opposite, or that two such hypothetical choosers would not choose exact opposites. If it is asserted that there is a nomological connection between having the restricted knowledge, etc., and choosing $x$, for some unique determinate value of $x$, the question arises how we may know that this is so, that there is such a nomological connection. By relying on cognitive psychology?

In fact, the very idea behind such definitions of goodness seems perverse. Alan Donagan has remarked, with respect to the ideal observer theory but with application to all types of "hypothetical choice" theories, that "if it were asked, 'Is 563 the sum of 179 and 384?' nobody would offer, as a step towards an answer, 'It is, if it is the sum that an ideal calculator would reach by considering the question as an ideal calculator would.' "[95] And Amartya Sen and Bernard Williams have written: "Is the mere fact that someone chooses something a source of value for the thing chosen? It is natural to think of choosing and valuing as related, but it is hard to avoid the suspicion that, in this representation, the direction of the linkage has been inverted . . . even when qualifications are added to the supposed choice in the form of 'under ideal conditions' or 'with full understanding.' "[96]

But to explain a conceptual scheme, which I have tried to do in this chapter, is one thing; to apply it and defend its application is something else. (As I warned at the beginning, I have been writing as if it does have application, but only for the sake of brevity of exposition.) I proceed now to its application and defense. Is there such a property as goodness? If there is, what sort of property is it? How is it related to the properties that exemplify it, what I have called the abstract goods? Is there the sort of intellectual intuition for ignoring the possibility of which I have chided Rawls, Brandt, and Foot? If there is, what is it? How do we, or at least how can we, know that there is such a property as goodness and that certain other properties exemplify it? And, finally, how do we, or at least how can we, know which actions are right and which are wrong, in other words, how do we, or at least how can we, know how to act? I shall discuss and attempt to answer these questions by considering the merits of several varieties of skepticism in ethics, in the sense of this phrase explained in chapter 1.

# CHAPTER THREE

# Our Awareness of Good

## 1. Emotivism and Prescriptivism

According to the most familiar variety of skepticism in ethics, the words "good," "right," "ought," "virtue," and "duty," or "evil," "wrong," and "vice," when used in ethical sentences, are not used to describe ethical facts, though in part they may describe, and their use may be motivated by the speaker's knowledge of, certain nonethical facts. Rather, their ethically characteristic use is to express an emotion or an attitude of approval or disapproval, or an interest, or to attempt to produce in the listener such an emotion or attitude or interest, or to commend or prescribe or condemn or prohibit a certain action and thus, by implication, to express an imperative, perhaps one subject to the condition of universalizability. (For my purposes here it does not matter which of these alternatives the skeptic selects; it does not matter whether he is, for example, an emotivist or a prescriptivist.) But though it is undeniable that these words often do have such a use, it is not true that whenever used their use is of the sorts mentioned. I may describe a certain action reported in the newspaper as wrong or bad, without having any appropriate emotion or attitude, without attempting to produce in the listener any emotion or attitude, and without commending or prescribing to him or her to refrain from the sort of action reported (unless the notion of commending or prescribing is a mere idling wheel here, automatically to be applied whenever an appropriate ethical sentence is used); nor need it be true that I even tend to have such an emotion or attitude toward actions such as the one reported.[1]

But even if ethical terms were always used for the expression or evocation of certain emotions or attitudes or interests, or for commending or condemning, or for prescribing or prohibiting actions, we would need further argument to show that this is not merely a part or an aspect of their use, indeed one to be understood, quite naturally, in terms of another part or aspect that is purely descriptive, namely, the attribution of an objective ethical property to whatever the sentence is about. To use Austin's familiar terminology, the fact that in uttering an ethical sentence one is performing a certain illocutionary act and perhaps even a certain perlocutionary act does not entail at all that one is not performing also an irreducibly ethical locutionary act.[2] *Prima facie*, I find a certain action morally repulsive and condemn it because I believe that it is wrong; and, typically, this is why I may also want my listener (there need not be one) to find it morally repulsive, and to condemn it and refrain from it.

But, clearly, a sufficient answer to the noncognitivist positions I have mentioned would be to provide an adequate argument for the existence of objective ethical properties, and this is exactly what I shall attempt to do in the later chapters of this book. As Stevenson admitted in his criticism of Moore, although his analysis of the use of "right," "with reference to emotive meaning and disagreement in attitude, stands as an alternative to Moore's non-naturalistic views, it does not positively disprove the view that 'right,' whether directly or indirectly, has to do with a non-natural quality."[3] Exactly the same can be said about R. M. Hare's view that the primary use of "good" is to commend and thereby to prescribe.[4] His argument against those who hold that it stands for a property, namely, that they cannot account for its action-guiding, motivating role, is at best question begging. The property *good* of which Moore spoke may be such that the awareness or thought of it is naturally action guiding or motivating. Indeed, this is obviously true of "natural" properties such as pleasure and health. We shall return to this point.

I do not propose to discuss in detail the adequacy of these noncognitivist positions as accounts of moral discourse. Over the years they have been subjected to sufficient criticism. It is significant that, in 1977, as firmly committed an opponent to the view that there are objective moral properties as J. L. Mackie found himself compelled to admit that the ordinary use of moral terms involves the belief on the part of the speaker that he is referring to such properties.[5] For my purposes here it is more important to observe how lacking the noncognitivist positions I have mentioned are in providing a detailed account of the nature of the emotions and of the moral attitudes, and of the psychological circumstances characteristic of the performance of the speech-acts of commending and condemning, an account that, I suggest, can only be phenomenological. What if to morally approve of a certain action should turn out to consist, at least in part, in being aware of the (real or apparent) goodness or rightness of the action? This is essentially a phenomenological question, though sometimes expressed as one concerning meaning, and it is appropriate to answer it by relying not only on one's own findings but also on those of a variety of other philosophers. I proceed to do so.

Sidgwick wrote: "The peculiar emotion of moral approbation is, in my experience, inseparably bound up with the conviction, implicit or explicit, that the conduct approved is 'really' right—*i. e.*, that it cannot, without error, be disapproved by any other mind."[6] G. E. Moore went further and suggested that to approve a thing is to feel that it has the property good.[7] But W. D. Ross added: "If we ask ourselves what approval is we find that the basic element in it is not feeling at all but the judgement that an object is good."[8] Nicolai Hartmann argued that "Nothing is ever loved, striven for, yearned after, except for the sake of some value immediately discerned (and felt). But, conversely, never is loving, striving, yearning presupposed in the case of a thing that is of value, or in the case of the value itself which is inherent in the thing."[9] Sartre described emotion as "a certain way of apprehending the world,"[10] a consciousness of the world as possessing a specific new aspect or quality,[11] rather than "a modification of our psychic being."[12] "If I abruptly perceive an object as horrible . . . The horrible is now within the thing, at the heart of the thing; it is its affective texture; it is constitutive of it."[13] "To feel sympathy for Peter is to be conscious of Peter as sympathetic."[14] Similar views about the emotions had been held by Brentano, Meinong, and Scheler. More recently, Renford Bambrough has pointed out that just as "to believe is (roughly) to hold to be true . . . to approve is (equally roughly) to hold to be good."[15] And in an important, even more recent book, Robert Sokolowski writes: "It is not the case that we first feel a need and then search for something to fill the need. . . . Rather something in the world simply begins to look good."[16]

Analogous views have been held regarding the closely related notion of desire, when it has been understood phenomenologically, and this is an appropriate place to return to the familiar suggestion, already mentioned in the previous chapter, that goodness is at most a relational property, roughly that of being an actual or possible object of desire. The view is, I suggest, phenomenologically unsound. Sartre argued that "the character of unreflected desire is to transcend itself by apprehending on the subject the quality of desirability. Everything happens as if we lived in a world whose objects, in addition to their qualities of warmth, odor, shape, etc., had the qualities of repulsive, attractive, delightful, useful, etc., and as if these qualities were forces having a certain power over us."[17] He also remarked that "if I desire a house or a glass of water or a woman's body . . . how can my desire be anything but the consciousness of these objects as desirable? Let us beware then of considering these desires as little psychic entities dwelling in consciousness; they are consciousness itself . . . for consciousness is on principle consciousness of something."[18]

The defenders of the relational view of goodness as object of desire, like the defenders of the first variety of ethical skepticism, which we considered earlier, seem to be in the grip of the eighteenth-century philosophy of mind that conceived of the emotions and the desires as (to use a combination of Sartrean and Rylean jargon) curious inhabitants of a ghostly realm that are, if at all, only contingently related to their objects. Even if they allow that consciousness *of* these objects is necessarily presupposed, they regard the emotional or conative character of such consciousness as only causally related to its objects. This is exactly what Sartre denies. At least in one sense of the vague word "desire," a desire is consciousness of the real or apparent goodness (desirability) of the desired object. I shall consider this view in greater detail in the next section and especially in chapter 5, section 3. Suffice it here to remark that if it is true that the notion of desire thus presupposes the notion of goodness, or at least of value in general, then any attempt to explicate the latter in terms of the former is radically wrongheaded. The same can be said about explicating ethical notions in terms of the notion of (human) needs. It should be evident that what one needs ("truly needs," we say, not just "thinks he needs") is either an intrinsic or an extrinsic good, and that one thinks one needs something only if one regards it as an intrinsic or an extrinsic good.

## 2. Moral Motivation

One of the main objections to ethical theories such as Moore's, Prichard's, and Ross's has been that they cannot account for moral motivation, for the motivating role of our (alleged) cognition of the primitive objective properties of goodness and/

or rightness.[19] It is curious that this objection is made by philosophers who also profess not only to disbelieve in the existence of such properties but even to fail to have any idea of what they might be. One is tempted to reply to them that if they had such an idea they would understand how the cognition of goodness and rightness would be motivating, and that in any case only one who does have the required idea has the right to have opinions about the connection between the cognition of those properties and moral motivation. Let us, however, consider the issue more closely.

First, we (including psychologists) know too little about the empirical facts concerning motivation in general to have justifiable opinions about what can and what cannot provide motives for certain actions. For all we know, that recognition of the objective goodness of a certain thing is quite naturally a motive for seeking it, is no more problematic than that infants willingly drink milk—food that is biologically good for them—but not, say, unsweetened tea. In the case of the abstract good pleasure and the abstract evil pain, the very question, Why do we prefer pleasure to pain, everything else being equal? strikes us as silly, since the answer is so obvious: because pleasure is good and pain bad.[20] A. C. Ewing remarks that "it may just as well be an ultimate fact about our nature that we desire what is good as that we dislike being burnt."[21] To say that these are ultimate facts, I assume, is not to deny that they may be biologically explainable.

But, second, if the view of desire suggested in the previous section is correct, then we do achieve a clear understanding of how the cognition of goodness can be motivating. If we assume that the desire to do $x$ is at least one paradigm of what we mean by a motive for doing $x$ (an assumption generally made by philosophers), and if we agree that at least one kind of desire consists in, or at least essentially includes, the awareness of the (real or apparent) goodness of the object desired, then of course the cognition of goodness is motivating! And then we can easily understand even the Socratic doctrine that virtue is knowledge, that one who knows the good necessarily pursues it. According to Nicholas P. White, for Plato "to apprehend the Good fully along with a situation in which it might be exemplified *simply is* to have a desire overwhelming all others to see that instantiation take place," and White suggests that this is Plato's version of the Socratic view that no one "willingly sins."[22] We can also understand Aristotle's view that we desire something because it seems good to us, and it is not the case that something seems good to us because we desire it,[23] Aquinas's view that "The will can tend to nothing except under the aspect of good,"[24] and Kant's observation that if we interpret the classical dictum "Nihil appetimus nisi sub ratione boni; Nihil aversamur nisi sub ratione mali" to mean "under the direction of reason we desire nothing except so far as we esteem it good or evil," then "it is indubitably certain."[25] The insistence that reason or cognition by itself moves nothing, that special motive-forces, namely, independent desires for the ends aimed at by action, are needed, derives its plausibility from an inadequate conception both of desire and of what it is to know that something is good.

In his insightful recent book *Reason and Value*,[26] E. J. Bond argues that values are objective and that desiring a thing is neither a necessary nor a sufficient condition of its being a value. Yet he retains the Humean view that there can be no action without desire by suggesting that while cognition of value cannot determine the will directly, it can do so indirectly by creating an appropriate reflective desire (p. 58, *et passim*). "For how [else] is the connection made between cognition and the will?" he asks (p. 12). But it seems to me no more puzzling to suppose that this connection is direct than to suppose, with Bond, that the connection between the cognition and the reflective desire it creates is direct. The truth seems to be that what he calls the reflective desire is nothing but the cognition, and the latter may be called desire only in order to acknowledge its directly motivating role.

Is the view of desire I have described really defensible? I shall say more about it in chapter 5, and it will be supported by the general phenomenology I shall defend in the final section of this chapter. But some remarks are in order here. We must begin by acknowledging that the English term "desire" (to say nothing of the term "want," badly mangled by recent philosophers) applies to a variety of cases that may well have nothing in common. To desire a long life, in ordinary circumstances, does seem merely to be vividly aware of the (real or apparent) goodness of a long life. To desire a woman of whose (real or apparent) desirability one is aware may be nothing but for one to be vividly aware of her desirability. In this case desirability does appear to be a property of the woman. And awareness of it should not be confused with mere thinking. To merely think of the woman as desirable need not be to desire her. (Aristotle explained cases of weakness of the will by noting that in such cases one's belief that what one does is bad, or will have bad, though remote, consequences, is like the belief of a man who is asleep or mad or drunk, or like the "belief" expressed by actors on the stage.)[27] But what of the very possible case of desiring a woman of whom one is aware as undesirable? This may well be like desiring a certain food one finds unpleasant tasting. What is characteristic of such a desire seems to be that it is a desire of something as a means, in the first case to the end of sexual, and in the second to the end of alimentary, satisfaction or pleasure. In such cases we may say that the ultimate object of the desire is the end, and the desire of the end is the same as the vivid awareness of its goodness as satisfaction or as pleasure (surely an intrinsic goodness). The desire for the means, on the other hand, is of a very different nature—it is in part awareness of the means-end relationship and in part awareness of the intrinsic goodness of the end. Such desire is compatible with the awareness of the means as intrinsically undesirable.

Inattention to the even more evident heterogeneity of the applications of the term "want" has led to facile arguments for psychological hedonism such as the following: (1) One freely chooses to do x only if one wants to do x. (2) One wants to do x only if one expects some pleasure in (from) doing x. (3) Therefore, one freely chooses to do x only if one expects some pleasure in (from) doing x.[28] The argument rests on equivocation in the use of "want," between what have been called its intentional sense and its inclinational sense.[29] In the former it is more or less a synonym of "(freely) chooses" or "would (freely) choose," and in that sense (1) is trivially true. In the latter sense it is a synonym of "has an inclination to choose x," and only in this sense is (2) even remotely plausible.

After all this has been said, however, we must admit that the questions of the motivating function of knowledge of goodness, of the nature of desire, and of the relation between "desire" and "reason" cannot be adequately answered until we have a theoretically defensible, even if sketchy, general phenomenology of the nature of consciousness, and also a reasonably detailed account of what goods there are. Abstract reasoning and randomly selected examples are not enough. We shall return to this question, therefore, in chapter 5, when we will be ready to give it a more adequate and detailed answer.

## 3. Is and Ought

According to a second variety of ethical skepticism, to be traced directly to Hume, [30] no ethical statement follows deductively (or indeed inductively) from any nonethical statement or set of nonethical statements. "Ought" cannot be inferred from "is." Indeed, this is so, though a defense of the claim would need to show the irrelevance of various counterexamples, such as the inference from "It is sunny outside" to "It is sunny outside or one ought to keep one's promises." But the skeptical conclusion, namely, that we cannot know or even have reason for believing any ethical statement to be true, does not follow from the deductive or inductive nonderivability of ethical statements from nonethical statements. Statements about shapes cannot be deductively or inductively inferred from statements that are solely about colors, and indeed *nonethical* statements cannot be deductively or inductively inferred from *ethical* statements. But this is hardly a ground for skepticism regarding geometry or, say, the empirical sciences.

Moreover, in addition to deduction and induction, there are valid inferences legitimized by what philosophers have sometimes called synthetic a priori connections. I can infer that this page is not blue from the fact that it is white. The inference is neither deductive nor inductive, but surely it is as valid as any deductive or inductive inference. Now, a statement attributing goodness to a property, for example, "Happiness is good," might be a synthetic a priori statement, like the statement that no surface is both white and blue throughout at the same time. If so, then that a certain person's life is at least partially good could be validly inferred from the premise that it is a happy life.

It is not just that ethical statements can be validly inferred from nonethical statements in this way. It is not clear that inferences of the converse sort, of what is from what would be good or ought to be, are never valid. A familiar example is the claim that the existence of the world follows from the goodness of its creator. A less familiar but extremely interesting claim is that, even if the world has no creator, it exists because it is better that something rather than nothing should exist. [31] The temptation to scoff at such an explanation of the existence of the world is more a sign of a narrow view of the nature of explanation than of any obvious difficulty in the idea. Whether the explanation is adequate is, of course, a different question.

## 4. Why Should I Do What I Ought to Do?

A third, and far more interesting, variety of ethical skepticism we owe chiefly to the existentialist philosophers, though something like an appeal to it is often made also by analytic philosophers. Let us admit, the skeptic would now say, that there is objective goodness, and that we do have knowledge of ethical facts. But while an analogous admission with respect to any other target of philosophical skepticism (for example, the existence and knowability of an external world) would constitute surrender, the skeptic would say, this is not so in the case of ethics. For ethics is concerned not only with knowledge and belief, but also with decision, with choice. It is a practical, even though not merely practical, discipline. The primary ethical problem is the justification of human decision. But any appeal to objective ethical facts, or to ethical knowledge, or to ethical evidence, itself constitutes a decision, the decision to make the appeal, to be guided by those facts, that knowledge, that evidence. Clearly, *this* decision cannot itself be justified by the ethical facts, or knowledge, or evidence. But nothing else can justify it. Yet unless it can be justified, no other decision or action can really be regarded as justified by the ethical facts, knowledge, or evidence, regardless of how objective and unquestionable these might be.

This skeptical challenge may be put more bluntly as the question, Even if I know what I ought to do, why should I do it? This question is, of course, ambiguous, and to appreciate its importance we must make clear that it is not intended here to be understood in any of the following three familiar ways. First, as demanding why I should sometimes sacrifice my own good for the good of others. This, the egoist's question, I shall consider in chapter 6. Second, as acknowledging the possibility (often actuality) of conflict between what I know I ought to do and my inclinations (whether egoistic or altruistic), and then demanding a reason for doing what I know I ought to do rather than following my inclinations. The demand is unreasonable because by hypothesis all the relevant reasons for either decision have already been taken into account, and therefore there is no room left for further deliberation. There is room only for decision.[32] Yet, because of the presence of contrary inclinations, it is natural to make this unreasonable demand. We *feel* a need for further reassurance that the ethical judgment is indeed true, if we are to accept it and act in accordance with it, even when all the reasons that can be given for regarding it as true have already been given. We have a special stake in the question of its truth. This is why we make epistemological demands on ethics that it would never occur to us to make on physics or mathematics. This is why we think that there is a special problem about the justifiability of ethical judgments. The feeling, of course, is unreasonable. Even outside ethics, if we prove to someone that a certain argument is valid and its premises true, this does not entail that he will accept the conclusion, and we can give him no further reasons for accepting it. He will either accept it or (if, for example, it is too painful) not accept it, or at least not act in accordance with it, but not as a result of further reasoning, whether his own or ours. It's just that the latter sort of case seldom occurs outside ethics, while in ethics it is common, for the reason I have given. The truth is that both in ethics and outside ethics argument comes to an end, and one either accepts the conclusion and, if possible, acts on it, or one does not. That this is so is an important fact, but it supports skepticism in ethics no more than it supports skepticism in logic.

The third misunderstanding of our question, Why should I do what I ought to do? consists in the supposition that the word "should" in it has a sense different from that of "ought." If the supposed sense of "Why should I?" is "Is it in my interest?" then the question is merely the first one we have discussed. If it asks generally what motivation I have, it has already been dealt with in our discussion of the second question. But it may be supposed that "should" here has an ethical sense, that it expresses, so to speak, "a higher ought" than that expressed by the word "ought" in the sentence. Indeed, this could be so, for the word "ought" in the sentence might be so understood that "what I ought to do" is a synonym of "what is generally believed that one ought to do," and then of course the whole sentence would be perfectly straightforward, but irrelevant. It would simply mean, Why ought I to do what is generally believed that one ought to do? To be relevant, the question must be so understood that in it "ought" has the standard ethical sense and "should" also has a purely ethical sense as expressing, so to speak, a higher ought. But what is this higher ought? The truth is that, once we have made the needed distinctions and avoided the usual ambiguities, we see that the idea of such an ought is vacuous.

For the question to be interesting, the skeptic must understand it as being simply, Why ought I to do what I ought to do? in which "ought" is used in the same sense in both of its occurrences. And the skeptic's challenge is that this question makes sense, has a point, and yet cannot be answered, even though it appears to be questioning an obvious tautology, that is, "I ought to do what I ought to do." (Or, "Given that I ought to do such and such, then I ought to do such and such." Compare the question "Is something that is such and such, such and such?" and the answer "Given that it is such and such, then it is such and such.") Sartre might explain the anomaly by drawing attention to the essential capability of man to decenter himself, to put a distance between himself and any reality, even if that reality is he himself.[33] And to join him in concluding that since the question cannot be answered, nothing justifies human decision, or to join Nietzsche in rejoicing in our freedom to legislate our values, would be merely to acknowledge that the skeptic has won.

But has he? What he really demands when he asks for an answer to the question, Why ought I to do what I ought to do? is an answer that would *compel* him to be moral, to do what he ought to do. Indeed, Sartre's insistence that values, though qualities of *objects*, not of any inner states of consciousness, are placed in objects *by* consciousness, and therefore are in some sense unreal, seems motivated entirely by his belief that if this were not so then one would not be free, that the reality of values is incompatible with human freedom, that if values were parts of reality then they would be "forces having a certain power over us."[34] According to him, the belief, characteristic of everyday morality, that values are parts of reality is nothing but a variety of bad faith, of the self-deception by means of which we attempt to flee from what he calls anguish. And anguish for Sartre is the consciousness of our absolute, "monstrous" freedom. Insofar as the self-deception is successful, he says, I find myself "engaged in a world of values." This is the immediate world with its urgency, and in this world "my acts cause values to spring up like partridges." But "my freedom is the unique foundation of values and . . . *nothing*, absolutely nothing, justifies me in adopting this or that particular value, this or that particular scale of values. As a being by whom values exist, I am unjustifiable. My freedom is anguished at being the foundation of values while itself without foundation."[35] In this part of his philosophy, Sartre, of course, followed Nietzsche, who had argued that the death of God, that is, our ceasing to believe in God and therefore to regard our beliefs about values as having the firm foundation of the authority of an omniscient and omnibenevolent being, liberates us by rendering us free to legislate our own values. Nietzsche seemed to rejoice in this newly found freedom, comparing it to the freedom of a bird that has been let out of its cage, but also seemed to have some misgivings, observing that the liberated bird now finds itself flying over an endless ocean and has no idea in what direction to fly.[36] There is much more to Nietzsche's and Sartre's views about values, of course, but these are the ones relevant to our topic here.

All this, I suggest, is a confusion, though an important one. At the bottom, it is a confusion of the question, What *ought* I to do? with the question, What *shall* I do?[37] The answer to neither question entails an answer to the other, although an omniscient and perfectly virtuous person would do (or at least try to do) only what he or she ought to do and everything that he or she ought to do, this being a trivial consequence of the concepts of omniscience and virtue. The answer to the original question, Why ought I to do what I ought to do?—the question that constitutes the foundation of the Nietzchean and Sartrean view under discussion— is simply: because it is what I ought to do. This question is quite different from the question, *Shall* I do what I ought to do? with which it is confused. Ethics neither does nor should attempt to provide us with an answer to the latter. There is a sense in which the individual person alone can answer it, and of course he answers it primarily in his actions, not words. Nietzsche and Sartre confuse the two questions and this is why they believe that the reality of values is incompatible with human freedom.

Indeed, a person is not free to violate the principle that one ought to do what one ought to do, since this principle is a mere tautology; a violation of it would be an action that is both one the person ought to perform and one that the person ought not to perform. No degree of freedom of the will can allow a person, even God, to perform a self-contradictory action. (I ignore here the uninteresting sense in which a person may violate a principle by denying it.) But a person may still *be* free to do and also free not to do what he ought to do, even what he *knows* he ought to do. And certainly he may want to do what he knows he ought not to do. We are free to be immoral; indeed, this is the most important manifestation of our freedom, and, if we follow Augustine, the source of our pride and therefore of sin. That our being immoral is an objective fact is no more incompatible with our freedom than is the recognition of this objective fact a guarantee of moral conduct. For knowledge of what we ought to be and do is only one motive among many for performing an action. There are also what Kant called our inclinations: desires, feelings, emotions, both egoistic and altruistic, even if, as I have argued, at least some desires consist in consciousness of the real or apparent goodness of their objects. (That an object is good does not entail that we ought to produce it; producing it may have very bad other consequences.) The moral life is typically a battle between virtue and such inclinations. Perhaps Socrates was right in believing that possession of the highest kind or degree of knowledge of what we ought to do would necessarily lead to our doing it. Yet it is not the reality of values that would have this miraculous result, but rather the possession of a miraculous kind or degree of *knowledge* of values.

John Rawls has argued, in connection with Kant, that "Heteronomy obtains not only when first principles are fixed by the special psychological constitution of human nature, as in Hume, but also when they are fixed by an order of universals or concepts grasped by rational intuition, as in Plato's realm of forms or in Leibniz's hierarchy of perfections."[38] I cannot discuss here whether this is adequate exegesis of Kant, nor can I attempt to deal with Rawls's own very difficult notion of autonomy. Suffice it to say that Kant's epistemology prevented him from taking seriously the alternative provided by Platonism. At least part of the explanation of his emphasis on the moral autonomy of the will is to be found in his belief that only thus could the necessary and a priori character of moral principles be understood. But Platonism suggests another, in my opinion far more comprehensible, way. If by the autonomy of the person (the will) is meant (Kant does not mean this) that the person *chooses* or *decides*, however consistently, what ethical judgments are to count as moral laws, without being guided by knowledge of objective moral truths, then the Platonist would say that the proper word is not "autonomy" but "anomie." (Indeed, Sartre too argued that values cannot have their foundation in "being" because this would "realize the heteronomy of my will."[39] But I believe he would have agreed that the correct description of what he took to be the actual situation is "anomie," not "autonomy," of the will). On the other hand, if what is meant by autonomy is that nothing restricts the person's freedom to accept or reject, or to choose to act in accordance with or in violation of, any proposed ethical judgments, whether or not these express moral laws, then the issue is that of free will; whether moral laws are fixed by an order of universals or not is irrelevant. It is worth noting that the Platonic Forms would belong to the intelligible, not the sensible world, and that the relationship of our intellectual intuition of them to the will would be totally unlike the relationship of our sensuous inclinations or even of the purely rational objects of volition (for example, perfection) to the will. It was in terms of the latter relationship that Kant in fact understood heteronomy.

To be sure, as I argued in the previous section, there is an intimate connection between the belief or consciousness that we ought to do a certain action and our doing it (or between the belief or consciousness that a certain thing is good and our having a "pro-attitude" toward it). This connection has received much emphasis in recent analytic ethics, but for the purpose of showing that ethical terms cannot be purely descriptive. The truth, however, I have argued, is that it is of the very nature of ethical belief or consciousness to constitute a motive, a desire, even if not a very strong one, for action. And sometimes this motive or desire does result in action. But this is so not because the belief is not about objective values, as even as astute a moral philosopher as J. N. Findlay has, surprisingly, argued,[40] but because of a deep, hardly understood, and seldom explored fact about human nature. It is not unlike the equally deep and also hardly understood and seldom explored fact that usually we aim at believing what is true, that usually we do accept the conclusions of arguments we regard as sound, not merely for prudential reasons but for the sake of truth itself. This is a fact not about the nature of truth but about the nature of human beings. In the eighteenth century Richard Price wrote: "As there are some propositions, which, when attended to, necessarily determine all minds to *believe* them: And as . . . there are some ends, whose natures are such, that, when perceived, all beings immediately and necessarily *desire* them: So it is very credible, that, in like manner, there are some actions whose natures are such that, when observed, all rational beings immediately and necessarily *approve* them."[41] I should only add that at least some rational beings also *act* on such approval.

## 5. *Phenomenological Skepticism*

The varieties of skepticism in ethics we have examined so far are perhaps not particularly serious, although the third has forced us to provide a needed clarification of the role of objective values. Far more serious is a fourth variety, which argues that there is not a real property such as goodness and therefore there is nothing real for which the words "right," "ought," "virtue," and "duty," all of which I have defined in terms of "good," may stand, because neither do we perceive such a property nor is it a datum of any mode of consciousness or awareness other than perception. As the passage from Stevenson with which this book began shows, were it not for this conviction, the first two varieties of ethical skepticism we examined would be mere observations about certain aspects of the uses of ethical terms and about the logical relations between ethical and nonethical statements. And were it not for this conviction, the confusions in which the third variety was found to be involved would be too evident to be made, at least in the case of Nietzsche, who regarded the death of God as having extraordinary implications for man only because he took for granted that values could have an objective foundation only in God. So we embark now on an examination of this crucial fourth variety of skepticism in ethics. Our examination of it will not be concluded until chapter 7, where we will briefly consider also a fifth and a sixth variety. But we shall find that the most serious is a seventh variety of skepticism, itself divisible into two versions; it will be the topic of the final chapter 8.

In 1739 Hume wrote: "Take any action allow'd to be vicious: Wilful murder, for instance. Examine it in all lights, and see if you can find that matter of fact, or real existence, which you call vice. . . . The vice entirely escapes you, as long as you consider the object."[42] He meant by "vice" and "virtue" roughly evil and good, not what we have defined these terms to mean.

But a very different view of the phenomenological availability of objective values was defended by the most important British twentieth-century moral philosopher, as well as by the most important continental twentieth-century moral philosopher. In 1903 G. E. Moore wrote: " . . . 'good' has no definition because it is simple and has no parts. It is one of those innumerable objects of thought which are themselves incapable of definition, because they are the ultimate terms by reference to which whatever *is* capable of definition must be defined. . . . There is, therefore, no intrinsic difficulty in the contention that 'good' denotes a simple and indefinable quality. There are many other instances of such qualities. Consider yellow, for example."[43] And in 1913 Max Scheler wrote: "Values are *clearly feelable phenomena.*" Also, "there are *authentic* and *true* value-qualities and . . . they constitute a special domain of objectivities."[44] And again, " 'good' and 'evil' . . . are *clearly feelable* . . . values. . . . All that can be requested is that one attend to seeing precisely what is immediately experienced in feeling good and evil."[45]

It is difficult to judge by examining their work whether Moore and Scheler were right, since both are extraordinarily obscure on this issue, though in different ways: Moore, as I noted at the beginning of this book, by failing to provide sufficient explanations, and Scheler by providing ample but often unhelpful explanations. Surely, the truth is that goodness is not given to consciousness in the simple and unquestionable way in which a specific shade of yellow, or a thrill of pleasure or a pang of pain, is given. And the further claim ordinarily made that goodness is necessarily given to consciousness as mysteriously supervening on some other and indeed categorially different, yet equally specific or determinate, property or properties[46] only compounds the phenomenological absurdity. (We must not imagine that we achieve understanding through a purely formal definition of supervenience such as the following: "a normative property G 'supervenes on' a nonnormative property H, provided only: H is necessarily such that whatever has it has G, but not necessarily such that whoever attributes it attributes G."[47] Formal definitions seldom produce understanding.) Moore's and Scheler's phenomenological claims strengthen the skeptic's case, since, at least on the surface, they are so obviously false. And if they were true, how would we explain the fact that so many philosophers have failed to find what Moore and Scheler so easily found?

But to reject this fourth variety of skepticism in ethics we need not compare goodness with a specific shade of yellow, or with a pleasure or a pain. Indeed, if only such as these could be objects of awareness or consciousness (I shall use these terms as synonyms), then goodness could not be. But to accept the antecedent of this conditional is in effect to accept Hume's general phenomenology. And our conception of consciousness and of its objects must be subtler than Hume's. That this is so is the lasting contribution of the continental phenomenological tradition, of Brentano, Meinong, Husserl, Sartre. As long as we regard consciousness as nothing more than simple sense perception and introspection, as Hume did, then of course it follows that virtue and vice, but also generic colors and shapes, numbers, material objects, and causal connections, are not objects of consciousness. We neither see them nor feel them as we see specific colors and shapes and feel particular pleasures and pains.

But what grounds do we have for so limiting consciousness? As Berkeley had found himself forced to admit before Hume, there is such a thing as considering or attending to the generic property of a triangle, to its triangularity as such, without attending to its specific property, namely, to its being a scalene, or an isosceles, or an equilateral triangle (one does this regularly in learning and teaching geometry).[48] Indeed, according to Berkeley, one cannot form an *idea* (i.e., an image) of a triangle that is not an idea of a scalene or an isosceles or an equilateral triangle. But even if this is so, the fact is that Berkeley acknowledges the existence of a consciousness of triangularity in general, a consciousness of a generic property. This consciousness, though hardly describable as purely intellectual intuition, one that is quite distinct from the perception of the triangular surface, is not mere sense perception. We do not *see* two properties, the isosceles triangle and the triangle in general, in a particular surface.

But it is to the European phenomenological tradition, not to Berkeley, that we must look for detailed applications of the broader, non-Humean conception of consciousness. Husserl argued repeatedly that even in sense perception the usual object is not just the front surface of a body, to say nothing of a mere colored expanse, but a body as a whole, as having a complete three-dimensional surface, and insides, and an immediate past and an immediate future, of all of which we are conscious, even if not in the "filled-out" way in which we are conscious of the front surface. Meinong argued that we can be conscious, at least in thought, of nonexistent objects, such as a golden mountain, and even know certain truths about them. Or, to take another, very different example, when I imagine Peter, as both Sartre and Ryle argued at great length, it is Peter I am conscious of, and not, as Hume claimed, an internal mental picture of Peter. But this imaginative consciousness of Peter is neither sense perception nor introspection. Nor, to take another example from Sartre, is the consciousness of Peter-as-not-being-in-the-café, when one looks for him in the café but fails to find him, sense perception or introspection, and it is certainly not merely the making of a judgment. And, as we have already noted, even in experiencing an emotion, according to Sartre it is the world, including one's body, that one is conscious of, and not some internal mental occurrence only contingently related to one's body and the world.

Once the constraints of the Humean conception of consciousness are thus loosened, his denial that we can find the vice, the evil, in a case of murder no longer appears obviously correct. To be sure, we don't see it as we see a specific shade of yellow, but are we not conscious of it, as well as of the virtue, the goodness, in a case of charity, perhaps somewhat in the way we are conscious of the triangularity of a scalene triangle we see?

But after all this has been said, we must admit that the fourth variety of skepticism in ethics has not been answered adequately. It does not suffice to render implausible the narrow, Humean conception of consciousness. An adequate answer must rest on an adequate *general* phenomenology, on an adequate metaphysics, and on an adequate epistemology. We require a phenomenology that would show on the basis of considerations concerning the nature of conciousness in general, rather than on the basis of specific and bare phenomenological appeals, that if there is what may be neutrally described as ethical or moral consciousness, it can only be a consciousness of objective ethical or moral properties, even if these be in some sense illusory, unreal, rather than of internal, subjective states, whether emotional or attitudinal. We require a metaphysics that would provide an adequate, intelligible, account of what the properties in question would be, if there really were such properties, in particular an account of goodness, and of the sort of relationship that is supposed to hold between goodness and the properties (what in chapter 2 I called "the abstract goods") exemplifying it. Only then would it be at all plausible to believe that these properties themselves have such a property as goodness, for only then would we find this belief *intelligible*. And we require an epistemology that would legitimize the claim that we do have *knowledge* of such a property as goodness and therefore that there really is such a property. For might not ethical consciousness still be an illusory consciousness, an ethical hallucination, as Sartre himself thought, even if metaphysics has assured us that its objects are intelligible, that they *can* be real? Or, might not the belief in the existence of an ethical consciousness of the required kind be a conceptual illusion, a phenomenological misunderstanding? Metaphysics tells us what is possible, not what is actual; and knowledge of what is actual can never be based on mere phenomenological appeals. This last point requires explanation.

A color is given phenomenologically as a property of an object, certainly not as a property of our consciousness of the object.[49] And there are no general *metaphysical* puzzles about the possibility of such properties of objects. But from this it does not follow (as the history of epistemology amply testifies) that the color given phenomenologically as a property of an object is the real color of the object, or even that any colors are real properties of objects. Indeed, four sentences after the passage I quoted earlier, Hume concluded: "Vice and virtue, therefore, may be compared to sounds, colors, heat and cold, which, according to modern philosophy, are not qualities in objects, but perceptions in the mind." And W. D. Ross, who accepted what he called "an objective view of goodness,"[50] defended a subjective view of beauty[51] explicitly on the grounds that there is a connection between beauty and such qualities as colors, regarding which he wrote: "For my own part, reflection on the facts of perception and of its illusions forces me to think that there is no such thing as objective colour."[52] Earlier, R. B. Perry had argued against "that pan-objectivism which, having concluded that the so-called 'secondary qualities,' such as color, have as good a title to extra-mental existence as the so-called primary qualities, such as figure, sees no reason why the so-called 'tertiary qualities,' such as good, should not be assigned the same status."[53]

But even if we can show that ethical consciousness is not an illusory consciousness, we would still need to show that the belief in the existence of an ethical consciousness *of the required kind* is not a conceptual illusion, the result of radical though understandable misclassification, like the classification of a shade of grey as white, of an ellipse as a circle, of the whale as a fish. Indeed, one can interpret the first variety of ethical skepticism that we considered in this chapter as claiming that a realist theory of ethics is based on just such a conceptual illusion, if not on a misclassification of the phenomenological facts then at least on a misclassification of the uses of ethical terms, of treating terms that are mainly nondescriptive as purely descriptive, on a mistake in what Austin called linguistic phenomenology.

I begin with the first question I have distinguished, namely, the general phenomenological question, What sort of "thing" must consciousness be if appeals to its data are to be legitimate in our inquiry?

## 6. The General Phenomenology
## Required to Rebut the Skeptic

The general phenomenology I believe we require was developed in great detail by Sartre in his early phenomenological writings. It corresponds to some extent to much of what Gilbert Ryle says in *The Concept of Mind* and elsewhere—not surprisingly so, since Ryle too had some knowledge of Husserlian phenomenology.[54] Corresponding to what Ryle called the myth of the ghost in the machine is what Sartre called the illusion of immanence. Ryle opposed "the notion that a mind is a 'place,' where mental pictures are seen and reproductions of voices and tunes are heard."[55] And Sartre wrote: "We pictured consciousness as a place peopled with small likenesses and these likenesses were the images. No doubt but that this misconception arises from our habit of thinking in space and in terms of space. This we shall call: *the illusion of immanence.*"[56] Sartre viewed his conception of consciousness as the logical development of Husserl's theory of the intentionality of consciousness, a development which required that consciousness be denied all immanence, that it be allowed no inhabitants, not even Husserl's transcendental ego or Husserl's *hyle*.

> All consciousness, as Husserl has shown, is consciousness of something. This means that there is no consciousness which is not a *positing* of a transcendent object, or if you prefer, that consciousness has no "content." . . . A table is not *in* consciousness—not even in the capacity of a representation. . . . The first procedure of philosophy ought to be to expel things from consciousness and to reestablish its true connection with the world, to know that consciousness is a positional consciousness *of* the world. All consciousness is positional in that it transcends itself in order to reach an object, and it exhausts itself in this same positing.[57]

This is why pure subjectivity is an impossibility.[58] Consciousness is not being in itself but a relation to being in itself, to the world.[59]

An immediate consequence of this conception is that a state of consciousness owes its distinctive character solely to its object, or more precisely to the object as it is given to that state of consciousness. The consciousness in itself has no character, no content, is pure transparence, translucence; if considered in abstraction from its object it is *nothing*, since "all physical, psycho-physical, and psychic objects, all truths, all values are outside it. . . . There is no longer an 'inner life.' "[60] Sartre's works abound with applications of this view, some of which I have already noted.

"*Representation*, as a psychic event, is a pure invention of philosophers."[61] "As soon as we abandon the hypothesis of the contents of consciousness, we must recognize that there is never a motive *in* consciousness; motives are only *for* consciousness."[62] "To have sympathy for Peter is to be conscious of Peter as sympathetic."[63] If I pity Peter there is for my consciousness the quality Peter-having-to-be-helped, and "this quality of 'having to be helped' lies in Peter."[64] "When I run after a streetcar . . . there is consciousness of the *streetcar-having-to-be-overtaken*."[65] To desire is to apprehend in the object the quality of desirability.[66]

If consciousness in general is as described by Sartre, then ethical or moral consciousness, the existence of which surely cannot be denied, may only be consciousness of ethical or moral objects or properties. It cannot consist in the occurrence of what Ryle would have described as ghostly episodes within oneself, having an intrinsic character, presumably "emotional" or "attitudinal," and only contingently related, if at all, to their so-called objects. To morally approve of something, we must say, can only be to be conscious of it as moral, to be conscious of its moral goodness, even if this were illusory. Ethical consciousness must be consciousness of certain objective values, of certain properties of objects, even if, as Sartre indeed thought, these were in some sense unreal, since there is nothing else it could be. And the values must be objective in the straightforward sense that they can be only *objects* of consciousness, they could not be *in* consciousness, they could not be *subjective*, since there is *nothing* in consciousness. Let me emphasize that this conclusion is intended to follow not from a specific phenomenological examination of moral or ethical consciousness, but from the phenomenological examination of consciousness in general.

The conception of consciousness Moore defends in his revolutionary article "The Refutation of Idealism,"[67] published in the same year as *Principia Ethica*, as well as in his unjustly neglected later article "The Subject Matter of Psychology,"[68] is strikingly similar to Sartre's. He rejects the mental contents theory, according to which "the object of an experience is in reality merely a content or inseparable aspect of that experience," and defends what has been called the act-object, or intentionality, theory, according to which the "peculiar relation . . . of 'awareness of anything' . . . is involved equally in the analysis of *every* experience. . . . [and is] the only thing which gives us reason to call any fact mental."[69] He even describes consciousness, very much as Sartre much later was to describe it, as something that seems to be "transparent,"[70] is "diaphanous," and thus seems to be "a mere emptiness."[71] And, applying this conception of consciousness to perceptual consciousness, he asserts: "There is, therefore, no question of how we are to 'get outside the circle of our own ideas and sensations.' Merely to have a sensation is already to *be* outside that circle. It is to know something which is as truly and really *not* a part of *my* experience, as anything which I can ever know."[72] It would be merely another application of the same reasoning to say that to be in a state of ethical consciousness can only be to be conscious of ("know") ethical objects or properties which in no sense are a part of the consciousness itself. One such property would be goodness.[73]

I noted in chapter 1 that such a conception of consciousness would be described by Hilary Putnam as magical.[74] The sarcasm of the description is quite unjustified, though it may be excused as just another manifestation of the reigning fashion in current philosophy. This is not the place to try to *show* that it is unjustified. To do so would require an examination of a whole world-picture. But, as I noted in chapter 1, the scientism and physicalism characteristic of this world-picture have been rejected by Putnam himself in his more recent writings.

Of course, the *metaphysical* status of consciousness as described by Moore and Sartre must be subjected to detailed examination, no longer one based only on phenomenology. Can consciousness be a relation to the world, if, as Sartre argued and Moore hinted,[75] there is no ego to serve as one of the two relata? But the present book is not the place for a discussion of this issue. For our purposes here it may be better to avoid the frequent illusions of understanding produced by the employment of such technical terms as "relation," and follow Heidegger in simply saying that a phenomenon is that which shows itself in itself. The task of a phenomenology of values would then be to let values show themselves in themselves.[76] That such Heideggerian descriptions do not fit in any of the familiar technical slots of philosophy is a merit, not a defect, if the facts about consciousness do not fit in any of those slots.

But it would be parochial to suppose that we should not have engaged in phenomenological discussions without first offering a metaphysical theory of consciousness, and especially a defense of the possibility or at least the relevance of phenomenological appeals. The truth is that thoroughgoing realists in ethics, such as Plato and Moore, have rested their realist views chiefly on their belief that they are *aware* of such a property as goodness. And the truth is also that their opponents have rested *their* views chiefly on their belief that they are *not* aware of such a property. Both have been confident that their respective beliefs are true, quite apart from any particular views about the nature of awareness or consciousness. That their disagreement about the phenomenological facts is genuine and important must be taken for granted by any serious study of the issue of skepticism in ethics. If a particular metaphysical theory or philosophy of mind does not allow us to do so, if it denies the legitimacy and relevance of phenomenological appeals, then so much the worse for it.

CHAPTER FOUR

# The Nature of Good

## 1. The Metaphysics Required to Rebut the Skeptic

Even though the conclusion that we are aware of objective ethical properties, and therefore that the fourth, Humean variety of skepticism is false, does *seem* to follow from a general phenomenology that I believe is superior to its existing alternatives and that seems supported by the phenomenological facts about consciousness, we require also an answer to the metaphysical question, What sort of property would goodness be if there were such a property? As we shall see, this answer will modify our phenomenological conclusion significantly. We require also an answer to the epistemological question, Do we, and if we do, how do we, *know* that there is such a property and that certain abstract entities exemplify it? But we will not attempt to answer it until chapter 7. It cannot be properly understood except on the basis of the detailed metaphysical discussions in this and the next two chapters. I shall continue to write as if the epistemological question has been answered, but only for the sake of expository simplicity. Everything I shall say in this and the next two chapters could be merely a description of a massive ethical hallucination.

It is appropriate and instructive to begin our consideration of the metaphysical question with G. E. Moore's classic discussion of it, which largely determined the course of British and American ethics in the twentieth century. Moore's answer was that goodness is a simple, indefinable, and nonnatural property. He rejected any accounts of it as a relational property, for example, that of being desired or that of being approved, on the grounds that they commit the naturalistic fallacy and, later, that they either lead to contradiction or make the fact of ethical disagreement incomprehensible. But we have already seen (chapter 2, section 7, and chapter 3, sections 1 and 2) that there are more convincing reasons for rejecting such accounts, namely, that at least some species of the psychological attitudes to which they appeal involve awareness of goodness and thus cannot be noncircularly mentioned in an account of goodness. So goodness, if there is such a property at all, is a monadic property. According to Moore, it is simple in the straightforward sense that it has no parts, and indefinable because a real definition (Moore had no interest in nominal definitions of "good") is an account of the parts of the thing defined and of their arrangement.[1] It is nonnatural in the sense that, though a property of natural objects, that is, objects that "exist in time," it cannot exist in time *by itself*. The natural properties of a natural object, on the other hand, can exist in time by themselves because they are "parts of which the object is made up rather than mere predicates which attach to it," since "they are in themselves substantial and give to the object all the substance that it has."[2] In another, later work, he asserted that goodness "depends *only* on the intrinsic nature of what possesses it" and "*though* this is so, it is yet not itself an intrinsic property,"[3] in the sense that, unlike the thing's intrinsic properties, it need not be mentioned in a complete description of the thing.[4] But he remained dissatisfied with all of these formulations.[5]

Moore seemed to regard simplicity and indefinability as logically equivalent, though I doubt he would have said they are the same property. (He was notoriously scrupulous about identifying properties, and in *Ethics* even took back his claim in *Principia Ethica* that "right" can be defined in terms of "good.")[6] But it is not at all clear that they are logically equivalent. If we say that a thing is simple if and only if it has no parts, much would depend on what we allow to be counted as parts. And if by "definition" we mean not what Moore seemed to mean, namely, a mere enumeration of parts and description of their arrangement, but what Aristotle and the medieval philosophers meant, namely a description of the thing in terms of its genus and differentia (Moore's example of a definition, that of a horse, on page 8 of *Principia Ethica* is just such a definition), then we must ask whether the genus and the differentia are parts, or correspond to parts, of the thing defined. (Throughout this book I shall mean by species, genera, and differentiae properties, not the open classes of individuals these properties determine.) Moreover, in some cases we can state the genus of a thing but not its differentia, while in others we can do neither.

Moore gave yellow as an example of a simple and indefinable, though natural, property. On the stipulation (explicitly made by him) that by "yellow" we should mean what today would be called a phenomenal property, it seems reasonable to hold that yellow has no parts. (If we distinguished its hue, degree of saturation, and degree of brightness and called them its parts, then at least these would have no parts.)[7] But we can assert that yellow is a color, just as blue, red, etc., are colors; in other words, we can state the genus to which it belongs. Indeed, we seem unable to find a differentia that can be nontautologically named. We could of course say that the differentia is yellow, but we would not regard "Yellow is yellow color" as a definition. Yet, if we introduced another word for that color, say, "wolley," could we not regard yellow as expressing the differentia of wolley and propose the definition "Wolley is yellow color"? Is the alleged indefinability of yellow a linguistic accident, or does it issue from the very nature of color? And why do shapes have definitions, indeed the standard examples of definition, for example, "A triangle is a closed plane three-sided figure," "A cube is a six-faced regular polyhedron"? Could it be because there is a sense in which shapes have parts, for example, a triangle consists of its three sides, a cube of its six faces? But does a circle really consist of the points mentioned in its definition? And can we not define a point as a dimensionless position in space, even though it follows from this definition that a point has no parts? And in the case of paradigmatic definitions, even if they are possible only for properties that in some sense have parts, we certainly do not want to say that the genus and the differentia mentioned in the definition are parts of what is defined.

Being a closed plane figure and being three-sided are hardly parts of being a triangle, not even in the sense in which the three sides of a triangle may be said to be parts of it. I shall return to this point.

Clearly, the simplicity and indefinability of goodness are not at all straightforward matters, as long as we are guided by the idea of the simplicity and indefinability of a property such as yellow. But it is not examples such as colors that are the paradigms of indefinable properties. The absence of suitable differentiae for them is hardly a matter of logical necessity. The paradigms of indefinable properties are the properties that would count as summa genera, not as infimae species—for it is a tautology that the former do not fall under a higher genus, and therefore that they are indefinable according to the classical conception of definition. Could it be that goodness is not definable because it is a summun genus? Now, what summa genera there are and whether a certain property is indeed a summum genus are, of course, not matters to decide from a purely logical point of view. Perhaps color is a summum genus, perhaps property, perhaps only being. Is goodness a summum genus, some of its subgenera being perhaps, as Moore suggests, personal affection, aesthetic enjoyment, knowledge, pleasure? If it is, then indeed it would be indefinable, in a perfectly clear, quite noncontroversial, not at all mysterious sense. And it would also be simple, for not even the distinction between the genus and the differentia of a property, which often produces the illusion of complexity, would be applicable to it; nor would it make sense to speak of its subgenera as parts of it, as long as we do not confuse properties, whether genera or species, with the open classes they determine. But the more important question seems to me to be not whether goodness is a summum genus and therefore indefinable, but whether it is a genus, a generic property at all. I believe that a Moorean ethics is defensible only if the answer to that latter question is affirmative. And if it is affirmative, then of course goodness cannot be an infima species. Moreover, the answer provides us with an immediate and reasonable explanation of a not at all mysterious sense in which goodness may also be described as a nonnatural property.

Moore's idea, mentioned earlier, that the natural properties of a thing are parts of it, that they constitute it, and therefore that each of them could be imagined as existing all by itself, is by no means novel. It is the usual conclusion reached by philosophers who reject the existence of a substratum in which the properties of an individual thing are supposed to inhere. It is the conclusion that an individual thing is in some sense a bundle or cluster of properties. Indeed, in 1899 this was exactly the view that Moore defended, although he considered the properties in question to be universals (he called them concepts but made clear that by this he did not mean any mental entities but rather "universal meanings"). "An existent is seen to be nothing but a concept or a complex of concepts standing in a unique relation to the concept of existence."[8] But he soon drastically revised this view. In 1901, in an article of great philosophical importance but now largely ignored, he argued that in addition to universals there are the particular properties (for example, this red, that red) which exemplify them. When we say, " 'The red at this place is the same as the red at that place' . . . we are asserting that two things numerically different have the same relation to one universal (a particular tint of red)."[9] The constituents of an individual thing would be these particular properties, not the universals they exemplify. He makes the distinction between particular and universal properties also in his article "Qualities" in Baldwin's *Dictionary of Philosophy and Psychology*. Presumably, then, in *Principia Ethica* it is such particular properties that are parts of an individual thing and might be supposed to exist in time all by themselves. Indeed, he remained sympathetic to this theory of universals in his 1910–11 lectures, which were published in 1953 as *Some Main Problems of Philosophy*,[10] though there (as he admits in the Appendix added in 1952) the discussion is marred by his giving patches of color as examples of particular "properties."[11]

While the particular properties of an individual thing would be in time, the universals they exemplify would not be in time. Therefore, by the definition of a nonnatural property given in *Principia Ethica*, they would be nonnatural properties and presumably what Moore called there "mere predicates." Of course, by "mere predicates" he did not mean mere words. There is such a property as goodness, according to him, even though it would be one of these mere predicates. It does not exist, but does have being.[12] In common with Meinong and the early Russell, Moore reserved the term "exists" for entities that are in time, for concrete entities.

Clearly, so understood, universals would not be perceivable through the senses, or at least in the same way as their particular property-instances would be.[13] Equally clearly, what universals are exemplified by, or in, a concrete entity would be completely fixed by what particular properties constitute it, by its intrinsic nature. A complete description of the latter would be a complete description of the entity in the sense that it would contain everything from which what nonnatural, universal properties the entity has could be inferred. But in this view yellow and pleasure, considered as universals, would be nonnatural properties, which Moore denied. Going beyond what Moore says, however, can we introduce a distinction between universals that would preserve the difference he claimed there is between such a property as yellow or pleasure, and the property goodness?

We can, if we recognize that the universals exemplified by the particular properties constitutive of a concrete thing form complex hierarchies, ordered in accordance with degree of generality. The particular color of a yellow object exemplifies an absolutely specific universal, an infima species, namely, the exact shade of yellow we would say it is. But it also exemplifies the generic universal Yellow. In a similar fashion, though farther removed, it exemplifies the generic universal Color, even the generic universal Property. The closer a universal is to the bottom of the hierarchy, that is, the less general it is, the more plausible it is to think of it as a part of the object, as perceivable through the senses, and thus as being *in nature*. This is surely true of the color yellow. But when we consider members of the hierarchy closer to its opposite end, the situation is quite different. Then we seem far removed from nature, and when we reach the genus Property we cannot even intelligibly think of it as being a *part* of the object. For, on Moore's bundle theory, are not *all* of its parts properties? And, surely, we cannot literally *see* Color as such, let alone Property as such, even if we are willing to say that we can literally see Yellow as such in yellow concrete objects.

Thus if Goodness is a summum genus (if it is, then Property would not be a genus), or even just a genus of a very high degree of generality, the description of it as nonnatural and not a part of any natural objects, though exemplified by some, becomes quite comprehensible. And our awareness of it, though not simple sense perception but deserving to be called *intellectual*, perhaps even intellectual *intuition*, would appear no more mysterious or doubtful than our awareness of color as such or of triangularity as such. Yet, understood in this way, the nonnatural status of a property would be a matter of degree, and Moore nowhere suggests that this might be so. But if we *add* such an account of the property goodness to Moore's account (there can be no question of offering it as an interpretation), then we can accept what Moore does say. We would also find the existence of such a property far less questionable. It would be no more mysterious or queer than its species. And we would achieve clear understanding of what might be meant by "good-making" properties. Instead of being puzzled by the nature of such a mysterious relation of "making" (or its converse, sometimes called "being consequential upon" or "supervening upon"), we would be guided by the paradigm of the relationship of the specific colors to the genus color.

And we would then see as grotesque, objections to the reality of goodness such as that of Ralph Barton Perry: "One who upholds this view of good must be prepared to point to a distinct *quale* which appears in that region which our value terms roughly indicate, and which is different from the object's shape and size, from the interrelation of its parts, from its relation to other objects, or to a subject; and from all the other factors which belong to the same context, but are designated by words other than 'good'."[14] W. D. Ross's timid reply that goodness is "discerned by intelligence" and that this is why it is "not as easily discerned as what is discerned by sense-perception" would hardly convince anyone.[15] More convincing might be Ross's further remark that unlike yellow, goodness is a consequential (or "supervenient," we might say) property. But this remark does not help at all if we have no idea of what relation the word "consequential" (or "supervenient") expresses. (I have already remarked that a purely formal definition does not provide us with such an idea.) The genus-species relation, I suggest, is exactly what should be expressed. Then we can answer Perry's objection by agreeing that there is no *specific* quale that "good" indicates, but pointing out that goodness can be found in "the region which our value terms roughly indicate" as the *genus* of some specific quale present in that region. If we find in a person the property of being compassionate, we should not expect to find *in the same way also* the property of being good. But we can find the property of being good *in* the property of being compassionate, as we can find triangularity in an isosceles triangle and color in a shade of yellow.[16]

Of course, the genus-species relationship is not reducible to formal entailment, except through tendentious definitions (in which way any statement could be "shown" to be a tautology). The word "yellow" is not introduced in our language by a definition and can be learned long before one has learned the word "color." And the word "color" is not introduced as the name of a disjunctive property, that of being either yellow or blue or red or . . . , for it is not synonymous or probably even coreferential with any such name we might actually construct. Therefore, "If S is yellow then it is colored" is not reducible to an instance of a logical truth, but the antecedent does entail the consequent (it is absolutely impossible that the former is true and the latter false), though not in virtue of their logical forms. And that the whale is a species of a (logical) genus other than that of fish is the result not of arbitrary linguistic convention but of the adoption of a classificatory scheme that is more adequate to the objective similarities and differences among species of animals. This is why R. M. Hare's familiar argument (echoing Moore's open question argument) that if "x is good" meant, say, "x is pleasant," then we could not informatively say that x is good because it is pleasant, and thus commend x,[17] is irrelevant to our view. We are defining neither goodness in terms of its species nor its species in terms of goodness.

I speak here of stipulative or lexical, nominal definitions, which alone can found formal entailments, not of real definitions. The difference between these, and the fact that there are real definitions, should be evident, even though it is usually denied. "The circle is a closed plane curve all points on which are equidistant from a point within it" neither reports a fact about language nor stipulates a linguistic convention. It tells us *what* the circle is, of which usually we have antecedently, perhaps even as children, an exact idea, and does so by telling us of what genus it is a species and what distinguishes it from all other species in that genus. It is the result of a discovery about the sort of shape we usually mean by the word "circle." It is necessary and a priori, but not analytic, for it is neither a law of logic nor deducible from one by substitution of synonyms; it is not a mere report or a mere stipulation that the definiendum and the definiens are (or are to be) synonymous. This is why it cannot found a formal entailment. "If S is a circle then it is a closed plane curve" does not express a formal entailment, just as "If S is yellow then it is colored" does not. The word "circle" is not a synonym of the phrase "closed plane curve all points on which are equidistant from a point within it." (When schoolchildren learn the definition they learn geometry, not English.) They stand for one and the same figure, as the names "Evening Star" and "Morning Star" stand for one and the same planet, and are no more synonymous than these latter names are. The conflation of reference and meaning is trendy today, but good philosophical sense must rebel against it. Coreference may be a matter of linguistic convention but need not be; synonymy, ultimately, must be. This is why the statement that a certain property is a species of the genus goodness, e.g., "Courage is a good," is not a tautology, even if necessarily true, and leaves the question whether it is true open, in Moore's sense, unlike, say, the statement that a bachelor is male. I shall return to this point in chapter 5.

The view of the nature of goodness I am suggesting entails that goodness is not an infima species, an absolutely specific property, and therefore is indefinable not for the reason that it is such a property. But, as I have noted, the important question, *pace* Moore, is not whether it is definable but whether it is a genus, a generic property. Only if it is the latter would the familiar phenomenological objections to Moore's ethics be met.

The view that goodness is a generic property was well expressed by Brand Blanshard, indeed in the context of a criticism of Moore:

Pleasure or happiness is commonly taken as a clear case of the intrinsically good. But can one draw a line within a given experience of pleasure between the pleasure and its goodness? Moore apparently thinks that one can, that the pleasure and the goodness are sharply distinct, though connected synthetically by a relation of entailment, as colour and extension are in "what is coloured is extended." I cannot think that this has caught the true relation between them. The relation is more intimate. The goodness of being happy is not some isolable quality supervening upon the happiness; the happiness is itself a kind of goodness; we call it *a* good, as we call love an emotion, meaning, I think, that it is one of the forms in which goodness presents itself.[18]

Blanshard referred with approval to H. W. B. Joseph's views on the subject. Indeed, we find Joseph writing:

Generic identity, it would seem, may show its differentiations with more or less suppression, if one may so put it, of the identity. Vertebrate structure is so one in vertebrates of different kinds that one may indicate the identity diagrammatically. Colour is not so one in different colours that the identity can be visually indicated. The completest differentiation is that of being, in being a substance, being a quality, being a quantity, etc.; so that Aristotle said being is not a genus. Good, if it is in all the categories, is almost as profoundly differentiated as being, and cannot be called by the name of one of them, a quality.[19]

But neither Blanshard nor Joseph made much of this conception of goodness in his ethical works, probably because both of them believed that a generic universal, so understood, "lies not in the reality thought about, but in our thought about that reality," that "the universal triangle or man or colour is not as such real," that one could not discern a self-identical "little hard nucleus" in all of the species of a generic universal.[20] Perhaps as a result, in part, of this belief, Blanshard held rather that "goodness is satisfactoriness, which consists jointly in the fulfilment of impulse-desire by the content it demands and the attendant satisfaction. A good is what *is* thus satisfactory. *The* good is what would be satisfactory in the end."[21] I shall return to Blanshard's reasons for rejecting generic universals in section 4 of this chapter and in section 8 of chapter 5, where further explanations of the view defended in the present chapter will be offered.

W. E. Johnson's distinction between determinables and determinates[22] corresponds to the distinction between genera and their species to which I have appealed here. But the extent of the correspondence is not clear. For example, Johnson would not agree that Property is a determinable. But we should note that Moore explicitly denied that he had thought of goodness as a determinable and of the properties that are good, which I have called abstract goods, as its determinates.[23] And, indeed, in his article "Identity," he appears to deny that there are generic universals at all, that, for example, "a number of reds of different tints" have something in common (p. 124), but seems mainly concerned to argue against the view that there are concrete universals, in the Hegelian sense. In 1910–11 he continues to adopt this position.[24] But not so in 1919, when he writes:

> This character wh. we express by "is a shade of blue," is, of course, something which is common to all shades of blue—something which they have "in common" . . . this character is not "in common" to both of 2 blue shades, in the sense that it is a part or constituent of both. . . . Obviously this character also is not identical with any shade which possesses it, nor yet with any other shade of colour that we *see*. It is not similar in shade to any shade that we *see*. So that, if it is "seen" at all, it is only in a completely different sense.[25]

This view is endorsed in 1953 (though with some hesitancy, characteristic of almost everything Moore wrote in his later years), in the Appendix to *Some Main Problems of Philosophy* (p. 378).

Thus we seem to find Moore not only accepting generic universals eventually, but also, judging from the passage just quoted, perhaps holding very much the classical view of the nature of the genus-species relationship and of our awareness of generic universals. But he did so fifteen years after the publication of *Principia Ethica*, and in print only in his posthumously published *Commonplace Book*. That he did not do it earlier is understandable. Generic universals are a much easier target for the nominalist than are specific universals, for reasons I shall explain in the next section. But then, in *Principia Ethica*, did Moore hold goodness to be an absolutely specific universal and that it was indefinable for that reason? If he did, then I believe his view cannot survive the common objection that we simply do not find such a property before our minds. But, once again, we can *supplement* his ethical theory by holding that goodness is a generic universal, and refrain from what could only be exegetic speculations. We can obtain no further guidance from Moore's discussions of this topic.

It may be noted that goodness would almost certainly need to be regarded as a generic property by theories other than Moore's or ours. If it is the same as pleasure, surely there are many kinds of pleasure. If it is the same as being an object of desire, surely there are many kinds of desire. If the reader finds what I say in this section (indeed in this whole chapter) too complicated and difficult, he or she should not expect to find an adequate account of the metaphysics of any rival theory of goodness to be less complicated or difficult. It is just that the rival theories known to me do not include the necessary metaphysical details and they ignore the difficult metaphysical questions. Were they fully worked out, they would, in the general structure of their purely metaphysical parts, parallel ours.


## 2. Universals and Intellectual Intuition

The nature of the genus-species relationship is one of the most difficult metaphysical topics. The reason, I suggest, is that it makes especially evident what I shall later call the transcendental character of the concept of identity. Clearly, we can, do, and must distinguish, for example, the property of being crimson and the property of being red, or the property of being an isosceles triangle and the property of being a triangle, as even Berkeley was forced to admit. But to be aware of both in a particular instance, say in a particular crimson surface or a particular triangular surface, is not to be aware of two properties that are distinct but coexemplified, at all in the way in which, say, the color and the shape of the surface are distinct but coexemplified. There is a clear sense in which the crimson color and the red color of the surface are one and the same property, since its being red consists entirely in its being crimson. But there is also a clear sense in which they are not one and the same property, since a scarlet surface is also red but is not crimson.

The fact is that the notion of a generic property and, therefore, the notion of a consciousness (or awareness) of a generic property are (even if usually unwittingly) understood analogically; they are extensions of the notion of a specific property and of the notion of a consciousness of a specific property. And the notion of a specific property is itself an analogical extension of the paradigmatic notion of an entity, namely that of an individual entity, while the notion of a consciousness (e.g., "seeing") of a specific property is an analogical extension of the paradigmatic notion of a consciousness of an individual thing. The analogical nature of these notions becomes evident when we consider what it is to regard properties as universals, as I have assumed all along that we should.

The notion of a universal property is based on the notion of the (numerical) identity of a property of one individual thing and a property of another individual thing. Indeed, the clearest and least questionable explanation of the technical term "universal" is that to say that a certain property of an individual thing is a universal is to say that it *can* be (numerically) identical with a property of another individual thing. (There need not be such a second individual thing.) If the identity is *specific*, such as (perhaps) that of the color or shape of this page and the color or shape of the next page, then we have a case of identity usually questioned only on philosophical grounds, but still defensible only by arguing that it is more like the paradigmatic case of identity, that of individual identity, say, the identity of the book you are reading now and the book you were reading a few moments ago, than it is like anything else.[26] And since it is the analogical notion of specific identity that grounds the notion of a *specific* universal, the latter is a notion of something that can be regarded as a single entity only analogically.

Now the notion of a *generic* universal is grounded in the notion of *generic identity*, in the notion that allows us to say, for example, that a scarlet thing and a crimson thing have the same general color though not exactly the same color, and that an equilateral triangle and a scalene triangle are the same general figure, though not exactly the same figure. Clearly, this notion is twice removed from the paradigmatic notion of identity, that of individual identity, since the qualifications just made ("though not exactly the same color," "though not exactly the same figure") are absolutely necessary. But generic identity is still more like identity than like anything else. And the *generic property* is more like a single entity than like anything else; for example, it is much less like a mere collection of entities, or even like a collection of entities entering in some relation to one another, as the so-called resemblance theories hold. It should be noted that if we regard what we have called generic properties as sets of resembling specific universals, and thus not as universals,[27] then, by thus allowing for a presumably irreducible relation of resemblance, we destroy the chief ground for accepting even the existence of specific universals, for not regarding *them* as mere sets of resembling *individuals* (whether ordinary or Stoutian). For that ground is that there is no relation of resemblance, unless by it we mean numerical identity (partial or complete) of properties. [28]

It is idle to try, as D. M. Armstrong has tried, to understand generic identity as a kind of partial identity. [29] Scarlet and crimson do not display the sort of complexity that would allow us to say that each consists of the property red, in virtue of which both are red, and of something distinct from it, in virtue of which they are different red colors. Nor can we regard an isoceles triangle as a composite of three-sidedness and equality of two sides. The equality of the sides is the equality of two sides of a three-sided figure, not equality of just any two line segments. And as John Cook Wilson observed, the triangularity of a figure does not consist in its three sides; "it consists in its having the three sides; they are not members of its triangularity." [30]

Nor is *attending* to its triangularity when looking at an isoceles triangular surface the same sort of consciousness as attending to its being an isoceles triangle, as we may recall from our study of geometry. Indeed, as I have pointed out, neither is the attending to the isoceles triangularity of the surface the same sort of awareness or consciousness as the attending to the individual surface itself, though it is more like the latter than is the attending to the generic property triangularity. To be conscious of a specific property as such is to be conscious of it as it would be wherever and whenever it is instantiated, indeed as it would be even if not instantiated at all. Following Husserl's terminology, we may describe such consciousness as somewhat empty, unfilled, while the consciousness of the surface is completely filled out. [31] Indeed, it is only on philosophical reflection that our consciousness of a *specific* property as such strikes us as somewhat empty. But that our consciousness, for example, of the generic property Property, that is, the property of being a property, is *almost* wholly empty, is immediately evident. Yet it is also evident that it is quite real. The reader may consider whether he or she has any difficulty in distinguishing between properties and individual things, in recognizing, seeing, certain things as properties and others as individual things. If this is true of our consciousness of the generic property Property, it is even more evidently true of our consciousness of generic properties of a much lower degree of generality, such as Triangularity, Redness, and Goodness. The latter consciousness is far less unfilled than the consciousness of Property, and thus its reality is far more evident. Yet, unlike our consciousness of a particular surface, it is not completely filled.

This is why, in addition to saying that a generic property is a single entity only analogically, we must say that our *awareness* (or consciousness) of a generic property is awareness also only analogically, indeed that it is twice removed from the primary, paradigmatic case, that of awareness of an individual thing. The intermediate case is that of awareness of the specific property as such, which is more like awareness of an individual thing than is the awareness of a generic property, yet still not the same sort of awareness as the awareness of an individual thing. The difference is evident from the fact that, as I have noted, to be aware of a specific property as such is to be aware of it as it would be wherever and whenever it is instantiated, indeed to be aware of it as it would be even if it were nowhere and never instantiated; nothing like this is true of our awareness of an individual thing. But both awareness of a specific property and awareness of a generic property are more like awareness of a single individual thing than like awareness of a collection of individual things, for the same reason that their objects are more like single individual things than like collections of individual things. We can call both kinds of awareness intellectual awareness or *intuition*, even when they occur in cases of sense perception. If we do so, then we would find an independent means of understanding the traditional idea of intuition in ethics, which has been rather unthinkingly derided in recent years. But it should be noted that what I have described is directly relevant only to the idea of intuition as a mode of awareness of properties, not as a mode of *knowledge* of truths about them. We shall not be ready to consider the latter idea until chapter 7.

Both awareness of specific properties and awareness of generic properties are present in the most fundamental kind of conceptual cognition, namely, in recognition,[32] the first, say, in the recognition of the color of a given individual thing as a certain familiar, even if nameless, specific shade of color, and the second in the recognition of it as *yellow*. For, in general, to *recognize* $x$ as $y$ one must be aware of both $x$ and $y$, though in very different ways. It is not to *recall* some $z$ such that one knows that $x$ is identical with $z$. This may happen even if $x$ is not recognized. For example, I may recall seeing someone last year whose identity with the person before me now, whom I do *not* recognize, I infer from their similarities. And I may recognize the person before me without recalling any past occasion on which I saw that person. Wittgenstein wrote: "It is easy to have a false picture of the processes called 'recognizing'; . . . as if I carried a picture of an object with me and used it to perform an identification of an object as the one represented by the picture . . . it is not so much as if I were comparing the object with a picture set beside it, but as if the object *coincided* with the picture. So I see only one thing, not two."[33]

It is the analogical nature of the notions of generic identity, of a generic property, and of our awareness of generic properties, that explains and excuses the fourth, Humean variety of skepticism in ethics, the opinion that we are simply not aware or conscious of, and therefore have no reason to believe that there is, such a property as goodness. (Of course, as we have seen, the notions of specific identity, specific property, and awareness of specific properties, are also analogical, but though Hume himself rejected them, they are seldom questioned, presumably because of their greater proximity to the paradigms of the concepts of identity, entity, and awareness.) We can now see that our metaphysical investigation has resulted in a major modification of the result of our phenomenological investigation, namely, that we are aware of goodness. A generic property such as goodness is an entity only in an analogical sense of "entity," and we are aware of it only in an analogical sense of "aware." This is a good example of why we should hold fast to the requirement that phenomenological appeals are not to be divorced from metaphysical considerations.

The reader may find disturbing our claim that thought and therefore talk about properties and about our awareness of them are through-and-through analogical in nature, and think that our metaphysical conclusion in effect cancels the phenomenological conclusion we reached in the previous chapter. But it does not, and any feeling of disturbance would be a symptom of a rather narrow view of what it is to think and talk about something. Indeed, the simple, paradigmatic cases of the application of a concept consist simply in our seeing the object of its application as unquestionably falling under the concept, and we are quite unaware that the property for which the concept stands is an entity only analogically. But the intellectually challenging cases, whether in philosophical or legal or scientific or mathematical reasoning, are precisely those which are not paradigmatic. With respect to such cases we must be willing to ask not so much, What *is* it? but rather, What is it *like*? To understand something is to see it in the light of other things, sometimes easily, sometimes not.[34] Is abortion homicide? Is school segregation incompatible with equality? Does quantum mechanics show that nature is non-deterministic, perhaps even that the elementary particles can be said to have free will? Is not-being-a-property-of-itself, itself a property?

Even with respect to questions encountered in everyday life, subtle thought often asks not what something is but what it is like. It may be unclear whether John really loves Mary, but perhaps quite clear that his attitude toward her, though considerably different from the paradigmatic attitudes of love, is more like the latter than like any other attitude. A very light shade of grey is not pure white but may be so much like pure white and so unlike paradigmatic greys that ordinarily to call it a grey would be grossly misleading. It would be easy to multiply examples such as these.

I hope the reader recognizes that the important qualifications made in the previous few paragraphs are not just needed because they are required for a defense of our notion of goodness as a generic property, but would need to be made in order to account for any notions likely to be of fundamental intellectual interest. I shall return to this topic in chapter 5, though in a different context. Suffice it here to say that if the reader takes my assertion that since goodness is a generic property it is, in a sense, not an entity and thus, in a sense, we are not aware of it, as constituting an admission that the skeptic has won, he or she would be reminded that exactly the same can be asserted also of triangularity and the color red, and of our awareness of them. Goodness and our awareness of it would be beyond the skeptic's reach if their reality could be questioned only by questioning the reality also of such properties as triangularity and the color red, and of our awareness of them.

The *general* conception of the genus-species relationship to which I have appealed is not new. It is the standard, classical conception. Aquinas held that "the unity of the genus comes from its indetermination or indifference; but not in such a way that what is signified by the genus is a nature numerically the same in different species, to which would be added something else (the difference) determining it. . . . Rather, the genus denotes a form (though not precisely any one in particular) which the difference expresses in a definite way, and which is the same as that which the genus denotes indeterminately."[35] He also held that "the genus . . . signifies indeterminately everything in the species and not the matter alone. Similarly, the difference designates the whole and not the form alone."[36] In twentieth-century philosophy we find John Cook Wilson writing:

> Now colour is not a member of red colour, for red colour is not a whole of which colour is a part in the sense that red contains something besides colour. On the contrary, red contains nothing except colour. Colour comprises everything in it. Red is not colour together with something which is not colour. In equilateral triangular figure, figure is not a member of equilateral triangular figure as a complex. For everything in the equilateral triangle comes under figure: it is altogether figure, and not figure together with something which is not figure.[37]

And W. E. Johnson wrote that color, though in a sense indeterminate, "is, metaphorically speaking, that from which the specific determinates, red, yellow, green, etc., emanate; while from shape emanate another completely different series of determinates such as triangular, square, octagonal, etc."[38] Similar views were held also by Aristotle, Hegel, Husserl, and, as we have seen, H. W. B. Joseph and Brand Blanshard. (I speak here of their *conceptions* of the genus-species relationship, not of their views on what status, if any, it has in reality. For example, as I read him, Aquinas denied that universals, whether specific or generic, exist at all except as particular ideas in a mind. And, as we have seen, Blanshard held that the genus exists only in thought, not in reality.)

The implicit common thesis of these views can be thought of as the most striking application of the Hegelian dictum that all genuine identity is identity in difference, the principle of the identity of identity and nonidentity.[39] The views I have mentioned, like the one I have explained in some detail, rest on the implicit acknowledgment of this principle in the case of generic identity, which grounds the existence of generic universals. But, as I have argued, the principle is certainly applicable, though less obviously, also to the specific identities in which the existence of specific universals is grounded. Even if the color of this page is exactly the same as the color of the next page, there is a sense in which they are distinguishable, and this is why the judgment of their identity is informative. For example, when you see the one, there is a clear sense in which it is false that you see the other, though also there is a no less clear sense in which it is true that you see the other. Indeed, as I shall argue in the next section, the Hegelian dictum applies even to individual identity, and this, I believe, is the lesson to be learned from Frege's account of informative identity statements in terms of the different modes in which the referred-to entity is presented. When Blanshard rejected the reality of generic universals on the grounds that he could not discern a self-identical nucleus in the species of a generic universal, he ignored the fact that no discernible nucleus of self-identity can be found in the subject matter of any genuine, informative identity statement, that such a nucleus exists only in the subject matter of empty statements of the form "x is x." As Wittgenstein suggested, philosophers' thinking about identity seems to be dominated by a picture that requires the genuine cases of identity to be cases of—nothing at all![40] He wrote:

215. But isn't *the same* at least the same?

We seem to have an infallible paradigm of identity in the identity of a thing with itself. I feel like saying: "Here at any rate there can't be a variety of interpretations. If you are seeing a thing you are seeing identity too."

Then are two things the same when they are what *one* thing is? And how am I to apply what the *one* thing shews me to the case of two things?

216. "A thing is identical with itself."—There is no finer example of a useless proposition, which yet is connected with a certain play of the imagination. It is as if in imagination we put a thing into its own shape and saw that it fitted.

## 3. The Account of Identity Required to Rebut the Skeptic

The assertions I made toward the end of the previous section are crucial to the main thesis of this chapter, for if true they render the idea of generic identity, and thus our view of the nature of goodness, intelligible and plausible. I shall try to explain them further by connecting them with the classic, Frege's account of the philosophically least questionable kind of informative identity statements, namely those about individual objects, in terms of his distinction between the entity referred to by an expression and the different modes in which that entity may be presented. *This* is his fundamental account, not, as usually supposed, that in terms of his distinction between the reference and sense of an expression, for he explained his notion of a sense in terms of the notion of a mode of presentation.[41] His account only superficially belongs in the philosophy of language. It is essentially metaphysical and epistemological.

For, what is a Fregean sense? The closest Frege came to an answer was in saying that the sense of an expression contains the manner, mode, in which the entity to which the expression refers is given, presented.[42] Elsewhere he wrote that "An object can be determined in different ways, and every one of these ways of determining it can give rise to a special name, and these different names then have different senses; for it is not self-evident that it is the same object which is being determined in different ways,"[43] that different signs designating the same object are not necessarily interchangeable because "it could be said that they lead to it from different directions,"[44] that "it is *via* a sense and only *via* a sense that a proper name is related to an object,"[45] that the sense of a proper name "serves to illuminate only a single aspect [or side]" of the thing referred to, that "comprehensive knowledge" of the thing referred to "would require us to be able to say immediately whether any given sense attaches to it. To such knowledge we never attain."[46]

For our purposes it is sufficient if we extract from all these assertions the idea, surely implicit in them, that there is no such thing as an object's being confronted in, or given to, consciousness *simpliciter*; that in each case it is given in a certain distinguishable way, *as if it were a different object*; that in the presentations of one and the same object there is not also presented a self-identical nucleus. This is why it is possible to informatively *identify*, and also, without contradiction, to *misiden-*

*tify*, an entity. Hence Frege's view that an identity statement can be informative only if the expressions flanking the identity sign express different senses. But the more fundamental view is that it is the difference between the two modes of presentation of the entity referred to that renders the identity statement informative. And by a mode of presentation Frege did not mean a sense datum or an idea, but, arguably, the entity referred to itself *as it presents itself*, if there is such an entity at all, there being no discernible self-identical nucleus in the modes of presentation of the same entity (if there were one, the identity judgment would not be informative); and he denied that one could have access to an entity except via a mode of presentation. That the entity is nevertheless distinct from its modes of presentation even if never itself presented as distinct, Frege presumably did not doubt. But he also never explained in detail what he took the connection between the two to be.

Frege also used another, much more suggestive, term for informative identity statements. He called them "recognition-statements."[47] He wrote to Russell that "a special act of recognition is required" if we are to recognize that the words "morning star" and "evening star" designate the same planet.[48] He described such statements as expressing the recognition of the same again.[49] And he argued that "for every object there is one type of proposition which must have a sense, namely, the recognition-statement,"[50] and that "if we are to use the symbol *a* to signify an object, we must have a criterion for deciding in all cases whether *b* is the same as *a*, even if it is not always in our power to apply this criterion."[51] If modes of presentation are what make recognition, and more generally identification, possible, then we can readily see that their metaphysical role is absolutely fundamental. For any metaphysics must regard its subject matter, presumably reality, as consisting of entities that are at least in principle recognizable, that can be encountered again or at least by more than one person, whether in perception or in thought, that can be identified not just in the sense of being singled out but in the more proper sense of being capable of being the subject of a true but informative identity judgment. Plato (in the *Theaetetus*) was perhaps the first to suggest this as a general requirement for any coherent view of reality.

What must modes of presentation be if they are to play this ontologically most fundamental role? It should be evident that the answer to this question cannot consist in classifying them as a subgenus of some higher genus. They cannot be individual things; they cannot be properties. The distinction between the mode in which an entity is presented and the entity itself cuts across the ontological categories and thus may be called transcendental, in the medieval sense of this term. Frege argued that the senses he called thoughts, and thus by implication all senses, since all other senses are or at least can be constituents of thoughts, are neither in the inner world nor in the outer world, but in "a third realm."[52] Yet, diverging from anything Frege said or would have said (for example, Frege denied that concepts, that is, properties, can enter in the identity relation and does not say in which of the three realms they belong), I want to suggest that, if properly understood, modes of presentation are that out of which both the inner and the outer world are constituted.[53]

My suggestion is not exegetical. The fact is that Frege did not say enough about the nature of a sense or about the nature of a mode of presentation. The vague familiarity of the idea of the manner or mode in which something is given or presented must not mislead us into thinking that we understand it. Nor is it at all clear how it may help us understand the possibility of informative identity statements. "The entity given in this manner is identical with the entity given in that manner" is itself an informative identity statement, and how are we to understand now *its* possibility? Surely not by postulating second-order, third-order, . . . modes of presentation! It would have been otherwise if Frege had said that in an informative identity statement the subject-terms refer directly to the modes of presentation contained in their senses, and only indirectly to the entity referred to, that they are to be understood somewhat as he claimed names in oblique contexts are to be understood. In such contexts, he held, names refer to their customary senses, and while he did not say so, it is not clear that, given his account of what a sense is, he would not have allowed that names in such contexts refer to modes of presentation, indeed, as I have suggested, to their customary referents, but only as these are presented in a certain way. In other words, he could have replaced the obscure notion of different modes of presentation with the notion of different *objects* corresponding to those different modes of presentation, somewhat *analogously* (but only analogously!) to the replacement, in some philosophies of perception, of the notion of the different modes of appearing of the same material entity with the notion of corresponding different objects, namely, sense data. But he did not. We must go beyond what Frege said or even could have meant, if we are to understand the nature of identity, and thus of generic identity and of the identity of goodness in its species.

What does the word "constituted" mean in my suggestion that both the "inner" and the "outer" world are constituted out of modes of presentation? Obviously, not the sort of constitution effected by part-whole relationships. It can only be the sort of constitution that is effected by identity, though not the empty identity expressed in "a is a" or "everything is self-identical" but rather identity that is inseparable from difference, the kind of identity grasped when we learn that 3 and 2 is 5, that this person is the same as the one we saw yesterday, that the color of this page is the same as the color of that page. We must not think of such identity as a relation, for it generates the members of all the ontological categories, including that of relations. And, for the same reason, it does not belong to any other category. We may call it a transcendental concept (but not in the medieval sense), since there is a sense in which it is *we* who introduce it into, and impose it upon, the domain of "modes of presentation," in order to render this domain orderly and thus allow it to be seen as a domain of recognizable, genuine *entities*. To suppose that we derive it from experience, where we find a certain relation ("identity"), which with respect to any "pair of objects" either holds or does not, would be both phenomenologically false and dialectically useless, since we need the concept of identity to identify also that *same* "relation" in the various "pairs" in which it holds. And this, I suggest, is the point at which conceptual irrealism must be accepted even in a realist ethical theory. I shall now try to explain this conclusion in some detail.

## 4. The Kernel of Irrealism in Our Account of Goodness

It should be evident that any ethical theory that reflects at all adequately everyday ethical thought would allow for a variety of species or subgenera of goodness, for example, existence (life), health, pleasure, desire-satisfaction, knowledge, self-control, friendship, *kinds* of actions such as promise keeping. But how could all of these be species or subgenera of the same genus? Are they not evidently heterogeneous? Aristotle seemed to think so,[54] and so did Aquinas and Scotus, who regarded goodness as one of the transcendentals, in the medieval sense of this term, not as a genus. We shall not be able to provide a complete answer to this question until we have examined what abstract goods there are (the examples I have given are intended here to be just examples). But for our present purposes it is sufficient to answer the question by pointing out that, as I have argued, even uncontroversial generic identity is not paradigmatic identity, but only analogous to paradigmatic identity, and, therefore, that generic properties are not paradigmatic single entities but are only analogous to single entities. If so, then there is nothing in the concept of identity that determines the point at which we may not attribute generic identity and must acknowledge heterogeneity. This is why, I suggest, the question whether goodness is a genus or a transcendental (in the medieval sense) has no cash value.

Of course, from this it does not follow that the classification of the abstract goods is a matter of caprice. That a certain property is a species or a subgenus of goodness is subject to justification. This justification involves an examination of the particular case, of the similarities and differences between it and the paradigmatic cases, the extent to which the resulting classification is illuminated by, and itself illuminates, the classification of other, nonethical properties, such as those we might regard as constitutive of human nature. In this chapter I have tried to show how it would be possible for goodness to be a real property, albeit a generic one, the species and subgenera of which are of great variety. To show that *in fact* it is such a property would be the task of an actual ethical theory, which I shall provide, at least in outline, shortly. But I must now introduce a necessary qualification of the thesis that goodness is a real property, necessary even if that thesis were made evident by a detailed ethical theory, though it is a qualification also of the thesis that, for example, triangularity is a real property. The qualification goes beyond that already made, namely that goodness, like any generic (or even specific) property is an entity only by analogy.

In defending the extension of the notions of identity, and thus of entity and of awareness of an entity, beyond their paradigms, I have appealed to the fact that extensions of the application of our concepts are common, indeed indispensable, in any serious attempt to understand a given subject matter. The justification of such extensions consists in our finding significant similarities between the cases in which they are made and the paradigmatic cases of the application of the concept. As long as the presence of the similarities is defensible, so are the extensions of the concept. But these similarities are themselves nothing but generic identities!

Now the notion of generic identity itself involves an extension of the application of a concept, although this time of the concept of identity itself. How do we defend, what justifies, this extension? We may point out the inadequacies, familiar in the literature on universals, of the alternative views on the topic of universals, those offered by the resemblance and the strict nominalist theories. But in order to have a positive account, we must appeal to the identity ("likeness," "analogousness") of what we wish to describe as generic identity with paradigmatic identity. This appeal itself involves a further extension of the application of the concept of identity. What justification can we have of *this* extension? Clearly, none. We cannot find a genuine justification of the extensions of the concept of identity by engaging in yet further extensions. But then neither can we find genuine justification of the application of the concept of identity to the paradigmatic, that is, standard and ordinarily uncontroversial, cases of individual identity. (That they are paradigmatic does not by itself provide such justification; the paradigms of a concept can be justifiably changed. For example, the identity of an individual through time is a paradigm of identity, but philosophers have not hesitated to question it!) Indeed, if we could find such justification, the ultimate nonjustifiability of judgments of generic identity might render these judgments suspect. But we could not.

Let us return to Wittgenstein's question quoted earlier (p. 72). How do we apply the concept of identity in the case of "two things," in the genuine cases of its application, those in which the application is informative, for example, to the color of this page and the color of the next page, or to the page you started reading and the page you are about to finish? By finding that whatever properties the one has the other also has? But does the color of this page have the property of being the color of the next page, which the next page does have? We can "find" that it does only if we independently find that the color of this page is identical with the color of the next page. And the same point can be made regarding the coincidence of the properties of the page you started reading and the page you are about to finish. Does the former have the property of being about to be finished? Only if it is independently judged to be identical with the latter. In the basic cases, identity is the criterion of coincidence of properties, not vice versa.

Could it be that we apply the concept of identity to the color of this page and the color of the next page, or to the page you started reading and the page you are about to finish, by detecting between "them" a relation called identity? But even if we detected *something*, how do we know that it is an *identity*? By finding that it is identical, whether specifically or generically, with some other relations already called identity? But which are these? And surely the appeal to a second- (and third-, fourth-, and so on) order relation of identity would be a mere fantasy. Surely the truth is that there is no relevant "something" that we can detect in a case of identity, no relation in the world that is called identity. Indeed, how could such a relation hold between "two" things and yet render them "one" thing?

Ultimately, that is, in the basic, noninferential cases, we apply the concept of identity not because we find in them something called identity, but because of the manner in which we conceive of them. We may say that the concept of identity is transcendental in the sense that, though it has application, it stands for nothing in the cases to which it applies. This is why there is ultimately no genuine justification of its applications, whether paradigmatic or nonparadigmatic. A few lines after the passage I quoted earlier, Wittgenstein says, about the justification for supposing that one is following the *same* rule, "If I have exhausted the justifications I have reached bedrock, and my spade is turned. Then I am inclined to say: 'This is simply what I do.' "[55]

It is thus that even a straightforward realism in ethics rests on a sort of *general irrealism*—irrealism with respect to the foundation of any conceptualization of the world, that is, the application of the concept of identity. But this sort of irrealism must not be confused with the sort of general irrealism that claims that there can be no appraisal of the adequacy of a conceptual scheme to reality, that we cannot justifiably criticize a conceptual scheme or the language that embodies it by comparing it with the facts. We can do all this on the basis of the extent to which the conceptual scheme or the language reflects the identities and nonidentities ("similarities" and "differences") involved in the facts. But these identities and nonidentities are not themselves elements in the facts. Given our concept of identity, whether a certain conceptual scheme or linguistic practice is adequate to its subject matter has, at least in principle, a determinate answer; the concept of identity provides the basis for such an answer. But whether our concept of identity itself is adequate to the nature of reality (in its paradigmatic as well as nonparadigmatic applications) is a question that can have no answer, since the concept of identity stands for nothing in reality. It is the basis of all criticism of the adequacy of any conceptual scheme or language as a representation of reality. This is why it is not itself subject to such criticism. Of course, this does not mean that its application is a matter of caprice, of whimsy, of purely "subjective" decision. We do have the concept of identity, and to have it is to be constrained in our applications of it. What we cannot do is to go beyond these constraints and discover an independent rationale for them, as we could in the case of other concepts. The absence of such a rationale makes itself felt in the relative freedom we enjoy in extending the applications of the concept and in the possibility of different but equally adequate classifications and of cross-classifications (the equilateral triangle is generically identical with the scalene triangle but also with the square, and pleasure is a good but also a psychological state). We shall return to this point at the end of the next chapter, after we have surveyed the main abstract goods.

So, there is a kernel of truth in irrealism with respect to ethics. The reality of the property goodness can be shown ultimately only by acknowledging the unreality of the "relation" of identity. But this fact is in no way peculiar to ethics. It holds with respect to any conceptual activity, for example, the geometry of the triangle. And the irrealism it implies is quite different from, indeed in a way antithetical to, the indiscriminate, wholesale irrealism that regards any established conceptual activity or linguistic practice as beyond realist criticism, beyond criticism based on comparison of it with the facts about its subject matter. (Indeed it is better to say that it is such criticizability that defines conceptual realism, realism with respect to the conditions 3 and 4 stated early in this book, p. 3, rather than the possibility of detecting an unconceptualized reality.) The difference could be illustrated as follows.

Given our concept of identity, it is an objective fact that a certain property of one thing is identical, whether specifically or generically, with a certain property of another thing, or that it is not, regardless of whether in ordinary speech we apply the same predicate to them or not. If they are identical but we have no common predicate for both, then we would be justified in introducing one. If they are not identical but we have a common predicate for both, then we might be justified in revising ordinary usage by replacing that predicate with two novel predicates. I suggest that among the concepts that do have application to reality, only the concept of identity (and concepts, such as the concept of existence, which may be understood in terms of it)[56] has nothing to compare it with in reality, although it is essential to any conceptual activity or linguistic practice. (A yardstick cannot be used to measure itself, but it can be used to measure other things.) It is not to be confused with any word or use of a word or linguistic practice, since it is presupposed in our recognition of words, without which recognition language would itself be impossible. Any essentially anthropological understanding of it, whether of the Wittgensteinean or some other variety, would be woefully superficial.

Nevertheless, isn't the view I have defended a form of idealism? A concept is not a word or a linguistic practice. And it is not a mental entity, for the Sartrean reason already noted in chapter 3 that there are no mental entities, if these are supposed to be inhabitants of consciousness. We can say that a concept is a principle of classification, but the principle is, so to speak, already in the world, already "classifying," sorting out, organizing, constituting the world. So understood, a concept may be thought of as a property or relation. The concept of identity, however, though classifying, sorting out, organizing, constituting the world on the most fundamental level, cannot be thought of as a property or relation. The concept applies to the world but does not stand for anything in the world. To say more about this, even if it were possible, would not belong in a book in ethics.

Would ordinary ethical thought find what I have said in defense of realism in ethics highly dubious and unclear, as I argued in chapter 1 it would so find defenses that appeal to shared language games or to causal explanations of ethical beliefs? It is already part of ordinary ethical thought that a variety of things are regarded as good, and my defense of realism, namely that such things have something in common, goodness, in the way the various colors have something in common, color, would hardly appear dubious or unclear. Of course, my *account* of this fact on the basis of a theory of identity is highly technical, and ordinary ethical thought would form no opinions about it. The nature of identity is not one of its objects of concern. It may seem, nevertheless, that our conclusions point to the desirability of a resemblance theory of universals, an alternative I have ignored here but discussed at great length elsewhere. Suffice it to suggest to the reader to consider whether irrealist conclusions would not also be inevitable regarding an irreducible relation of resemblance.

What I have said so far in this section provides us now with an answer to another objection by Brand Blanshard to generic universals, which we could not have considered earlier. It appeals to the indeterminacy of the classification of specific properties in some cases. He asks: "Where does blue end as it passes through violet and purple toward red on the one side, and through peacock blue toward

green on the other?"[57] There is no fact of the matter here, I suggest. With respect
to a pair of specific shades, we may impose the concept of identity and classify one
of them as blue, or withhold that imposition and rather impose the concept on
another pair containing that same shade as a member, with the result of classifying
it as red, or do neither. Of course, the problems of indeterminacy and vagueness
face us even if we do not accept generic universals. But the view of identity on
which this acceptance rests provides us with an explanation of these problems,
whether they arise regarding the classification of properties or regarding the identity
of an individual through time. (When does a series of minute changes in a table
make it cease to be a table?) It is worth remarking that indeterminacy and vagueness
need not be present in the classification of the species and subgenera of goodness
as goods, just as they do not arise, for example, in the classification of colors *as
colors*, rather than as blue or red or green.

The role of the concept of identity is to allow us to see, or think of, two things
as being one thing. An identity judgment is informative because indeed it is about
two things. It is true if and only if our concept of identity does allow us to see the
two things the judgment is about as one thing. This is how the concept of identity
is used and this is why we need it. These are the phenomenological facts about its
application. But to understand its application and avoid the misleading implication
that two things can be one thing, we may adopt the following terminological convention. Let us call the two things the identity judgment is about *objects*, being
guided by the idea of an intentional object, of the accusative of a mental act, of
an object as given or presented to consciousness; and let us call the one thing the
judgment is about, if it is true, an *entity*, being guided by the idea that an entity,
unlike a mere intentional object, is a being, a part of reality, and therefore recognizable, more generally, identifiable, at different times or by many persons.
Objects would *correspond* to Frege's modes of presentation, and entities to his entities
referred to. (I have already pointed out that in oblique contexts, where the dis-
tinctness of what I have called objects is most striking, Frege did claim that names
refer to their ordinary *senses*.) But just as he denied that senses are either in the
inner or in the outer world, and thus in effect that they are a category of things,
so we must deny that the distinction between objects and entities is a distinction
between two kinds of things. It is a distinction of reason. The domain of objects is
the domain of the primary applications of the concept of identity and thus of our
whole conceptual apparatus. The domain of entities is the conceptual result of these
applications. Even in the case of individual entities, identity involves difference,
the difference between the objects whose identity constitutes the individual entity.[58]

## 5. Summary

Let me summarize the (unavoidably) rather complex and difficult argument of the
previous sections of this chapter. I have suggested that goodness is a generic property,
on a very high level of generality, its species being, perhaps, personal affection,
aesthetic appreciation, pleasure, knowledge. This is why many fail to find it, and

also this is why "the naturalistic fallacy" is so easily committed. I have urged that it would be idle to look for goodness in any concrete entity as a specific property distinct from, though supervenient upon, the specific properties the thing exemplifies, in the sense in which the color of a surface is distinct from its shape, and the macroproperties of an object are perhaps supervenient upon its microproperties.[59] Moore's unfortunate comparison of goodness with the color yellow suggests that goodness is such a distinct property, and, not surprisingly, most of his readers have been unable to detect it. Or, in common with most of Moore's predecessors, they have confused it with one of its most prominent, most easily detectable, species, say, pleasure, a confusion of the sort that Moore called "the naturalistic fallacy."[60] This fallacy is quite understandable in the light of the extreme generality of goodness. Also understandable is the claim of even as astute a moral philosopher as Nicolai Hartmann that the concept of good as such has no content.[61] The concepts of an individual thing, of property, and of relation also may seem without content. But they do have content. We can understand how all this is possible if we understand how generic identity is possible. And we can understand *this* if we understand the nature of identity. Indeed, generic identity does involve diversity and, as Blanshard pointed out, there is no hard self-identical nucleus in its terms. But this is so even in the paradigmatic cases of individual identity, with which Frege was concerned. In the terminology I have suggested, the objects a statement of such identity is about are diverse, though only *qua* objects; this is why the statement is informative. And the entity the statement (if true) is about is not a self-identical nucleus in the objects but a conceptual result of their identity, a way in which they may be seen and understood. If this is true of individual identity, then the fact that it is true of generic identity, and in particular of the identity of goodness in its species, should no longer be a cause of concern for us.

Let us briefly return to Moore. What I have described as species of goodness, or as abstract goods, correspond to what in *Principia Ethica* Moore described as the things that have intrinsic value. He pointed out that the question "What is good?" may mean either "Which among existing things are good?" or "What *sort of* things are good?" and that to answer the former question we must first know the answer to the second question.[62] And he sometimes used the word "quality" or "property" for things that have intrinsic value.[63] The criterion Moore proposed for identifying the things that have intrinsic value was whether "if they existed *by themselves*, in absolute isolation, we should yet judge their existence to be good."[64] According to him, "personal affections and aesthetic enjoyments include *all* the greatest, and *by far* the greatest, goods we can imagine."[65] Knowledge, "though having little or no value by itself, is an absolutely essential constituent in the highest goods, and contributes immensely to their value."[66] Similarly, "the mere consciousness of pleasure, however intense, does not, *by itself*, appear to be a *great* good, even if it has some slight intrinsic value," and while pleasure by itself may too have some value, the organic unity of it and the consciousness of it has much greater value.[67] And freedom has no value in itself even though, possibly, without it "nothing very good can exist in this world."[68]

I shall not discuss here Moore's views on what things are good; I shall do so, briefly, in the next chapter. Despite their enormous influence on British intellectual life, and unquestionable intrinsic importance, they are not worked out in detail.[69] But Moore's method of absolute isolation can be easily accepted as a method of testing whether something is a species (or subgenus) of goodness, though it was not so understood by him. For to judge whether or not the existence of a *particular* property (which is what Moore must be talking about, if he is to be consistent) all by itself, in absolute isolation from everything else, would be good, is surely to judge whether the universal property of which it is an instance is (a) good. Indeed, the question whether it would be good if, say, a particular concrete pleasure should exist (occur) all by itself has a clear sense only if understood as the question whether pleasure as such is (a) good. On the other hand, in answering the latter question we may find it useful to ask the former question, in order to make sure that we do not confuse the intrinsic goodness (if any) of pleasure with the contributions (whether causal or noncausal, by way of being elements in what Moore called organic unities) that particular pleasures may make to the total goodness in the universe.[70]

Toward the end of the next chapter we shall return to the topic of the present chapter. For, some problems concerning the nature of goodness arise only, or at least especially clearly, when the main abstract goods have been identified and systematized. We turn now to this task.

# CHAPTER FIVE

# The System of Goods

## 1. The Principle of Division for the Genus Goodness

Moore was well aware that some of his "attributions of intrinsic goodness . . . do not display that symmetry and system which is wont to be required of philosophers" but claimed that this was no objection.[1] A similar claim was made almost thirty years later by Ross.[2] But symmetry and system are required in philosophy no less than in any other cognitive discipline. In any case, even if Moore and Ross would be right if the attributions of intrinsic goodness were understood as something other than the subsumption of certain species or subgenera under their proper genus, no such disavowal of systematic ambitions would be legitimate for us. Indeed, once we recognize that generic identity is not a kind of partial identity, we cannot hope to *prove* that any such subsumption is correct. We can hardly prove that yellow, blue, and red are colors, if they are such *not* in virtue of possessing a common absolutely specific element. A judgment such as that yellow is a color could not then be analytic in the Kantian sense, and the vague sense of "true in virtue of its meaning" would be irrelevant, for surely we could *see* that yellow, blue, and red have "something in common," though not a common part, which yellow and, say, triangularity do not have, that they "belong together" in a way the latter do not, even if we lacked a vocabulary for colors and shapes. Similarly, to move to a level of abstraction closer to that of the attributions of intrinsic goodness, ultimately we must *see*, not *prove*, that, say, colors and shapes belong to a common genus, to which dogs, trees, and rocks do not belong. Only when we see this can we grasp the rather technical philosophical notion of a property.

But while our systematic requirements cannot be satisfied by deductive proofs, neither can they be satisfied by mere listings of properties, however evident phenomenologically it may be that these are species or subgenera of the genus goodness. We must be able to state, or at least have some conception of, a principle governing the logical division of that genus and thus allowing us to see how its species issue from it, perhaps also to discover species hitherto unknown to us, and to validate the claim that the relationship between goodness and what I have called abstract goods is indeed a genus-species relationship. I shall attempt this task in the present chapter, though mainly to show that our systematic requirements can be met, not to provide a complete system of ethics. And I should remind the reader, as I have repeatedly done already, that nothing I shall say takes for granted that there is such a property as goodness and that the other properties I shall discuss are indeed species or subgenera of it. Only in chapter 7 will we be ready to argue for these propositions. Until then we shall be engaged, as we have been so far, in their detailed phenomenological and metaphysical elucidation. Such an elucidation is necessary if in chapter 7 we are to know for the truth of exactly *what* propositions we are to argue. But, as before, for the sake of simplicity of exposition I shall continue to write as if the epistemological problem we shall face in chapter 7 has been solved.

In the case of some genera, for example (phenomenal) color, a principle of logical division perhaps cannot be made explicit, but that we have some conception of it is confirmed by the fact, made familiar by Hume, that we can infer the existence of a shade of blue we have never experienced. Moreover, it is clearly internal to the genus, applicable only to that genus. In the case of other genera, a principle of logical division can be stated with great precision but is often, perhaps always, ultimately external. For example, the division of the genus triangle into the species equilateral, isosceles, and scalene triangles is governed ultimately by the principle, of much wider field of application than the subject matter of geometry, that any three magnitudes are such that either all three are equal or only two are equal or no two are equal, a clearly external principle of division.

Can we find a principle of division for the genus goodness? I believe that we can find at least an external principle if we follow the example set by Plato, Aristotle, the medieval philosophers, and indeed, more recently, also by Rashdall and Ross.[3] Precisely because abstract goods are properties, they can be correlated with certain other properties of the concrete entities exemplifying them, which properties are on an equal level of generality, and if the order and mutual connections of these latter properties is clear, then some clarity might be reflected upon the order and mutual connections of the former properties. Usually, the properties in question have been identified as certain aspects of human nature, often described as parts of the soul, and the Platonic division of the soul into three parts with a good corresponding to each is perhaps the most familiar philosophical story. But an even richer story is available in the more general classical-medieval doctrine of the hierarchy of being, of which the Platonic doctrine is only a part. Following Aristotle, Aquinas observed that "in natural things species seem to be arranged in a hierarchy: as the mixed things are more perfect than the elements, and plants than minerals, and animals than plants, and men than other animals."[4] And much of his moral philosophy consisted in identifying the elements in the nature of man and their hierarchy.

When we rely on the hierarchy of being as the key to the classification of goods, we achieve the level of abstraction the notion of goodness requires, and can speak of ethics, or, more precisely, of the theory of good and evil, as the science of being *qua* goodness, just as metaphysics has been described as the science of being *qua* being. We also achieve welcome philosophical contact, though perhaps not agreement, with Plato's doctrine of the Form of the Good as the Form of Forms, and the medieval doctrine of Good as one of the transcendentals, another transcendental being Being. And we can do justice to the classical idea that the goodness of an entity consists in its conformity to its nature. The good in question, we may say, is not the nature of the entity, but the realization of the good or goods corresponding to that nature. It is this realization that we should mean by the term "conformity." And, as we shall see, such realization need not be so different from what Aristotle and Aquinas meant by perfection or absolute, "second," actuality. But whether or not it is different, we can be confident that our principle of division for the genus goodness has not been selected without a good reason. It would be rather surprising if the abstract goods were not closely related to the most general characteristics of the beings capable of having them.

The idea of the hierarchy of being involves no mystery. It is straightforward and, at least in the part of it I shall consider, quite in conformity with the scientific facts known to us; and so is the related nonnormative notion of perfection or degree of reality. We may describe it, very roughly, as follows. At the bottom there is the level of inanimate being: planets and stars, clouds and rivers, mountains and pebbles. Its most general property, let us say, is just that of being an occupant of space. At the next level is living being, for example, plants. It shares the general property of inanimate being but also has its own characteristic property, namely, what we call life. For that reason it is more "perfect," has "greater," "higher" reality, than inanimate being—it has the most general property of the latter but also a property the latter does not have. At the third level there is sentient being; it is also a living being and one that occupies space, but more perfect because it has a third property, sentience. We have thus reached the level of (at least most) animals.

But there are yet higher levels, determined by additional general properties. An obvious such property, possessed by many animals, is that of (being capable of) desire. Sentience without desire seems conceivable.[5] But the converse is not the case. What would it be for an animal to desire food but to be incapable of tasting or even feeling or seeing what it eats? How would it differ in this respect from a plant that can be said to nourish itself but surely not to desire food? I speak here only of the bodily desires; the so-called higher desires, for example, the desire for knowledge, are better describable, as I suggested in chapter 3 and will argue in greater detail shortly, as cases of consciousness of the intrinsic goodness of a (believed to be) realizable future state. Hunger and the desire for knowledge are so dissimilar phenomenologically as to prohibit their being lumped together. And by "desire" I shall always mean conscious desire or a disposition to experience certain conscious desires. Appeals to the "unconscious" would better be appeals to the physiological.

The nature of the property of desire suggests that the fourth level of the hierarchy of being will be that of beings possessing rationality. By its very nature desire tends to lead to activity, namely, the activity aiming at the desired object or state, and the most primitive manifestation of rationality is the capacity to render such activity, which of course is concerned with means-ends relationships, more effective. Yet desire without even such minimal rationality is conceivable, and therefore the presence of the latter in an entity does enrich the reality of the entity and thus determines a genuinely higher level in the hierarchy of being. But such limited rationality should be sharply distinguished from a much higher kind of rationality, characteristic, as far as we know, only of human beings. Rationality in general, including that possessed by cats and apes, would be better called intelligence, as it is by psychologists, and the sort of intelligence of which only human beings are capable would be better described as reason or intellect.

The distinctive mark of the intellect is the capacity of entertaining, making, and appraising universal judgments and especially abstract singular judgments. A merely intelligent animal, say a cat or an ape, may well be capable of entertaining, making, and appraising singular judgments, such as that expressed by the sentence "That is milk," or even existential judgments, such as that expressed by the sentence "There is milk behind the door." If we define a human being as a rational animal, we must mean by "rational" what traditional philosophers meant by it, namely, intellectual, and not what many contemporary writers on ethics seem to mean, namely, just intelligent, capable of means-ends calculations. So understood, the property of rationality is clearly additional both to the property of being capable of desire and to that of mere intelligence, and is possessed only by some beings that possess the latter. I shall focus here on rationality, not intelligence in general. For the sake of clarity I shall often use the term "intellectual" for that property.

Now intellectual activity, and surely much of merely intelligent activity, often involves the making of decisions, choice between alternatives, even when there is no desire (in our strict sense of bodily desire) for the chosen alternative, or when the desire for it is the weaker one. A scientist must choose between accepting the theory he has devoted his life to refuting, the evidence for which he knows is now overwhelming, and preserving his deeply held convictions by ignoring the evidence. No desire in the strict sense need be present, and while we may disapprove of his choosing the second alternative, it is, or could be, purely intellectual in motivation. But the sort of case that connects the property of having an intellect with that of desire in the strict sense is exemplified by a person told by his physician to reduce his weight, who is facing a choice between abstaining from the chocolate mousse being served at the table and eating it. To suppose that in this case there is a conflict between two desires, the desire, say, to increase one's chances of living a long life and the desire to enjoy the dessert, is to rely on a use of the word "desire" that is justified at best by remote family resemblances. The difference between one's attitude toward the mousse and one's attitude toward increasing the probability of living a long life is so extreme as to forbid the facile application of the same concept to both. The latter is clearly an attitude of the intellect (which is not to say that it is always justified), and the former is clearly quite independent of the intellect. If we call the attitude of the intellect a dictate of reason, then we have before us a conflict between reason and desire, not between two desires.

Now, one has a natural capacity sometimes to do what reason dictates rather than what desire prompts. It is this capacity that is the clearest example of what we call will, whether or not its manifestations in decisions and choices are causally determined or not. It is a dramatically novel and yet fundamental property, inseparable from the possession of intellect yet clearly distinguishable from it. A will without intellect is inconceivable. The exercise of a will is most clearly manifested precisely in cases of a conflict between intellect and desire, and in subtle cases, like that of the scientist mentioned earlier, a conflict between two aims of the intellect, one of which may be of a higher order. This is why Aristotle defined choice as deliberate desire, Aquinas defined the will as the appetite of reason, and Kant held that "the will is nothing but practical reason."

But the presence of intellect without will is not inconceivable, and for that reason beings possessing the latter are on a higher level in the hierarchy of being than beings possessing only the former. It is possible that some intellectual beings lack will and thus have a nature less rich than that of intellectual beings that do have will. Whether in fact there are such beings is irrelevant here. It may be doubted that there are, on the grounds that an intellect without will would have no significant function, since it could translate its dictates into action only in the rare cases where there is no conflict. If so, we might have a biological reason why it would be *causally* impossible for a being to be intellectual but lack will. None of this should suggest to the reader that I subscribe to the view, which I questioned in chapter 3, that reason by itself can lead to no action. That view has a point only if understood as suggesting that something distinct from reason, usually some desire, leads to action. But the will is logically inseparable from the intellect. It *is* the intellect in its practical employment, as Kant argued. What is conceivable but perhaps biologically not possible is that reason should have only theoretical employment.

There is yet another fundamental property, which I shall call sociality and one, but only one, aspect of which Aristotle perhaps meant when he said that man is a political animal. By sociality I mean one's relationships with other beings that possess intellect and will, but relationships that logically presuppose the presence of these characteristics, as purely sexual or cannibalistic relationships do not. Thus sociality determines a level of the hierarchy of being that is higher than those determined by intellect and will, for it is *logically* possible that some intellectual and volitional beings do not enter into such relationships. Of course, this may be *causally* impossible. There can be no intellectual activity that does not employ concepts, one cannot possess a stock of concepts that is adequate for anything deserving to be called intellectual activity except through the mastery of a sufficiently rich language, and one cannot, at least as a matter of fact, master such a language that is not public and the mastery of which is not achieved through relationships that are social in the sense I have indicated. And, needless to say, any advanced intellectual activity, such as scientific investigation, is as a matter of fact either directly a collective effort or presupposes the results of others' past efforts, and thus is social in nature.

I have identified seven levels in the hierarchy of being, although as far as we know the three highest (those characterized by possession of intellect, of will, and sociality) are occupied by the same beings, namely, human beings. The medievals identified two even higher levels, namely, those of the angels and God. (In fact, each angel was supposed to occupy a distinguishable level.) But I shall not discuss how if at all they fit in the hierarchy of being. If we now consider a being that has all seven characteristics corresponding to the seven levels and thus, unless there are those additional two (or more) levels, is the most perfect being, the being richest in reality, namely, human being, we can express all the distinctions we have made as distinctions between the most general aspects or characteristics of human nature. A human being occupies space, lives, is sentient, has desires, has the sort of intelligence deserving to be called intellect, is capable of volition, and is a member of a society of such beings.

But this assertion should not be misunderstood. From an ethical point of view, the relevant characteristics are those of being a social, intellectual, volitional, desiring, sentient, living, spatial being, not that of being a member of the biological species Homo sapiens. Only thoughtless sentimentalism (not very unlike that of those who deplore the killing of baby seals but eat milk-fed veal) would cause us to regard a race of biologically human beings who, for permanent genetic reasons, lack the first three of the above characteristics in the same way as we regard human beings who do not. (This remark has no bearing on the question of how we should regard fetuses, infants, imbeciles, and those in irreversible coma. This question, I suggest, must be answered mainly by applying something like the classical notions of actuality and potentiality, and of privation; *ex hypothesi*, these have no relevant application to the case I am imagining.) And only lack of ethical imagination would cause us to refuse to so regard beings (say, from outer space) who do have those characteristics but are not human, perhaps biologically have nothing in common with humans. It was not through ignorance of the purely *biological* facts that Aristotle distinguished sharply between Greeks and barbarians, between masters and slaves, between men and women. Nor is it through knowledge of these facts that we ourselves may agree in opposing racial, ethnic, and sexual discrimination. Unless we smuggle into our biological conception of human being another, very different conception, the characteristic of belonging to the same biological species is simply not sufficiently fundamental for ethics.

If this is not evident, the reason perhaps is that although the difficulties taxonomy faces are well known, they do not happen to arise with respect to Homo sapiens. As David L. Hull has remarked, "very few properties are needed to distinguish modern man from any other known species. However, if a species of ape were to begin to develop along the same lines as man, acquiring comparable properties, the definition of Homo Sapiens would have to be expanded to exclude this new form if Homo Sapiens is to be kept minimally monophyletic."[6] We may view this biological fact as a piece of good fortune for us, as is the fact that there are not major differences between nationalities, races, and sexes, of the sorts Aristotle believed there were. Had it been otherwise, clear thought would have required painful changes in the moral and political attitides most philosophers hold today.

Therefore, our sketch of the hierarchy of being is a sketch concerned with properties that may be exemplified by (possibly the same) individual things, not with the classification of *actual* individual things in any of the empirical sciences. In this sense our sketch is a priori. That there are the seven properties I have identified, and that individuals may be classified hierarchically in accordance with the exemplification by them of these properties, can be known to be true a priori, even if there were no individuals exemplifying them. This is why the view I have developed must not be confused with the classical view that in our identification of the abstract goods we are to be guided by the empirical facts about "human nature," and therefore is not open to the familiar modern objections to this view. This is why also it is not open to the objection that it ignores the details of current science, for example, that in some cases it is unclear whether an organism should be classified as a plant or an animal. The view I have outlined involves no claim to represent all of the levels of the hierarchy of being as they are empirically determinable, or to describe in adequate empirical detail those it does represent. Neither physics nor biology is a part of it! But there can be no reasonable doubt that the seven properties it identifies are genuine and that they are roughly as described. Nor, of course, need we doubt that in fact they are exemplified in nature.

## 2. Existence and Health

Many, if not all, of the most general abstract goods identified in the history of ethics and readily acknowledged by mature everyday thought can now be seen to correspond to the seven properties defining the hierarchy of being. The good corresponding to the first (occupancy of space) is surely just existence as such, or continued existence. In the case of living beings, we usually mean their existence *qua* living, not *qua* inanimate objects, that is, corpses, and the good in question is usually described as life. And, indeed, Hobbes held that self-preservation is the primary goal of all rational individuals.[7] But according to Augustine, *all* things have in common the fact that they were created by God, and the good that they all, including pebbles and mountains, have in common is the sheer fact of existing. The theological appeal is unnecessary. On the contrary, it has been generally supposed, beginning perhaps with Plato in the *Timaeus*, perhaps even with Genesis, that the reason God created the universe is precisely that the existence of the universe is an intrinsic good. Thomas Aquinas also argued directly for the intrinsic goodness of existence: "Just as it is impossible . . . for anything to be a being which does not have existence, so too it is necessary that every being be good by the very fact of its having existence, even though in many beings many other aspects of goodness are added over and above the act of existing by which they subsist."[8]

The intrinsic goodness of existence as such is evident in the attractiveness of the claims of certain conservationist and environmentalist movements, as long as we understand their goal of the preservation of the environment, including other species of life, as motivated by the belief that this is an intrinsic good, rather than something conducive to human interests.[9] It is the belief that, in Ramon M. Lemos's eloquent words, even inanimate objects have "a natural right not to be abused or destroyed," or at least that we have a natural obligation not to abuse or destroy them except insofar as this is "necessary for or contributes to the preservation or enhancement of the life of some living being."[10] It is also evident in the power of the view that it is better that there be something rather than nothing, that there be a universe even if it should contain no human beings or any other sort of life.[11] And let us consider how we would view the wanton, pointless destruction of a mountain, or lake, or even another planet, if this latter action became possible technologically.

But, the reader may protest, what is the *argument* for the view that there is an intrinsic good that even inanimate objects possess? I believe that it is just as improper to look for such an argument as it would be to try to prove that blue is a color. (In the preface to *Principia Ethica*, Moore asserted that ethical propositions regarding what kind of things are good in themselves are incapable of proof and disproof, that no relevant evidence can be adduced for them, though they may be self-evident.) Of course, if systematic considerations count as an argument, then there is the required argument, that represented by this whole chapter, just as we may say that systematic considerations constitute the argument for counting blue, and, say, not just yellow or red, as a color. And, as we have seen, the view in question has roots in ordinary consciousness. Beyond this, perhaps it is best to resort to rhetoric, as Henry More did when he wrote that to deny that God "takes pleasure that all his creatures enjoy themselves, that have life and sense and are capable of enjoyment," that "they are not in the least made for themselves," is "provinciality and ignorance."[12] It is also mere provinciality to refuse to say this also about in-animate things. But it is not difficult to understand why such provinciality is natural. Dietrich Von Hildebrand wrote: "[The] value of being as such . . . is so formal and so far remote from the qualitative values that it never in a single created individual being discloses itself in its full depth and grandeur."[13]

It must not be supposed, however, that there are genuine arguments to the contrary. A familiar sort of such an "argument" is the following:

> A mere thing, however valuable to others, has no good of its own. The explanation of that fact, I suspect, consists in the fact that mere things have no conative life: no conscious wishes, desires, and hopes; or urges and impulses; or unconscious drives, aims, and goals; or latent tendencies, direction of growth, and natural fulfillment. Interests must be compounded somehow out of conation; hence mere things have no inter-ests. . . . Without interests a creature can have no "good" of its own, the achievement of which can be its due. Mere things are not loci of value in their own right, but rather their value consists entirely in being objects of other beings' interests.[14]

What is the argument here? If the vague term "interests" (which, except in the philosophy of law, we would do well to avoid) is understood in the manner suggested in the passage quoted, then the argument is the blatantly question-begging claim that mere (that is, inanimate) things have no good of their own because they are mere things, because they are inanimate. If the term "interests" is so understood that whatever can have a good of its own has interests, then the argument rests mainly on the premise that interests must be compounded of conations, which, on this interpretation of the term "interest," is again mere question begging.[15]

The good corresponding to being a living thing is surely health, including bodily integrity. This is universally recognized as a good, and often mentioned as such in classical Greek ethics. The quibble that the notion of health is in part "normative" need not concern us. It would be extraordinary if the subgenera of goodness should be nonnormative, that they could be characterized without even implicit appeal to their genus.[16] This does not render the assertion that health is a good analytic. (See above, pp. 63–64.) If we were to *define* health as the good corresponding to life, which I have *not* done, this would be a real definition, not a nominal definition, and as such the relationship it asserts to hold between the species defined and its genus is better described as synthetic a priori, certainly not as analytic. The difference can be explained as follows. In its ordinary applications, the concept of health is governed by considerations such as physical vigor, freedom from infection, regularity of heartbeat, normality with respect to a sufficiently large population, etc. This is quite unlike the paradigms of a nominal definition and of the resulting genuinely analytic statements, such as the definition of a bachelor as an unmarried man and the statement that all bachelors are unmarried men; in its ordinary applications, the concept of bachelor is governed precisely by the consideration whether the person is an unmarried man, a fact to the significance of which Hilary Putnam has repeatedly drawn attention.[17] A simple way of seeing the difference is to note that one who does not possess in one's vocabulary the word "bachelor" or a synonym of it cannot know that all bachelors are unmarried men, while one who does not possess in one's vocabulary the word "health" or a synonym of it *can* know that health is a good. Only philosophers who hold that all thought and knowledge essentially involve the use of language would deny this. What I have said about health I would also say, but will forbear from in effect repeating myself, about any other abstract good the notion of which may be called "normative." Indeed, we would do well to avoid the vague term "normative" when we do ethics.

## 3. Pleasure and Satisfaction

The good corresponding to sentience, I suggest, thus acknowledging the element of truth to be found in hedonism and classical utilitarianism, is pleasure. (Of course, like all the other properties defining the hierarchy of being, sentience is itself an important extrinsic good, namely, a means to the preservation of the animal's life. But it is with intrinsic goods we are concerned.) I use the word "pleasure" here in what I believe is its only clear and phenomenologically distinctive sense, that of *bodily* pleasure, but sometimes I shall use it also in its vague broader sense, suitably qualifying it when necessary, because otherwise a whole new technical terminology would need to be invented. The so-called higher pleasures, for example, those of intellectual work, as well as some others not describable as "higher" yet also not as "bodily," are best understood as one's consciousness of the goodness of the state or activity described as pleasant. (One is pleased or pained when one is conscious of the goodness or badness of one's intellectual work, but the pleasure or the pain is hardly other than the acute consciousness of the goodness or the badness.)

The reader may find what I have said high-handed. But surely it is evident that, like the concept of desire, the ordinary concept of pleasure is at best governed only by family resemblances. We express it commonly not only in speaking of a pleasant sensation (for example, a sexual one), but also in speaking of taking pleasure in something, being delighted, enjoying, being happy, liking, feeling good, and so on. The idea that all the applications of these notions have something in common simply does not survive even a perfunctory phenomenological investigation. It is especially obvious that they do not have in common a certain distinctive sensation, if for no other reason than that, unlike sensations such as bodily pain, most are inherently intentional, as Ryle has pointed out.[18] (But I do not agree that there are no sensations of pleasure. The pleasure characteristic of orgasm is surely a sensation.) A sufficient reason for refusing to classify the bodily pleasures and the so-called higher pleasures in the same genus (one lower than that of goodness) is that the former have (or at least are experienced as having) spatial location, for example, in the mouth, in the genitals, or in a larger part of the body, or in the body as a whole, while the latter do not.[19] (I shall ignore the suggestion that what all have in common is something called a "hedonic tone.")

The view of some psychologists that pleasure is to be understood in terms of desire, perhaps as a state one desires to continue,[20] can be evaluated only after an account of the notion of desire is provided, and that, as I have argued and will argue again shortly, is also a prime example of a notion governed only by family resemblances. In any case, it is not difficult to think of counterexamples. Many pleasures are such that it is essential to them to be of short duration, perhaps almost momentary, and either in fact we do not desire them to be otherwise, or it is even incoherent to speak of such a desire. The pleasure of orgasm may be an example of the first kind; that of winning a game (not that of having won a game, which is very different) is presumably an example of the second kind. If the concept of pleasure is to have a place in an ethical theory, it must be regimented, but only for phenomenological, not scientific, reasons. What I am engaged in is precisely such a regimentation, as I have already done with the concept of desire, and I feel no qualms over doing this. Let me provide some details.

The bane of the history of ethics has been the indiscriminate use of the notion of pleasure, which reached its culmination in the absurdity of Mill's subsuming under it such things as virtue and money, and in his doctrine of qualitative differences between pleasures. The absurdity of the latter consisted not in his recognition of fundamental differences between the states in question but in his insistence that these states nevertheless belong to the same genus, namely, pleasure.[21] Let us first note the diversity there is among the bodily pleasures. In addition to those that are (experienced as) located in particular parts of the body, there are *bodily* pleasures the location of which is either the whole body or an indeterminately large part of it. (An example might be the pleasure of orgasm.) Such pleasures may be passive (for example, the comfort of being in a warm bed during a cold night) or, more often, active (for example, the pleasure of exercise). Bodily pleasures may also be *caused* by intellectual activities; an example would be the *bodily* excitement one sometimes experiences when successfully engaged in a heated argument. In all of these cases, the pleasure is inseparable from sentience even if a necessary condition of its occurrence is a condition or activity that is by no means purely or even at all sensory. And that condition or activity may be a logically, not causally, necessary condition. Some pleasures of exercise may be logically possible only if one is exercising or at least is under the impression that one is exercising; their character may be logically dependent on the circumstances in which they take place, as Aristotle in effect argued in Book 10 of the *Nichomachean Ethics* with respect to pleasures in general. I shall come back to this point.

But when we speak of pleasures or "enjoyments" that are nonbodily, we must have in mind states of a totally different kind. And I suggest that these states consist in one's consciousness (perhaps, I should add, focused, attentive, acute, vivid consciousness) of the goodness of certain objects, conditions, or activities.[22] I have already mentioned the example of the pleasures (and pains) of one's intellectual work. Other examples would be the pleasures of friendship, of loyal participation in a worthwhile common enterprise, of raising a child, of listening to a symphony. Of course, in all of these cases, bodily pleasures may also be present and this would in part explain what I branded as the indiscriminate use of the word "pleasure."

Take the last example. There is no doubt that listening to a symphony often causes a number of bodily pleasures, for example, certain thrills in the spine. But even if these pleasures are, in their intrinsic character, logically inseparable from their causes, and thus are not *merely* caused by them, they differ fundamentally from certain other states, which are often described as the *appreciation* of the music, of its structure, coherence, elegance, subtlety, etc. It is these latter states that presumably are to be classified as "higher pleasures." But are they not simply the consciousness (attentive, acute, vivid) of the sheer goodness of (the good qualities of) the symphony? To describe such consciousness as sentience would obviously be misleading, even though it may involve sentience. And to classify it with the bodily pleasures would be to suggest that there is similarity where there is none.

Perhaps the consciousness of the goodness of something (not merely of something that is good) is always *itself* good, and if so, we may, for lack of a simpler terminology, express this fact by describing the consciousness as a pleasure. But if we do so, we must recognize that this would be merely a matter of terminology, as may easily be seen even in the case of particular *bodily* pleasures, say those of orgasm. There may, though usually would not, occur consciousness of the goodness of such a pleasure when the pleasure is occurring, and that consciousness, let us suppose, would be good in itself (though it might be rather distracting!). But it must be sharply distinguished from that of whose goodness it is consciousness, the pleasure of orgasm. Unlike the latter, it is a reflective and rather abstract state that may well be describable as intellectual. To call both *pleasure* would be to disguise the fundamental phenomenological difference between the two.

Of course, the contention that consciousness of the goodness (*qua* goodness) of good things is itself something *good* would be substantive, not just verbal. But if we accepted it, then we would achieve a welcome clarification of the concept of a great good that has been accorded primacy in much of traditional ethics, namely, happiness. We can say that happiness is, essentially, the consciousness of the goodness of what has been (or is confidently expected to be) realized—but only if the latter is lasting, extensive, and not marred by much pain or consciousness of the badness of other states that have been (or are expected to be) realized. But insofar as the good of happiness, so understood, is derivative from the goodness of the goods of whose goodness happiness is the consciousness, it need not be included in our list of fundamental abstract goods, it does not properly belong in their hierarchy. I shall return to this topic.

The good corresponding to bodily desire is surely satisfaction—the satisfaction of the desire, especially the calm, stable sort of satisfaction due to the temperance or moderateness of the desire, very much what Plato and Aristotle called *sophrosyne*. It has been regarded as the only good by many utilitarians, and by many who have been misleadingly called hedonists. It must not be confused with pleasure. Pleasure may but need not accompany the satisfaction of a desire. It may occur even if there is no relevant desire, and a desire may be satisfied even if no pleasure is experienced. One may enjoy a new scent without having wanted to smell it, or even to smell anything at all.[23] And a hungry person may satisfy his hunger and thus attain a state of satisfaction even if he does not experience the gustatory pleasures characteristic of eating (perhaps he has lost his sense of taste or the food is revolting), or even the possibly pleasant, but sometimes painful, sensation of a full stomach. Indeed, no pleasure at all need be felt. To describe the state of satisfaction itself as pleasure would be incoherent, since the former consists simply in the *cessation* of the desire, while pleasure, whatever it may be, is certainly not the mere cessation of something. If this seems implausible, the reason is probably that one confuses the satisfaction of the desire with some, perhaps common, accompanying pleasure, for example, the possibly pleasant sensation of a full stomach and of general bodily comfort.

Moreover, one may desire and experience gustatory pleasures even if not hungry, as is evident in the case of the satiated gourmand who continues to eat. We should keep in mind that hunger is the desire for food,[24] or for eating, not for gustatory pleasure. A hungry person may eat food he finds revolting and also eat even if doing so causes painful sensations (for example, if the food is too hot). Nor is hunger the desire for the cessation of a pain. An unsatisfied desire may be said to be painful in the sense that it is something bad of whose badness one is conscious, but not in the literal sense of being a bodily pain. Hunger may be accompanied by pains in the stomach, but it is not the same as those pains. And the desire that the pains cease is not the same as hunger, which is the desire to eat. The desire to avoid pain would be understood in the same general way as the desire for pleasure, which we shall consider shortly. On all this there is much good sense to be found in Bishop Butler.

It is sometimes argued that what one desires is always pleasure, on the grounds that even if ostensibly one desires something else, say *x*, one would not desire it if *x* were not at least generally pleasurable to oneself. But even if this subjunctive conditional were true (how we may determine that it is true is seldom discussed), its truth would have no tendency to show that what one desires is not *x* but a certain pleasure. The general pleasurability of *x* may be a necessary condition of one's desiring *x*, but surely there are many other necessary conditions. Are all these also what one desires when one desires *x*?

In our ethical theory, the notion of desire has been restricted to the bodily desires, for reasons similar to those I gave for restricting the notion of pleasure to the bodily pleasures. (But, as with "pleasure," for expository convenience I sometimes use "desire" more broadly, suitably qualifying it when necessary.) Indeed, the use of the notion of desire (or want, or conation, or preference, etc.) in the history of ethics has been even more indiscriminate than that of the notion of pleasure. As we have seen, one reason for this has been the para-mechanical as-sumption that mere consciousness of something cannot prompt decision and thus action, that the presence of a "real motive force" is necessary, and the related failure to acknowledge the will not only as a property distinct from desire but as one presupposing the presence of intellect. Hence the purely technical sense in which many writers[25] use it, roughly that of a motivational state. There is nothing wrong with such a technical notion, as long as we remember that it covers a great variety of states that in any other respect need have nothing in common, and that the really interesting and controversial questions concern the identification of these states and the account of their similarities and differences.

But perhaps the chief reason for the indiscriminate use of the concept of desire has been the failure to recognize the existence and nature of our consciousness of the goodness *qua* goodness of good things. For, as I have suggested, in the case of the so-called higher, or nonbodily, desires, what there is seems to be simply the (vivid, acute) consciousness of the (actual or apparent) goodness of something. What distinguishes it from the consciousness we describe as a "higher pleasure" is that it is consciousness of the goodness of things not yet realized, while in the case of a "higher pleasure," one is conscious of the goodness of something that has been realized. (Though, if a confident expectation of its realization is present, then there may be the "pleasure," i.e., the consciousness of the goodness, of that *expectation*.) To desire to complete one's work is to be conscious of the goodness of the com-pletion, or the goodness (real or imaginary) of the work to be completed. To desire (want) to act as one ought to act is to be conscious of the goodness of acting as one ought to act. A variety of bodily sensations may accompany such occurrent "higher desires," though they are not logically or even causally necessary for the latter. But neither in the case of the higher pleasures nor in the case of the higher desires need the state of whose goodness one is conscious involve oneself. One can take pleasure in another person's present health and desire another person's future health.

The view of desire and of pleasure I have defended is not unlike, though by no means the same as, Aristotle's. In sharp contrast with the indiscriminate use of these notions in modern ethics, Aristotle distinguished kinds of desire and kinds of pleasure so different from one another as to prompt us (though perhaps not Aristotle) to regard them as generically different. Corresponding to each part of the soul there is a distinctive desire (*oreksis*), and in the case of the rational part, the corresponding desire (*boulesis*, usually translated as wish but probably better as just rational desire) has as its object the good (or at least the apparent good).[26] Obviously, this latter desire, if occurrent, involves awareness of something as good. Although Aristotle might not have agreed, it is unclear that it need involve anything else. With respect to pleasure, Aristotle held (in Book 10 but not in Book 7 of the *Nichomachean Ethics*) that pleasure perfects the pleasant activity by supervening upon it "like the bloom of manhood to those in their prime of life."[27] And indeed, at least with respect to some activities, our awareness of them as good may be thought of as "supervening" upon them, without affecting their essence yet rendering them more valuable. One who is aware of one's work as good is in a better state than one who is not, is more likely to be absorbed in it and to persevere, even if one does not have any experiences even remotely resembling, say, gustatory or sexual pleasures.

If what I have claimed regarding the "higher" desires and pleasures has not been generally recognized and perhaps seems to the reader implausible and indeed dogmatic, the reason, I think, is to be sought in our failure to make clear and explicit what is involved in being conscious of the goodness of a thing and to distinguish levels of intensity, vividness, and clarity of focus in such consciousness. There is, first, consciousness of a good thing. There is, second, consciousness of the qualities of the thing that are good and in virtue of the goodness of which it itself is good. There is, third, consciousness of the goodness of these qualities. [28] Only the third is at issue in our proposed account of the nonbodily desires and pleasures. And within this third kind of consciousness, further distinctions should be made. As with any other consiousness, it may be attentive or inattentive. It may be sharply focused upon its object (clearly bringing it out as the figure against the ground, in gestalt terminology) or not sharply focused. It may be preoccupying, central, vivid, dominant in the total conscious life of the person at the time, or incidental, peripheral, blurred, subordinate to others, one among very many. It is in such differences, I suggest, that the so-called differences in strength of the nonbodily pleasures and desires consist, when the object remains constant, and in terms of which the so-called conative nature of nonbodily desire is to be understood.

The reason consciousness of the goodness of a state not yet realized has been described as desire is probably that, like bodily desire, it may be said to aim at what is not yet realized, in the sense that it may lead, for reasons hardly known to us (see above, chap. 3, section 2), to actions that tend to realize the state. Yet the enormous difference between bodily desire and the aiming at a good that is not yet realized, but of whose goodness one is conscious, is evident. First, what bodily desire aims at need not be good or even thought of as good. It must not be confused with its satisfaction. Hunger has eating as its aim, and it has it even if satisfaction does not and is not expected to result from the eating. Sexual desire, in one of its forms, has orgasm as its aim, not the satisfaction that may or may not follow. But eating and sexual orgasm are neither good nor bad in themselves. They may cause, but are not the same as, the satisfaction of the corresponding desire, which is a good. And they may cause, or even be logically necessary conditions for the nature of, certain pleasures, which also are good. But it is not that satisfaction or those pleasures at which the desires aim.

Second, the good corresponding to bodily desire, which I called satisfaction, is simply the cessation of the desire. Hunger is the desire to eat, but its satisfaction does not consist in eating; a hungry person may eat any amount of food and still be hungry—at most we can say that one's hunger is satisfied when one has eaten enough, but enough for one's hunger to be satisfied, that is, to cease to exist. And while we would not call its cessation satisfaction if achieved by taking a pill rather than by eating, there *need* not be a phenomenological difference between such a state and one achieved by eating. This is why diet pills can be effective. (But there *might* be such a difference, though this would not affect the argument. The memory of the manner the satisfaction was achieved might modify the experience, and so might any accompanying pleasure or pain.) But in the case of a "higher desire," in aiming at a good not yet realized but of whose goodness one is conscious, one is of course aiming at that good, at its realization. If one is aiming at understanding a difficult point in mathematics, the good involved is not the cessation of one's aiming (this might be positively bad, as a case of weak will or perhaps insufficient intelligence), but one's understanding of the point. This is why, while we can say that in the case of the bodily desires their good is satisfaction, to say this in the case of the "desire" for mathematical understanding would be grossly misleading. The former can achieve their good simply by ceasing to exist. The latter cannot. The good of satisfied bodily desire can be intelligibly described as the good of freedom from desire; hence the intelligibility, indeed plausibility, of Stoic ethics. But the good of satisfied "desire" for mathematical understanding cannot be intelligibly described as the "good" of sheer lack of curiosity or as achievable by drastic prefrontal lobotomy.

A higher desire so understood must not be confused with a wish, even though in some cases to wish something is to desire it. I may wish that something had happened in the past or that it were happening now, and I suggest that such a wish does consist in the consciousness of the goodness of its object. What distinguishes it from a higher desire is precisely its counterfactual nature; the idea of its satisfaction has no application and therefore no relevance to ethics. This is why desire in the ethically relevant sense is future oriented. But this does not mean that the satisfaction of a (future-oriented) "higher desire" is a distinguishable abstract good (as the satisfaction of a bodily desire indeed is). For it simply consists in the coming into being of the good that is desired, and to speak of the goodness of the satisfaction is to speak of the goodness of what has so come to be, for example, mathematical understanding.

Our discussion of the so-called higher desires may throw light on the nature of two kinds of desire that seem intermediate between them and the bodily desires. They are the desires for (bodily) pleasure and the second-order desires for the satisfaction of some first-order desires. I have already argued that the former must not be confused with the bodily desires themselves, which aim, say, at eating or drinking or sexual intercourse, not at the pleasure that may or may not accompany these. Yet there is desire for pleasure. The satiated gourmand may continue to eat in order to experience further gustatory pleasures. A person whose sexual desire is fully satisfied may continue to engage in pleasurable sexual activities. What does the desire for pleasure consist in, then? I have suggested that it consists in the consciousness of the goodness of a possible future pleasure. Is it a bodily or a higher desire? It is a desire for a bodily state, if we follow my suggestion that when speaking strictly we shall understand by pleasure only bodily pleasure. But it is much more like the higher desires in all other respects. It involves not only considerable abstraction but *thought of the absent*, which is a mark of a level of intelligence that, even if not limited to humans, is hardly present in most animals. Unlike the bodily desires, for example, hunger, thirst, sexual excitement, it is not a *feeling* but rather a *thought*. I would suggest a similar account of second-order desires for the satisfaction of a first-order desire, for example, one's desire that one's hunger, whether present or future, be satisfied. It is not the same as one's hunger; the object of the latter is eating, and in any case one may desire that a future hunger be satisfied, which of course one does not now experience. Nor is it a desire for gustatory pleasure, for it may be present even if for some reason one does not enjoy or expect to enjoy eating. It consists, I suggest, in the vivid consciousness, thought, of the goodness of the satisfaction of the first-order desire.

There are, of course, a number of questions about desire that I have not considered. For example, can one desire what one *knows* will occur? Can one desire what one *knows* will not occur? This is not the place to discuss these questions, important though they may be to the phenomenology of desire.[29] How we answer them would not affect, I believe, the adequacy of what I have said.

We can now expand on what was said earlier about the concept of happiness. If we describe the realization of the goods, of whose goodness one had been conscious even before their realization, as the satisfaction of one's higher desires, and include in these the desires for pleasure and the second-order desires for the satisfaction of first-order desires, then we could say that one's happiness includes, essentially, the satisfaction of one's desires, both bodily and higher, a view indeed often held. But it includes also the consciousness of the goodness of what has been realized, even if one had not been previously conscious of it, had not "desired" it. But such realizations must be frequent and not accompanied by much pain or consciousness of the badness of other bad things that have occurred or are expected to occur. Happiness, so understood, would still be a derivative good, not belonging to our hierarchy of abstract goods but entirely to be understood in terms of it. The concept of happiness is heterogeneous; it is a mongrel concept, and thus, I suggest, inessential for an ethical theory, though it is useful.

But what if the thing of whose goodness one is conscious is only imagined to have been realized? Would there still be a higher pleasure, a good? Or would what has occurred be just a false, an unreal, pleasure, and thus not really a good, as Plato and Aristotle held? The question is difficult because the answer to it would depend on one's metaphysics of imaginary, nonexistent objects. I shall not try to settle it here. Suffice it to say that even in such a case a good has been realized, namely a *real* consciousness of goodness, even though this goodness is that of an unreal object and thus perhaps itself unreal, just as imagining something is a real state, even if what is imagined is not a real thing.

If what I have said about the notions of pleasure, desire, and happiness is correct, then what is the explanation of the prominence of these notions in the history of ethics? It seems to me not difficult to find. Bodily pleasure and the satisfaction of bodily desire are the most obvious goods, presumably because their goodness is appreciated even in earliest childhood. The notion of happiness as the characteristic of a life or a period of life that is *generally* pleasant and satisfied, is an obvious first move toward greater sophistication, one that can be made easily even in early adolescence. It is not surprising that these three naturally and quite justifiably commendatory notions should later tend to serve the task of commendations for which they are in fact not suited. It is natural that the discovery of new goods should be greeted as the discovery of new pleasures, or satisfactions, or kinds of happiness. But then the resultant confusions become quickly evident, and an attempt is made to restore conceptual order by insisting on "qualitative" differences between pleasures, as Mill did.

## 4. Knowledge

The abstract good corresponding to the intellect, I suggest, is what may be called theoretical knowledge, in the sense of entertaining and accepting on grounds of evidence (including self-evidence) universal propositions and especially abstract singular propositions, but also including the deeper understanding that the very entertainment of such propositions constitutes, an understanding to be found not only in philosophy, mathematics, and the sciences but also in the really great works of art. (As my use of the terms "entertaining" and "accepting" suggests, by knowledge as an abstract good I do not mean a disposition, which as Aristotle remarked may be present even in sleep, but the characteristic manifestations of the relevant dispositions.) This suggestion is quite familiar from the history of ethics, and central to Plato's and Aristotle's ethical views. If we wished, we could say that there is also an abstract good corresponding to intelligence in general, namely, knowledge in general. But the general notion of intelligence, especially as applied to the lower animals, is too indeterminate to be of much use to us. And the corresponding general notion of knowledge may not convey a clear sense of any intrinsic goodness. Is a cat's knowledge of how to catch a mouse an intrinsic good? Indeed, is a fisherman's skill an intrinsic good? And would memorizing the contents of a telephone book be good in itself? The good corresponding to the intellect, not to mere intelligence, is obviously very different from anything of that sort. What is the difference? I have already touched upon it in the methodological remarks I made in the previous chapter. Let me explain it now in greater detail.

In its logically primary and philosophically most significant sense, knowledge is knowledge that something is the case, it is propositional knowledge. And it is convenient, at least provisionally, to regard the logically simplest case of knowledge as consisting in knowing that a certain concept is applicable to a given object. Whether concepts are understood as words, or as meanings or uses of words, or as a certain sort of mental entity, or as principles or ways of classifying objects, to know that $x$ is (an) $F$ is to know that the concept of (an) $F$ is applicable to $x$. To know that this page is white is to know that the concept of (something) white is applicable to this page.

But there are two very different ways of determining, coming to know, that a certain concept $F$ is applicable to a given object $x$. First, we may take for granted the content of the concept $F$ and attempt to determine whether $x$ has the property or feature in virtue of which $F$ would be applicable to it; the attempt would be needed if the property or feature in question were hidden from us or perhaps simply not noticed sufficiently or at all. I shall call the result of such a determination *information*. Epistemology has concerned itself almost exclusively with knowledge as information. Second, we may take for granted certain properties or features of $x$ and attempt to determine whether they render $F$ applicable to $x$; such an attempt would be needed if the properties or features were unfamiliar, or if the content of $F$ were insufficiently clear and distinct, or if $F$, though clear and distinct, were not standardly applicable to $x$. I shall call the result of such a determination *under-standing*.[30] Another way of explaining the difference between information and understanding would be to say that to seek information is to attempt to determine which of two given and clearly understood contradictory propositions is true, while to seek understanding is to attempt to discover, formulate, or become clear about a pair of contradictory propositions such that one of them may be seen to be true. But what is obviously more fundamental and, I suggest, of far greater *intrinsic* value is the discovery of the pair of propositions, or the coming to grasp them more clearly, not the seeing of the truth of one of them, which may or may not follow. For this reason I shall often apply the term "understanding" to the grasp of the propositions even when neither is (yet) seen to be true. The former is a cognitive achievement independent of, but presupposed by, the latter. Without it the seeing cannot take place. Without understanding there can be no information. (I do not mean to deny, of course, that understanding may not presuppose information contained in *other* propositions. Obviously, scientific understanding rests largely on such prior information.) Let me try to explain the distinction with some examples.

If one tries to determine whether the whale is a fish and takes for granted that the concept of fish is that of a certain kind of nonmammal, one is presumably trying to determine whether or not the whale has the characteristics of being a mammal; one's investigation would require the observation and perhaps dissection of whales, and one's goal would be information about the whale. If one tries to determine whether the whale is a fish but takes for granted that it has mammalian characteristics, then one is presumably trying to determine whether the presence of such characteristics renders the concept of fish inapplicable; one's investigation would require an account of the concept of fish, presumably in the context of a general inquiry into the most appropriate, most illuminating classificatory system of animals, and one's aim would be the understanding of the whale.

Other examples are plentiful. Whether the United States is a democracy may call for information, to be achieved by determining whether, for example, blacks are free to participate in elections, or how the major parties nominate their presidential candidates. But it may also call for understanding, to be achieved by a judicious account of the concept of democracy, though one that is neither an exercise in introspection nor a mere listing of reminders of how we use the word; such an account would be part of the determination of the most appropriate and most illuminating classificatory system of forms of government. Whether a certain man is honest may call for the sort of information that detectives can provide about his activities and psychiatrists about his motives. But it may also call for a deepened understanding of what honesty is. To wonder about the color of the hat wrapped in the box is probably to seek information. To wonder whether the color of the hat before one's eyes is white or just very light grey is probably to seek understanding.

How do we achieve understanding, an illuminating description, an appropriate classification, a justifiable placement of something in our conceptual framework? By attending to the similarities and differences (identities and nonidentities, whether specific or generic) between it and other objects. For to find that a concept already in our possession is applicable to x is to find that x is sufficiently similar to the paradigmatic objects of the application of that concept to be countable as one of them. And to find a concept that, though not straightforwardly applicable to x, is nevertheless more suitable than any other available concept is to find that x is more like the paradigmatic objects of the application of that concept than it is like the paradigmatic objects of the application of any other concept, though not so much like them that we should be willing to include it among them. (This, the reader may recall, was the nature of our argument for generic identity.)

As I remarked in chapter 4, it is the latter case that is likely to be intellectually challenging. Indeed, we may be faced with such a challenge even if we do possess a concept paradigmatically applicable to the object. For the concept we possess may leave unclear, indistinct, unilluminated the *place* of the object on the logical land-scape of the world, its similarities to and differences from other objects, or perhaps even mislead us about them. We could then engage in conceptual revision. But we could also simply note such similarities and differences, without making our language reflect them.[31]

It is often said that the appraisal of *degrees* of similarity is subjective, a function of our interests and attitudes, and thus that it cannot provide us with knowledge of what something is objectively. (This view is not to be confused with the irrealism with respect to the concept of identity, which I defended in chapter 4.) But the premise is at best a wild exaggeration. To begin with, there are unquestionably objective appraisals of degrees of similarity. That the hue of a certain shade of blue is more like the hue of a certain second shade of blue than it is like the hue of a certain third shade of blue could be determined as objectively and unquestionably as anything could. But let us suppose that we compare complex objects that may be similar in some respects but not in others. How do we appraise the *general* similarity of such objects? Obviously not just by counting respects of specific simi-larity. But can we then offer an objective appraisal of a general similarity?

The question presupposes that respects of similarity cannot be ordered with respect to degree of importance or fundamentality according to an objective cri-terion. And the reason this presupposition seems not implausible is the extraordinary generality of both the question and the presupposition. When applied to specific cases, however, the implausibility of the presupposition is quite evident. That of three shades of color the first is more like the second than like the third, because the first two are closer in hue, even though the first and the third are both liked by Mary but the second is not, is an objective judgment in no sense influenced by our attitudes and interests, even if Mary were the one making the judgment. It is an objective fact that similarity in hue is a more fundamental similarity between colors than similarity with respect to being liked by Mary. That a cat and a dog belong together in our classificatory scheme, in a way that a cat and a pencil do not, even though the cat and the pencil are the same in color while the cat and the dog are not, is again, I suggest, a perfectly objective fact about degrees of fundamentality of similarity, however difficult it may be to make precise the criteria for determining such degrees.

I have engaged in this discussion of knowledge as understanding in order to make clear how knowledge may be seen to be a great intrinsic good. As long as by knowledge we mean mere information, for example, knowledge of the contents of a telephone book, we might be inclined to agree with Moore that it is good almost solely as a means or as a contributory factor in organic unities that are good.[32] But we are not likely to be so inclined with respect to knowledge as understanding. In order to explain the distinction, I have relied on rather pedestrian examples of understanding. But it is easy to see that understanding is especially required on the highest levels of knowledge, and that there its goodness, its intrinsic value, is, as Plato might have said, dazzling. That material objects consist of $n$ rather than $m$ kinds of micro-particles is information the intrinsic value of which may not be evident. But, given that at least some of these kinds of micro-particles do not fit the fundamental categories in terms of which we understand macro-objects (for example, they do not seem to be subject to causal laws as these are ordinarily understood), the great task (so far unfulfilled) of understanding them can easily be seen to aim at an achievement of extraordinary intrinsic value.

And when we come to philosophy, where the aim is almost always understanding and the topics are by definition the most fundamental ones, the value of knowledge as understanding is immediately evident. For on those levels understanding becomes indeed describable as wisdom, which was how the good of the intellect was described in classical philosophy. On those levels the difference between understanding and mere information is so great that, sometimes, though by no means always, the connection between the former and truth is itself no longer clear, if for no other reason than that it becomes appropriate to seek understanding of what truth itself is. For example, one who grasps Kant's philosophy is not likely to ask whether it is true (the question may strike one as silly), though not because one does not care about truth. And we can now see more clearly that certain aesthetic achievements are also cognitive achievements, though obviously in a sense that requires careful explanation. Dante's *Divine Comedy* and Dostoevski's *Crime and Punishment* exhibit great understanding but probably contain little information. The good corresponding to the intellect may be exemplified not only by the theoretical disciplines but also by the arts.

## 5. Fortitude and Friendship

We can be brief about the abstract good corresponding to the will. Surely, it is what we call firmness or strength of will, fortitude. (Again, the abstract good is not fortitude as a disposition but rather the manifestations of the relevant disposition.) In the paradigmatic case, one has strong will not when one follows the promptings of bodily desire (one need have no will at all to do so) but when one follows the dictates of reason, of the intellect. The will is not what Plato meant by the spirited part of the soul, and firmness of will may not be what he meant by courage, but the similarity in both respects should be evident. The will is the natural ally of the intellect, and its good consists in *actually* functioning as such an ally. This good may well be described as courage, in the broad sense of this term that would allow us to say, for example, that one is courageous when persevering in a difficult activity despite persistent pain or great misfortune. We may add that the necessary correlate of an *effective* will is freedom from external constraint, which is the ordinary sense of "freedom," and, not surprisingly, this has also been regarded as a great good. But the rationale for so regarding it, I suggest, is the one I have just given, and it does not support the common modern view that freedom from external constraint is a distinctive abstract good.[33] Thus I find myself in agreement with Moore.[34] I shall have a little more to say about this topic in connection with justice.

It is as an aspect of fortitude that virtue or good will (in the sense defined in chapter 2) would fit in our system of abstract goods. It is one's fortitude in willing and doing what one knows or at least believes is right, *because* of this knowledge or belief. But not all fortitude is virtue, in this sense, though it is still a good. For reason may require actions on grounds other than that they are right, and fortitude may also be manifested in willing and performing those actions. Presumably, this would occur only through a defect of reason, namely, ignorance of or inattention (even if unavoidable) to right and wrong, in general or on the particular occasion. There would be no action that a cognitively fully competent reason (one fully competent also in ethical knowledge) would require except on the grounds that it is right. And a will of perfect fortitude would never fail to ensure the performance of the action on those grounds. (Let us remember that a right action is always one that can be done.) This is why it has been said that virtue, so understood, is the highest good. Hastings Rashdall held that "goodness in the narrower moral sense— the right direction of the will—is itself the greatest of goods, and must always be paramount in the ideal man."[35] It is fortitude of the highest order. But there are other goods, which may be greater, namely, the goods corresponding to sociality and to the property of being a society. And even when reason is defective, fortitude in obeying its dictates remains admirable in itself, though we may deplore its consequences. The general's errors do not detract from the intrinsic goodness of the soldier's valor. The goodness of an abstract good does not entail that all of its concrete instances are unqualifiedly good.

We cannot be brief about the good corresponding to sociality. Augustine called it love, both of all creatures made in the image of God and of God himself. G. E. Moore regarded what he called personal affection as one of the two great goods (the other being aesthetic appreciation, which, as we have seen, need not be very different from the sort of understanding found on the highest levels of theoretical knowledge). Benevolence, usually regarded in modern but not in ancient ethics as one of the two main social virtues (the other being justice), may reasonably be described as a generalized form of love, in the not at all unfamiliar broader and deeper, nonsentimentalist and adult sense of the word. But that sense may also be conveyed by the word "friendship," as well as by the word "brotherhood." I suggest that it will be least misleading if we describe the abstract good corresponding to sociality as friendship. (Again, as with knowledge and fortitude, not friendship as a disposition but its actual practice.) "Love" suggests a special emotion or sentiment, the intrinsic goodness of which may be doubted (even though it can be a very great extrinsic good). And its Christian sense, though of great philosophical interest, has no place in a purely philosophical theory. "Brotherhood" is acceptable but obviously metaphorical. "Benevolence" suggests a certain sort of motive, indeed characteristic of friendship and included in it, but the motive may be present and the social relationship for which it is the motive may still be absent—and it is only a relationship that can be the good corresponding to the relationship of sociality. But this does not imply that genuine friendship requires reciprocation, though we would agree that ideal friendship does. We know well that one can be a friend of a neighbor, regard him as an end and with respect, and act toward him accordingly, even if the neighbor does none of these with respect to oneself. (In holding this we do achieve some common ground with the Christian conception of love.) "Friendship" is, of course, a word with a variety of uses, but I believe the reader can identify the use to which I shall be appealing in these pages. To try to define it would be as pointless as to try to define "health" or "pleasure."[36]

When we do describe the good corresponding to sociality as friendship, we establish once again contact with Plato and Aristotle. In The Republic Plato held that the function of the philosopher-kings is to care for and be friends of the rest of the citizens. And the attention Aristotle devoted to friendship in the Nichomachean Ethics is well known.[37] We also achieve, I believe, a much sharper focus upon the good distinctive of sociality. If we imagine a small and isolated society of human beings, surely the social ideal for them would be that they be friends. If this ideal is realized, then whatever is desirable about other social ideals, such as justice and fidelity in words and deeds, would also be realized. A true friend not only would not seek an unfairly greater share of a divisible good for himself; he is likely to try to give his friend the greater share. As Aristotle remarks, "Friendship seems to hold a state together, too, and lawgivers seem to pay more attention to friendship than to justice; for concord seems to be somewhat akin to friendship, and this they aim at most of all. . . . And when men are friends, they have no need of justice at all, but when they are just, they still need friendship; and a thing which is most just is thought to be done in a friendly way."[38] (Aristotle distinguished such true friendship from "friendship" for the sake of pleasure or mutual advantage.) It is characteristic of some forms of Christian ethics (for example, Augustine's) that the basic principle is "Love, and then do as you please," which of course entails that (Christian) love already includes whatever is of ethical value in "justice."[39] A similar view was held by Hume.[40] But we need not agree with Aristotle that friendship requires the presence of some other, "closer," or "personal," relationship, such as living together or at least seeing each other often. One can be a friend of one's students even if unable to recognize them and even if one teaches them only by correspondence.

It is of the very essence of this notion of friendship that it includes the Kantian notion of regarding a person as an end and never merely as a means. As Aristotle again remarks, "Those who wish the good of their friends for the sake of their friends are friends in the highest degree."[41] According to Aquinas, "That which is loved with the love of friendship is loved simply and for itself."[42] And Hastings Rashdall pointed out that "the most rudimentary family affection implies a certain consciousness (wholly unanalyzed no doubt) of the claims or rights or intrinsic worth of other persons."[43] Nor are the love and benevolence involved in friendship incompatible with the Kantian ideal of freedom from inclination. For if we suppose that they are directed upon beings that are intellectual and volitional *qua* intellectual and volitional, then they are not mere inclination or sentiment, what Kant called "pathological love," as perhaps is the case with love and benevolence toward the lower animals. Friendship involves some *admiration* of the other person (at least it is incompatible with *contempt*), a good opinion of him or her, an appreciation of at least some aspects of what he or she is, but *qua* a volitional and intellectual being; this is why purely sexual love is not friendship. And, indeed, Aristotle insisted that perfect friendship, as distinguished from friendship for the sake of pleasure or mutual advantage, involves mutual recognition of goodness, that it is possible only between good men.[44] If we regard (as Aristotle would) the properties of being intellectual and volitional as fully actualized only when their respective goods are achieved (I shall return to this point), then we can say that perfect friendship is possible only between beings who have achieved such goodness. When so understood, the abstract good corresponding to sociality seems indeed to include the second of the two great goods Moore identified, namely, personal affection, for, as Moore insisted, affection involves the appreciation of the other person as "of great intrinsic value," and as possessing good qualities.[45] Such affection is not clearly distinguishable from regarding its object as an end and never merely as a means.[46]

But our describing other persons as ends, or as having intrinsic worth, or as objects of special respect, does not involve the postulation of an additional abstract good. For so describing persons need merely be a way of acknowledging that they alone have the capacity for all the great goods we have identified, especially those of fortitude and knowledge, and therefore that the promotion of their good is of special ethical concern, since it consists in the promotion of those goods. As Hastings Rashdall pointed out, "When we say, 'Every one to count for one,' we are no doubt thinking merely of human beings; but why are the lower animals to be excluded from consideration? . . . The lives of animals cannot be thus lightly treated except upon a principle which involves the admission that the life of one sentient being may be more valuable on account of its greater potentialities."[47] Unless so understood, I suggest, the view that each person is an end, or has intrinsic worth, or deserves special respect, has no clear rationale or even content.[48]

My use of the word "friendship" is obviously both broader than the ordinary use and narrower than the Christian use of "love." It is broader than the ordinary use in that it applies to social relationships that may be "impersonal," such as (sometimes) that between a teacher and a student, and in that it need not involve special emotion or sentiment. But it is narrower than the Christian use of "love" in that it applies only to social relationships. It is the good of sociality. Perhaps one can, in general, abstractly, love all volitional and intellectual beings. And one can certainly acknowledge their great intrinsic worth and therefore acknowledge that one ought to preserve it and increase it. Insofar as Christian love, and generally benevolence and altruistic emotion, involve this acknowledgment, they may be good in themselves simply as consciousness of goodness (see above, p. 92), and of course good as means, that is, as motives, for doing what one ought to do.[49] But they need have nothing to do with sociality. Membership in the class of volitional and intellectual beings is not the same as entering into a social relationship, for the class may exist even if its members do not enter into such relationships. On the other hand, there is the intrinsic good of being an object of another person's special care and concern in an actual social relationship. This good is simply the good of friendship.

But though my use of "friendship" is, in the respect noted, broader than its ordinary use, in another respect it is much narrower. Most of what we call friendships would not fit my account; they are more properly describable as acquaintanceships, though perhaps ones involving a modicum of affection. Thus, what I have been describing may be called genuine friendship, which indeed is rare though not unrealizable. (Thus we need not disagree with Aristotle's remark that "It is impossible to be a friend to many men in a perfect friendship,"[50] as long as we regard the impossibility as factual, not conceptual.) But this is not a difficulty for our theory. Genuine knowledge as understanding, true fortitude, perfect health, are also rare. An abstract good need not be easy to achieve, yet our conception of it remains practical as a guide to the approximation of it. On the other hand, it is also reasonable to allow for broader uses of our notions of the abstract goods, guided by the notion of the highest or ideal species of each, but allowing that there are other, "lower," species as well. This would be in effect to acknowledge that at least some of the abstract goods we have identified are *subgenera*, not *species*, of goodness. I shall return to this point in the next chapter.

It has been argued by John Rawls[51] that benevolence is not a substitute for justice, since by itself it provides no principles for the adjudication of cases of conflict (should I help Brown or Jones, given that I cannot help both?), or guidance as to what is to count as a good. But the argument does not apply to the view defended in this book. Our notion of friendship presupposes the general conceptions of goodness and of those of its species or subgenera that were discussed earlier. And while our theory does not automatically resolve all possible particular cases of conflict (no theory, including Rawls's, can do that; even the most elaborate legal code cannot), it does contain the general principles that would guide such a resolution. I shall attempt to show that this indeed is so in the next chapter. But, of course, Rawls and many others have had more general reasons for denying that benevolence is a substitute for justice, to which I now come.

I endorsed Aristotle's view that among friends there is no need for justice, thus implying that justice is not a distinguishable good of sociality but an aspect of friendship. Is this not too cavalier a way of dealing with one of the great issues in ethics? Is not justice a good distinguishable from friendship? The question admits of no straightforward answer because there are many concepts of justice. But insofar as justice is an intrinsic good, it still need not be a distinctive intrinsic good. Even if not an *aspect* of friendship, it might be just a very imperfect *form* of friendship. It might be related to friendship as mere information is related to understanding, in the case of knowledge. But let us consider some of the various concepts of justice.

Plato devoted *The Republic* to an investigation of justice, though since the Greek term he used was *dikaiosyne*, it is probably better to say that his topic was rightness. In any case, his conclusion was that justice, whether in the state or in the individual soul, was, if not reducible to, at least inseparable from, the presence of the other three virtues, namely, wisdom, fortitude, and temperance. If so understood, it would be misleading to describe justice as an additional abstract good. (To say, as Plato did, that it is the three parts of the state, or of the soul, performing their proper functions in harmony, is to make explicit its special, second-order status.)

One can also think of justice as the structure of society that would be most likely to promote the goods the realization of which depends at least in part on the structure of society. This seems to be the view suggested by John Rawls's assertion that in their deliberation on the principles of justice the original contractors "are moved solely by the highest-order interests in their moral powers and by their concern to advance their determinate but unknown final ends." "They are not required to apply, or to be guided by, any prior and antecedent principles of right and justice."[52] If this is all there is to the value of justice (I am not suggesting that Rawls thinks that this is all there is), then it is a purely extrinsic good and not in competition with friendship as the good corresponding to sociality.

Justice may also be understood as the performance of the actions I have called duties, such as telling the truth and paying one's debts, but also the duties of the legislator and the judge. So understood, it is the goodness of those actions that have intrinsic goodness. It is especially evident that justice in this sense is not needed among friends as something *additional* to friendship. The reason, I suggest, is that the intrinsic goodness of such actions is due in part to their consisting in treating another person as an end, not as a means, whatever one's motive may be for doing so, and therefore it may be thought of as an aspect of the goodness of friendship.[53] On the other hand, in the absence of perfect friendship, justice in this sense would still be an intrinsic good, and for systematic reasons it may be described as a primitive, indeed embryonic, species of friendship.

Justice can also be understood as impartiality, as equality of treatment or at least of consideration. But such equality seems to have intrinsic value only in the absence of relevant differences. As Rashdall wrote, "No positive proof can, as it appears to me, be given that the higher good of few and the lower good of many may not come into collision. And when they do come into collision, there are some cases in which we should, I think, prefer the higher good of the few. How far then does this admission modify our acceptance of the Benthamite principle of equal consideration? Only to this extent—that . . . we may say 'Every man's good to count as equal to the *like good* of every other man.' "[54] If we understand equality of treatment as Rashdall did, then the claim that it has intrinsic value rests *in part* on what, in the conceptual scheme explained in chapter 2, is a tautology, namely, that one ought not to promote a good lesser than another that one could promote, everything else being equal. I shall return to this point in the next chapter. But it is worth remembering also that although a right action, or one that ought to be performed, can be said to be good in a sense different from that in which what it promotes can be said to be good, it can be said to be good also in the latter sense, that is, good in itself. (See above, pp. 27–28). The intrinsic value of equality of treatment would be due, in part, to the intrinsic value of right action.

But the claim that equality of treatment, as understood by Rashdall, has intrinsic value may rest also on another view: that in the absence of relevant differences, preferential treatment is unjustified. Is this view implied by the nature of friendship? I suggest that it is. Preferential treatment of some of one's friends, in the absence of relevant differences, is incompatible with one's being a genuine friend of those who do not benefit from the treatment, with regarding them as ends and with concern for their good. But what does a true friend do if equal *treatment* of all his friends is not possible? He can still achieve equality of *consideration*. He can flip a coin—a fair coin! But if equality of consideration with respect to one's friends has intrinsic goodness, the reason is that it is implied by the nature of friendship, by one's unswerving concern for the good of all of one's friends, even when that good cannot be achieved.

So far I have tried to show that whatever is intrinsically valuable about justice would be present in friendship, and therefore that justice need not be regarded as an additional abstract good. But suppose that friendship is absent. Would not justice as impartiality then be a distinctive, though second-best, good? Would not impartiality of treatment or at least of consideration still be required? Yes, it would be, but not because it constitutes a distinctive good. The principle of impartiality (or the related principle of the universalizability of one's maxims of conduct) is of great importance to ethics but has no ethical substance at all since it is not a principle of ethics. Insofar as it is defensible, it states, as Sidgwick formulates it, that "it cannot be right for A to treat B in a manner in which it would be wrong for B to treat A, merely on the ground that they are two different individuals, and without there being any difference between the natures or circumstances of the two which can be stated as a reasonable ground for difference of treatment."[55] Sidgwick claimed that this was the only element in "the common notion of Justice" that "could be intuitively known with perfect clearness and certainty."

So stated, the principle is indeed self-evident and must be acknowledged by any adequate ethical theory. But it is not a principle of ethics. It is merely an application to ethics of the general principle that what is true of one case must be true of all other cases that are exactly like it in all relevant respects. If the predicate "ought to be benefited in manner $m$" is applicable to A, and A and B do not differ in any relevant respect, then it is also applicable to B, for the same reason that if an object is blue then every other object exactly like it in all relevant respects would also be blue. That the predicate is ethical is quite irrelevant.[56] Of course, it may be that while *each* of A and B ought to be benefited in manner $m$, it is impossible that *both* be so benefited. In the terminology proposed in chapter 2, this case would be more properly described as follows: both benefiting A and benefiting B would be *right*, but neither is something one *ought* to do since it is impossible to do both;

yet one ought to do one or the other. I have suggested that among friends the decision may be made by flipping a coin—and this is not a flippant suggestion. It may be made in this way also among nonfriends.[57] But among nonfriends it may be made in many other ways, the obvious one being to be guided by personal preference. This is so because among nonfriends there is no *wrong* or *bad* way of resolving the problem, since by the hypothesis on which this discussion is based, there is no relevant difference that would render any particular way wrong or bad. The principle of impartiality does not prohibit certain decisions that ordinarily would be called partial. It does not prohibit my benefiting A rather than B just because I like A but not B, *if* I cannot do both. It prohibits this only if by doing so I would produce less good than I would if I benefit B. But if my relationship to both A and B is that of perfect friendship, decisions on such grounds would be prohibited, not by the principle of impartiality but by the very nature of friendship. They would need to be made by "flipping a coin." What is true among friends need not be true among nonfriends.

An alternative account of the ethical significance of justice as impartiality is that it is included in fortitude. It is a dictate of reason that if there are no relevant differences between A and B, then whatever is true of A is true of B and vice versa, including the property expressed by "ought to be benefited in way *m*" (assuming that it is possible to benefit both). One who violates this principle because of irrelevant differences between A and B (for example, one likes A but not B) displays lack of fortitude by violating a dictate of reason. But, as I have already noted, this dictate of reason is not itself ethical in content. Indeed, Hastings Rashdall even held that it, as well as the principles of prudence and benevolence, is essentially "mathematical in nature."[58]

Another familiar view is that justice is the proportionality of goodness to merit and of badness to demerit. Indeed, according to Kant, the *Summum Bonum* is, roughly, the combination of perfect virtue and the good of happiness. But the view makes no sense if the goods in question are fortitude, knowledge, or friendship. For, surely, by merit is meant the possession of one or more of just these goods, including Kantian good will (which, if the reader will remember, may be regarded as an aspect of fortitude). This is why the view in question ordinarily regards the "reward" as being pleasure or satisfaction, and the badness to be apportioned to demerit as pain or dissatisfaction. (Kant viewed happiness as the total satisfaction of one's needs and inclinations.) If justice is so understood, I find no reason for regarding it as an intrinsic good, though it may be good as a means, for example, in punishment. The attraction of the view that it is an intrinsic good seems to me due to preoccupation with the goods of bodily pleasure and satisfaction and to the all too natural sweetness we all find in the taste of revenge. I see nothing intrinsically good about good people having pleasant or satisfied lives (other than the intrinsic goodness of pleasure and satisfaction) and evil people having painful or dissatisfied lives. On the contrary, the idea that friendship, knowledge, or fortitude should be rewarded with bodily pleasure or satisfaction seems to me incoherent. Surely they are their own reward. If Kantian good will is an intrinsic good, it too would be its own reward. This is not to say, of course, that pleasure and satisfaction are not *additional* goods.[59]

But isn't it evident that a *distribution* of goods can be intrinsically good or bad even if it does not violate the principle of impartiality of treatment or at least of consideration in the absence of relevant differences, and even if the question of merit does not arise? Wouldn't it be better that five people be moderately pleased than that one be greatly pleased and the remaining four not pleased at all? If we say that it would be better, perhaps the reason is our concern for the four persons as ends, not merely as means. If so, distributive justice would be an aspect of friendship. Usually, however, when we make such judgments we regard the moderate pleasures of five as constituting together a greater hedonic good than the great pleasure of one, and often we are right to do so. Or we take into account the fact that the moderate pleasures may be essential as means to much greater goods, or as contributing factors in organic unities that are much greater goods. (Let us think of why a relaxing hour now and then is so very valuable.) Or we may confuse the state of not being pleased in a certain way with a state of being pained in some way, and then we would be guilty of a misunderstanding of the question. It is worth noting that this familiar conception of distributive justice has a clear application only to goods such as pleasure and satisfaction. Not surprisingly, it is at home mainly in political economy and in political philosophies such as Bentham's. It has no place, for example, in Plato's, Aristotle's, or Hegel's political philosophies, for reasons I shall discuss in the next chapter.

Nevertheless, our view on justice does lead to some painful conclusions. One is that sometimes an innocent person ought to be executed. But does anyone seriously believe (and not merely profess to believe) that this would not be so if it were the only means of, say, avoiding disaster of enormous magnitude? Another conclusion is that great inequalities in income and wealth are intrinsically neither bad nor good. A third is that there is no such thing as inviolable human rights. A fourth is that there is no particular political system that is intrinsically good or bad. Friendship requires neither a capitalist democracy, nor a socialist democracy, nor a communist dictatorship, nor a capitalist dictatorship, nor a Platonic Republic. (Any one of these may, of course, be very good or very bad as a means.) A fifth conclusion is that we cannot regard certain distributions or possessions of goods as intrinsically good ("just") because of the manner in which they have or might have come to be, whether that manner is one's own labor (or some other ground of "entitlement")[60] or a manner freely agreed upon in advance by all concerned.[61] The painfulness of these conclusions is considerably tempered when we remember that friendship involves regarding the individual as an end and never merely as a means. But even this has to be qualified. Unlike Kant, we cannot interpret the phrase "never merely as a means" to exclude any particular *treatment* of the individual as a means. For example, friendship does allow the sacrifice of one's friend for a greater good, perhaps simply the rescue of several other friends. What it requires is that one *regard* the person sacrificed as having great intrinsic value, that the sacrifice be done with a very special regret.

It may seem that having a voice in the selection of one's government, as in a democracy, is a case of being regarded with respect, as an end and not merely as a means, and therefore that such a political system is an intrinsic good. But a communist dictator or a Platonic philosopher-king can also regard each citizen with respect, or as an end. Respect for a person as a person does not entail respect for every characteristic of the person. In particular, it does not entail respect for every citizen's political judgment. Respect for our friends, our regarding them as ends and not merely as means, does not require that we regard them as competent in politics, any more than it requires that we regard them as competent in medicine. This must not be taken as an expression of a particular political attitude. Equality in voting rights, for example, can be sufficiently justified in terms of its consequences, and especially in terms of the familiar consequences of its absence, and therefore vigorously, passionately supported. But we need not regard it as an intrinsic good. When John Rawls writes of "our conception of persons as free and equal, and fully cooperating members of a democratic society,"[62] he assumes a political posture that of course has its attractions for us. But that is all it is: a political posture, not a reasoned philosophical position. His frequent description of it as a Kantian view is misleading. In Kant (assuming that it can be attributed to him), it was (logically) grounded in a metaphysical conception of the person, which was arrived at in the laborious metaphysical and epistemological investigations that begin with the transcendental aesthetic. I doubt that Rawls accepts Kant's metaphysics and epistemology. But with what does he replace them as the ground of his democratic conception of the person? We may like this conception, but as long as it is philosophically ungrounded, it remains just a likable political opinion, the one that happens to be most widely shared in the United States and a few other countries in the second half of the twentieth century.[63] Of course, probably all that Rawls wished to do was to elucidate this opinion and to connect it with other opinions we have. And, as I have already noted, democracy can easily be defended as a great instrumental good. But this is not the issue. The issue concerns its status as an intrinsic good, as an abstract good, as something to be sought for its own sake. The distinction must be made even if we agree with Rawls that its instrumental value includes fostering what he regards as the great individual good of self-respect.

The distinction between intrinsic and instrumental value is not clearly observed even in W. K. Frankena's instructive discussion of justice in his 1966 Lindley Lecture, "Some Beliefs about Justice."[64] Frankena regards the basic principle of social justice to be that of equality, which he defines as follows: a good "is to be so distributed, that everyone has an equal chance of achieving the best life he is capable of."[65] He notes the similarity of this view to what he takes to be Aristotle's view ("at his best") that "the ideal state [is] one in which each member enjoys the highest happiness—the most excellent activity—he is capable of attaining."[66] (This is not inconsistent with Aristotle's defense of slavery, since he believed that a natural slave can enjoy the best life he is capable of only as a slave.) Frankena admits that justice so understood can be given a utilitarian justification but also holds that a deontologist can say that it is right in itself. He prefers the deontologist's view but suggests that both the utilitarian and the deontologist may agree that "The Ideal is that state of affairs in which *every person* (or perhaps every sentient being) has the best life he is capable of," on the grounds that the deontologist could plausibly argue that justice (in the sense of equal treatment) is right because it is a constitutive condition of the Ideal.[67] But surely it is at most a causal, not a constitutive, condition of the Ideal as the latter is described by Frankena. Equal treatment may be the case and that Ideal still not be achieved, and the Ideal might be achieved through other means.

## 6. The Good of a Society

The property of sociality, exemplified by certain individual beings, gives rise to an ontologically very different order of being, namely, that of societies. Examples would be families, universities, orchestras, football teams, corporations, nations, indeed ideally humankind as a whole as long as our reservations about the notion of a human being are remembered. The claim I have made is of course controversial. This is not the place to defend it, and it is not essential to our inquiry. But perhaps I should suggest that the question whether a society is an entity of a different ontological kind from the kinds to which its individual members and their relations belong should be understood as asking whether a society has any properties (monadic or relational) that are not properties of individual persons or genuinely reducible to such properties. It seems to me clear that the answer is, yes. A university grants degrees, nations are at war, clubs have traditions. Even if the statements I have just made can be shown to be logically equivalent to statements solely about individual persons (no one has shown this, for no one has written the required statements), this need not mean that what the former statements assert is the same as what the corresponding latter statements would assert. Logically equivalent statements need not describe the same state of affairs. "ABC is an equilateral triangle" and "ABC is an equiangular triangle" are logically equivalent but do not assert the same thing, they do not describe the same state of affairs.[68]

Now friendship may be the good of an individual *qua* social, but do not societies themselves have their own good, one that is not reducible to the goods of the individuals who constitute them? When philosophers, including Plato, Aristotle, and Aquinas, describe the aim of the state as the common good, they presumably regard the state as a means, however important it may be, to individuals' goods, and when they describe the good state as the one that achieves this aim, they may be taken to be describing only its goodness as a means. But what would the good state be as an *end*? What is the intrinsic good of a society *qua* a society? The question is generally ignored in recent writings in ethical theory, though it was central to Hegelian and Marxist ethics. For example, John Rawls barely mentions "the claims of culture," the promotion of the arts and the sciences, and only to add that the principles of justice do not permit these claims if the grounds given are that such institutions are intrinsically valuable.[69] And Richard B. Brandt merely assumes in passing that the desire to have "art galleries and fine operas" is a form of benevolence.[70] But an important theme in normative thought has been that the promotion of the arts and the sciences is something that a good society ought to do for *their* sake, quite independently of considerations about justice or welfare-maximization, that at least in part their flourishing is constitutive of its goodness. More generally, it is the theme that society, to be really good, to be what it ought to be, must attain something more than the individual goods of its members.

Perhaps the crudest example of such a belief is traditional imperialism, the belief that the good ("greatness") of one's country consists in global power, even if achieved at great sacrifices by its individual members. Another example is the intellectually exciting Marxist (or perhaps pseudo-Marxist) thesis that the good of a society is its transition into a society on the next higher level of historical development. A third, much more recent, is the belief that mankind "has its destiny among the stars," that its good includes "the conquest of space." A fourth, already mentioned, which is not so common in ordinary thought but quite common in the thought of highly educated people, is that the good society is one in which the arts and the sciences flourish. Literally visible examples of such flourishing are state-sponsored works of great architecture, almost always the result of much sacrifice of the good of individuals.

Indeed, Sidgwick observed, without endorsement, that "an ideal constitution of society may be conceived and sought with many other ends in view besides the right distribution of good and evil among the individuals that compose it: as (*e.g.*) with a view to conquest and success in war, or to the development of industry and commerce, or to the highest possible cultivation of the arts and sciences."[71] To ignore this important theme in ethical thought is to exhibit the sort of obsession with the good of individuals, usually on the lowest levels of existence, health, pleasure, and satisfaction, that ought to be an embarrassment to modern ethics. An extraterrestrial civilization that learned about us might marvel at our lack of imagination and societal ambition if we remained preocccupied with such involuted aims. (In his *Autobiography* John Stuart Mill writes that during his period of depression he wondered what the point of life would be if the utilitarian ideal should ever be achieved.)[72] Much of contemporary ethics remains wedded not only to the Benthamite principle that "pleasure is in *itself* a good: nay, even setting aside immunity from pain, the only good,"[73] but also to the Benthamite principle that "the community is a fictitious *body*, composed of the individual persons who are considered as constituting as it were its *members*. The interest of the community then is, what?—the sum of the interests of the several members who compose it."[74] This conclusion is not surprising since the poverty of the first principle fits well with the superficiality of the second. One need not accept Hegel's metaphysics or the details of his political philosophy in order to take seriously his view that

> In contrast with the spheres of private rights and private welfare (the family and civil
> society), the state is from one point of view an external necessity and their higher
> authority; its nature is such that their laws and interests are subordinated to it and
> dependent on it. On the other hand, however, it is the end immanent within them,

and its strength lies in the unity of its own universal end and aim with the particular interest of individuals, in the fact that individuals have duties to the state in proportion as they have rights against it.[75]

What is the good of a society *qua* a society? It is easy to reject the claims of imperialism as at best immature, and of Marxism as resting on an inadequate metaphysics, namely, dialectical and historical materialism. Space exploration, and the arts and the sciences, have much greater appeal, but we must wonder whether the appeal of the first is not of the same kind as the appeal of imperialism, and whether the appeal of the second is not due to the appeal of knowledge as the good of an *individual qua* an intellectual being. And Hegel's view that the state is the culmination of the development of "objective mind," and that it is transcended by "absolute mind," the moments of which are art, religion, and philosophy, rests, like Marxism, on a very questionable metaphysics. The self-evidence of the seven abstract goods we identified earlier, namely, existence, health, pleasure, satisfaction, fortitude, knowledge, and friendship, seems simply not to be found in any suggested good of society as such. Perhaps the reason is that we do not yet have the sort of clear conception of what it is for something to be a society of intellectual and volitional beings that would suggest a self-evident conception of the good corresponding to the property of being such a society. And this itself may be due to the possibility that only humankind as a whole can have such a good, but humankind as a whole is not, or at least is not clearly, a society yet. That there is such a good is perhaps more a matter of faith. But, as Nicolai Hartmann put it, "it is faith on the grand scale, faith in a higher order, which determines the cosmic meaning of man."[76]

One final remark. It is often said that morality is necessarily social. This may be a mere stipulation of how the vague word "morality" is to be used. If intended as a claim about how the word is in fact used, it is obviously false. Among the paradigms of what we call moral or immoral are the refraining from and engaging in some sexual and other sensual practices that affect no other person. In any case, a consequence of our discussion in this chapter is that there is far more to the subject matter of ethics than what is necessarily social in nature. Friendship and the good, if there is one, of a society (*qua* a society) are only two of the goods we have identified. A Robinson Crusoe could face a formidable array of ethical problems, such as whether to devote his life to mindless sensual pleasure or to some intellectual endeavor, and could experience shame over his lack of fortitude, or pride over the moderation of his desires. These are problems and experiences that are of direct interest to ethics and, I suggest, quite intelligibly describable as moral. But they are not social.

## 7. The Limitations of Our System

I have identified seven abstract goods, guided by the conception of the hierarchy of being. All seven are familiar properties, and in no obvious way incompatible with the scientific picture of the word. Those involving consciousness could not be given a physicalistic account only if the facts of consciousness cannot. But if the latter is the case, then physicalism is unacceptable for reasons far more general than the concerns of ethics. Nothing in our system of abstract goods, including their genus, is mysterious, or supernatural, or even unobservable. (That they are universals has no such implications. Universals, both specific and generic, are needed in the physical sciences as well.)[77]

But the higher levels of the hierarchy of being are occupied by characteristics of great complexity and variety. We should expect the corresponding abstract goods to exhibit equal complexity and variety. Obviously, there are many kinds of intellect, each of which manifests itself in highly complex ways. We should expect therefore that there would be corresponding variety and complexity in the abstract good of knowledge, even when restricted to understanding. For example, a mathematically brilliant accomplishment in quantum mechanics, deep appreciation of the subtlety of a symphony, and the genuine profundity of a philosophical work are all very different; and even an adequate description of just one of them would be extremely complex. Sociality has specific forms, such as one's family, one's country, humankind, professional organizations, legal and political institutions, various forms of purely personal relationships. We should expect therefore that our notion of friendship should allow for corresponding distinctions. Fidelity in word and deed, loyalty, respect for others, one's duties to one's family as contrasted with one's duties to strangers, need not be denied the status of abstract goods just because they are so different from one another, and they should not for just that reason be regarded as not falling under the genus I have called friendship. A central thesis of this book is that we respect generic identity, but both as identity and as generic, in our thought about goodness and in our thought about the subgenera of goodness. We must avoid the error of supposing that such generic identities are not really identities at all, but also we must avoid the error of supposing that they are really specific identities.

Because of its complexity, the system of abstract goods can be adequately described only by very detailed examination of each level in the hierarchy of being and of the good corresponding to it. I have not attempted such an examination here. What would be required is not another chapter or even another book, but a series of books. It is encouraging that now, when the obsession with "meta-ethics" seems to have ended, such books have begun to appear.[78]

There is a further, related qualification that must be made here. We may be confident that the seven abstract goods I have identified are indeed goods. And their system corresponds convincingly to what we know about the hierarchy of being. But it would be presumptuous to suppose that what we know is very much. It is possible, perhaps probable, that elsewhere in the universe there are beings with at least some aspects of their nature totally different from those of ours, and with goods corresponding to those aspects also totally different from our goods. It may well be that our seven abstract goods are merely a minor segment in the real hierarchy of abstract goods. Moreover, if certain metaphysical and epistemological assumptions are granted, we can readily allow for goods other than those I have discussed. For example, if we accept Augustine's theology, we would find self-evident his view that the highest, indeed ultimately the only, good for a human being is the vision of God in afterlife. It is also quite possible that further scientific investigation of nature and further phenomenological investigation of such aspects of oneself as the emotions may suggest additional abstract goods. If we wish, we could describe all this as an admission of a kind of skepticism in ethics. But it is hardly the kind of skepticism with which this book is concerned. It is merely the admission that in ethics, just as in science, there is much that we do not know. We may still live in the prehistory of ethics. But then we may still live also in the prehistory of physics.

I have considered in this chapter the question, What are the (main) abstract goods? The answer to this question suggests what would be the answer to the question, What are the (main) abstract evils? Corresponding to the good of existence would be the evil of nonexistence or cessation of existence, death in the case of living beings. Corresponding to the good of health and bodily integrity would be disease and mutilation. Pain would correspond to pleasure, dissatisfaction to satisfaction, ignorance to knowledge, weakness of the will to strength of the will, friendlessness and especially enmity to friendship. I shall not discuss the abstract evils in detail, though such a discussion must be provided by a complete ethical theory. Toward the end of this chapter, I shall touch upon the question, which I mentioned in chapter 2, whether an evil is the privation of a good, and in the next chapter I shall make a few remarks about some of the abstract evils.

## 8. Is Good a Genus or a Transcendental?

I conclude this chapter by returning to the topic of chapter 4, for there are questions about it that we could not have considered before the exposition of the system of abstract goods in the present chapter. I have argued that goodness is a generic property, its species or subgenera being at least existence, health, pleasure, satisfaction, fortitude, knowledge, and friendship. But is it possible that these should be species or subgenera of the same genus? For, do they not belong to very different logical categories? Some seem to be properties of individuals, others properties of properties, and still others relations. Perhaps some are properties of states of affairs. Health is a property of individuals. Fortitude is a property of a property, namely, of the sort of capacity we call will. Friendship is a relation. And the good of society as such, if there is one, would perhaps be a property of a state of affairs. How can such properties and relations fall under the same genus, how can they exemplify one and the same higher property? If our ontology is that of classical logical atomism, based largely on Russell's and Whitehead's *Principia Mathematica* and its theory of types, the answer must certainly be that they cannot. But perhaps we have allowed ourselves too long to remain in the grip of *Principia Mathematica*. It is characteristic not only of goodness but of many of our most fundamental concepts that they do not accord with logical atomism, or indeed with Russellian logic at all. Being, or existence, I suggest, is predicable of individuals, of properties, of properties of properties, of relations, of states of affairs. We may also speak of knowing, or being aware or conscious of, any of these. Numerical concepts are also applicable to all of them—they all can be counted. And perhaps they all can be objects of aesthetic appreciation. If this is true of these notions, why should it not be true of goodness?

But even if we free ourselves from the grip of *Principia Mathematica*, the puzzle of the apparent *logical* heterogeneity of the abstract goods remains; if it is not merely apparent, then of course goodness cannot be a genus. Should we try to resolve it, as the examples we just gave of other concepts with logically hetereo-geneous application may suggest, by adopting a version of the medieval doctrine that goodness is not a genus but a transcendental, that its predication, whether univocal (Duns Scotus) or analogical (Thomas Aquinas), is not the predication of a common genus but rather ranges across the categories, the summa genera? As I observed in chapter 4, to what extent viewing goodness as a transcendental would differ from viewing it as a genus is unclear, since even if a genus it is one on a very high level of generality, and the distinction between genera and transcendentals on such a level is by no means evident. The reason is that, as I have argued, a generic universal is an entity only in an analogical sense. If so, what would be the cash value of distinguishing between saying that goodness is a generic universal and saying that it is a transcendental? (It should be noted that to say that goodness is an entity only analogically is not to subscribe to the view that the notion of it is applied to the abstract goods only analogically, not univocally. It is the notion of entity that is applied to the generic universal analogically, not the notion of that universal itself when it is applied to the subgenera and species of the universal. To take an extreme example, "Either $F$ or $G$ or $H$" is applied to $F$'s, $G$'s, and $H$'s univocally even if $F$'s, $G$'s, and $H$'s have nothing in common.) Nevertheless, let us consider the medieval view more closely.

Duns Scotus held that "Whatever pertains to 'being,' . . . in so far as it remains indifferent to finite and infinite, or as proper to the Infinite Being, does not belong to it as determined to a genus, but prior to any such determination, and therefore as transcendental and outside any genus."[79] I shall ignore here his inclusion among the transcendentals of disjunctive predicates such as "possible-or-necessary" and predicates applicable to both God and only some of the creatures, such as "wisdom," and will consider the view only with respect to the notions of being and those that are (according to Scotus) coextensive ("convertible") with it, namely, goodness, unity, and truth. (Scotus did not add beauty to the list.) The genera outside which something must be in order to be counted as a transcendental are, of course, Aristotle's categories. The underlying premise is that they are the summa genera. And this premise is taken for granted because it was thought that Aristotle had proved in the *Metaphysics* (998b 21–26) that being cannot be a genus. For if being is not a genus, then surely anything coextensive with it would also not be a genus. Aristotle argued, on the grounds that a genus is not predicable of the differentiae that determine its species, that being cannot be a genus because the differentiae that would determine its species would have to be other than being and therefore would have no being. I am skeptical about the adequacy of this argument but shall not discuss it here. For in the *Nichomachean Ethics* Aristotle argued not only that goodness differs from category to category (1096a 24–29), some of these differences being obviously due to the fact that in some categories (for example, place and time) an item is good only as a means or a contributory factor, but also that intrinsic goods such as honor, intelligence, and pleasure do not have a common goodness since they have different accounts or definitions even *qua* intrinsic goods (1096b 25). Aristotle did not develop his point further. But in effect he did deny that goodness is a genus. Therefore, even if the Aristotelian argument that being is not a genus, and therefore that goodness (since, like being, it is supposed also to range across the categories) is not a genus, is inadequate, the problem we face remains with us. We must have a positive reason for regarding goodness as a genus.

In chapter 2 I distinguished several, though intimately related, senses of the word "good": the sense in which it is predicable of abstract entities, the sense in which it is predicable of concrete entities, and the sense I expressed with the word "virtue." If these senses are different, then we cannot suppose that the application of the word to all three kinds of entities is the attribution to them of the same property, and therefore the subsumption of them in the same genus. But the issue before us concerns only the first sense. It is whether the *abstract entities* that are said to be good, what I have called the abstract goods, have a common property in the sense of falling under the same genus. If we stay with Aristotle's view of what categories, i.e., summa genera, there are, then our answer can only be negative. Exactly in which categories our seven abstract goods would belong is not so clear, but surely at least some would belong in the category of quality (e.g., health) and others in the category of relatives (e.g., friendship). But there are many reasons, quite outside ethics, for abandoning the Aristotelian categories in favor of the familiar contemporary categories of individuals, properties, and states of affairs. And if we do so, then we may remark that all of our abstract goods are properties in the wide contemporary sense in which also relations are properties, and that even if they do not fall under the common genus Goodness, surely they do fall under the common genus Property. But if so, then what general reason is there for denying that they fall under the same subgenus of the genus Property, namely, the subgenus Goodness? Indeed, as we have acknowledged, some of them are properties of individuals, others are properties of properties, and still others are relations; perhaps some are properties of states of affairs. But properties nonetheless they all are. I shall remind the reader that we have decided to ignore the Russellian theory of types.

Yet, obviously, this remark does not suffice. I have argued that, like intentional, numerical, and perhaps aesthetic properties, the property goodness is exemplified by entities of great logical variety. But I have also argued that it is exemplified by these entities in the sense that it is the *genus* to which they all belong, that the properties and relations exemplifying it are generically identical, on a level of generality lower than that of Property. And how could that be? The genus Property is naturally regarded as first divisible into the subgenera Monadic Property and Relation or, perhaps, into the subgenera Property of Individuals, Property of States of Affairs, Property of Properties, Property of Properties of Properties, etc., the division between monadic properties and relations occurring within each of these subgenera. But however we divide the genus Property there seems to be no place in the resulting first subgenera of it for the genus Goodness. To regard goodness as a genus with the sort of subgenera I have suggested would involve a drastic cross-classification of properties, a violation of every standard principle of the logical division of the genus Property under which goodness supposedly falls. In this crucial respect goodness seems to differ fundamentally from intentional, numerical, and aesthetic properties. None is regarded as the *genus* of the things exemplifying it. (By aesthetic property I mean here being an object of aesthetic appreciation. If there is such a monadic property as beauty, it would perhaps confront us with the same logical problems as goodness does.)

What this objection draws attention to is not so much a difficulty for our theory as a fact that must be recognized concerning all classifications of properties. Although some classifications are objectively more adequate than others, there need not be a uniquely adequate one. Nor need we deny the legitimacy of cross-classifications. The reason is twofold and familiar to us from chapter 4. To speak of generic properties, I argued there, is to speak of generic identities, and a generic identity is an identity only by analogy. It is an identity only in the sense that it is more like a paradigmatic case of identity than it is like anything else. It is possible therefore that one property may be regarded as generically identical with another in one context but not in another context. It may be "like" paradigmatic identity in one context but not in another. The ultimate explanation of this fact is that, as I argued in chapter 4, the concept of identity is transcendental (though not in the medieval sense); it is imposed by us on the objects of our experience and thought, not derived from some element in them that might be called "identity," not standing for any such element, and for this reason even the paradigms of its application can be violated without misrepresentation of any "facts" about them. This is why there need not be a uniquely adequate classification, and this is why cross-classifications are allowed. Nelson Goodman writes: "Is a circle more like a thin ellipse or a regular hexagon or a sphere? Is a cube more like a square or a tetrahedron? Is a long rectangle with a tiny corner clipped off more like the unclipped rectangle or a regular pentagon? Any number of equally reasonable principles give different similarity-orderings of shapes."[80] The dream of the highest universal that differentiates itself into subgenera and ultimately into infimae species, which perhaps differentiate themselves into their instances, is just a dream, though a wonderful one.

With respect to their purely formal characteristics, properties of individuals, properties of properties, properties of states of affairs, and relations can all belong at most to the genus Property. But with respect to their correspondence to levels in the hierarchy of being, they may belong to a genus of lower generality. Like everything else, they can be seen in different ways, in terms of different similarities, and in some of these ways they may be seen as generically identical, but not in others, at least not with the same degree of generality. It is with respect to their correspondence to the levels of the hierarchy of being that the abstract goods can be seen as generically identical, and goodness can be seen as a (generic) property, not with respect to their formal, logical characteristics. Goodness is by no means unique in this respect. Spatial relations and spatial monadic properties (for example, figures) surely belong to the genus Spatial Property, even though there would be no such genus if the genus Property were first divided into Monadic Property and

Relation. Spatial relations and spatial figures are more easily seen to be kinds of the same generic universal than, say, spatial figures and tastes are, even though both of the latter are monadic. An example on a much lower level of generality would be the fact that the equilateral triangle may be seen as a species of the genus Equilateral Figure, rather than of the genus Triangle, perhaps with equal adequacy. This means that it would be seen as generically identical, say, with the square rather than with the isosceles and scalene triangles.

What I have said in the preceding two paragraphs must not be misunderstood. To say that A and B may be generically identical in one context but not in another, that they can be classified in different yet equally adequate ways, is not at all to say that their generic identity or their classification is relative to our interests or to our linguistic resources or practices. Three shades of color A, B, and C may be such that A is more like B than like C in hue, but more like C than like B in brightness. Both are objective facts about the shades, and the different classifications of the shades that these objective facts would ground are no less objectively adequate. Perhaps they are even equally adequate. But even if they are equally adequate, each is far more adequate than classifying the shades in accordance, say, with Mary's preferences in colors. That one person may classify them according to hue and another according to degree of brightness is no more relevant or indeed philo-sophically interesting than that one person may prefer to study the causes of a certain disease while another prefers to study its effects. Such differences in pref-erence or interest do not render the facts medicine is concerned with "relative to human interests." On the other hand, if the person interested in the etiology of a disease is also interested in jazz, this fact would not render the classification of medical etiology and jazz in the same (low-level) genus at all adequate. Indeed, such a classification would be bizarre, because the judgment of generic identity on which it would need to be grounded would be bizarre. It would be bizarre because it violates our concept of identity, even though this does not consist in its failing to correspond to an entity in the world called identity.

Indeed, in some cases, like those cited earlier from Blanshard, we may find that our concept of identity has neither clear application nor clear nonapplication. (For example, we may be unwilling to assert of a certain two shades that both are yellow but also unwilling to deny that they are.) We could apply it or deny it verbally, but not genuinely, as long as there is nothing in the concept that suggests which we should do. Let me explain. Even though the concept of identity is transcendental, in the sense I have explained, this does not mean that its application is arbitrary. It is governed by paradigms and by considerations about the proximity of the subject matter under investigation to the paradigms, as well as by general systematic considerations, such as those that have been central in our investigation of goodness. Mere interest in applying it (or denying it), even if legitimized by linguistic convention, is not what matters. For the interest may be perverse, and the convention *mere* convention. But there can be cases that neither clearly fall, even analogically, under the concept of identity nor clearly fail to do so. In such cases we are free to apply it or to withhold it. Were identity a real element in the world, such applications and withholdings could not both be permissible.

## 9. Aristotelian-Thomistic Reflections

If we understand the question whether goodness is a genus in the manner suggested in the previous section, then our view achieves considerable similarity to Aristotle's and Aquinas's, since we can now more confidently hold what I suggested earlier, that the claim that being and goodness are transcendentals and not genera rests on a distinction that, given the nature of generic identity, has no cash value. According to Aquinas, "goodness and being are really the same, and differ only in idea. . . . The essence of goodness consists in this, that it is in some way desirable."[81] If he meant that goodness is a relational property, that of being capable of being desired by someone, then the view would be far removed from ours—it would be more like Ralph Barton Perry's. But of course Aquinas does not mean this. He goes on to say: "Now it is clear that a thing is desirable only in so far as it is perfect, for all desire their own perfection. But everything is perfect so far as it is actual. Therefore, it is clear that a thing is perfect so far as it has being; for being is the actuality of every thing. . . . Hence it is clear that goodness and being are the same really."[82] The perfection of a thing is to be understood in terms of the Aristotelian distinction between actuality and potentiality, and the notion of desire Aquinas employs is metaphysical, not psychological, and is to be understood in terms of the Aristotelian notion of a final cause.[83]

But we need not subscribe to the Aristotelian metaphysics in order to attach sense to saying that the abstract goods I have identified are the highest actualizations of the sorts of entities capable of having them, and thus to attach sense to saying also that they are what those entities by their very nature "desire" or "aim at." We *could* say that existence is the minimal actuality, which even inanimate objects can have; that health is the fullest actualization of living beings *qua* living; that pleasure and satisfaction are the fulfillment of the natures of sentience and desire; that fortitude is the fullest actualization of the will; knowledge, of the intellect; friendship, of sociality. My point is not that our abstract goods coincide with Aquinas's, but that their relationship to the levels of the hierarchy of being is, though not the same, not unlike what he thought it was. The characteristic determining each level may be said to be most fully, most clearly, exemplified only if the corresponding good is exemplified. Insofar as a plant is diseased, it is not fully living. Insofar as an intellect lacks knowledge and understanding, it is not fully, actually, but in a clear sense only potentially, an intellect.

If we understand the subject matter of ethics in this manner, then indeed we can say that while metaphysics is the science of being *qua* being, ethics is the science of being *qua* goodness. And if we take into account the Aristotelian-Thomistic distinction between first and second actuality (for example, between having knowledge and the exercise of it),[84] we may even say that the characteristically human good is happiness, in the Aristotelian sense of *eudaimonia*. For happiness, according to Aristotle, is living in accordance with virtue. The characteristically human abstract goods we have identified are not Aristotelian virtues, since they are not dispositions. But they coincide with the manifestations of at least some of the

Aristotelian virtues, and it is these manifestations, as constitutive of a kind of life, that Aristotle called *eudaimonia*.

When I began my exposition of a conceptual scheme for ethics in chapter 2, I noted that if evil is the absence (more precisely, the privation) of goodness, then it could be defined in terms of goodness, and therefore the concept of it would not be one of the primitive ethical concepts. Can we achieve further, though still only partial, agreement with Aquinas by saying that the evils corresponding to the goods of existence, health, pleasure, satisfaction, knowledge, fortitude, and friendship consist simply in the absence of the corresponding good? (More precisely, in the absence of a good that by nature *can* be present in the entity from which it is absent. According to Aquinas, "Because evil is the privation of good, and not a pure negation . . . therefore not every defect of good is an evil, but only the defect of the good which is naturally due."[85] Blindness is the absence of sight but only in beings capable of sight, and the absence of sight is an evil also only in beings capable of sight, not, for example, in stones, which cannot be described as blind.) Unfortunately, such an account does not seem to fit the case of pain, which is not merely the absence of pleasure, or the case of enmity, which is not merely the absence of friendship. Aquinas held that "the evil which comes from the withdrawal of the form and integrity of the thing has the nature of a pain."[86] It may be that pain is always the result of disease, that is, the absence of health, as this statement suggests. But it does not follow that it itself is that absence. Neither pain nor enmity seems to *be* the absence of a good. Yet surely they are evils. If so, we cannot in general regard evil as the privation of good.

Insofar as we may understand the abstract goods in the somewhat Aristotelian-Thomistic manner suggested in this section, we can also understand better a qualified use of "good" that is quite familiar and prominent in ethical discussions. It was crucial to Aristotle and Aquinas, and classical Greek and medieval ethics generally, because of its intimate connection with their metaphysical essentialism. The use I have in mind is that in which to say that something is good is to say that it is a paradigm of its kind. The notion of a paradigm of its kind has a clear application to human artifacts, since they are designed to serve a certain purpose that is known to us, and a paradigm of such a kind is simply something of that kind that has the distinctive characteristics in virtue of which it serves that purpose especially fully or effectively. But it also has application, though not so clear, to natural kinds, insofar as we can form a conception of what is distinctive of a natural kind. In the case of artifacts we have a clear conception because, guided by our purposes, we ourselves endow them with their distinctive characteristics. In the case of natural objects, we do not have that source of a clear conception, but this does not mean that we cannot form one on the basis of other considerations.

We can understand, for example, what it is for something to be a good horse, *qua* a horse, quite apart from our liking it or the uses to which it may be put. It is not difficult to grasp that a good horse is one that has the characteristics distinctive of a horse to a high degree. What those characteristics exactly are may not be evident to philosophers, but they should be evident to the zoologist or the veterinarian. If we can discern the good of the genus Living Being, namely, health, why could we not discern the more specific good of a certain species of living (nonrational) being? Presumably, the latter would be simply the kind of health and bodily development appropriate to that species, including its manifestations in behavior, and thus would fit in our hierarchy of abstract goods. Roughly, a good horse would be a healthy and properly developed horse.

The use of the notion of good in speaking, for example, of a good liar or a good burglar, would be understood along similar though more complicated lines. Being good at lying or burgling is presumably a manifestation of a certain kind of knowledge and fortitude and thus would fit in our system of abstract goods, and to that extent would be genuinely good. But insofar as its concrete exemplifications are incompatible with the concrete exemplifications of a higher kind of fortitude, namely virtue, they would be more bad than good.

# CHAPTER SIX

# The Quantities and Degrees of Good and Evil

## 1. My Own Good and the Good of Others

Our account of the hierarchy of being and of the abstract goods corresponding to its levels allows us now to consider the question mentioned in passing there about the resolution of possible conflicts, as well as to offer a more detailed view on the topic of egoism, which we touched upon in chapter 2. I should remind the reader, however, that the purpose of this and the previous chapter is not to present and defend a complete ethical theory but to display in detail the metaphysical intelligibility of such a theory. Its chief thesis is that goodness is a generic property; therefore we must be concerned with the possibility of identifying and systematizing the species and subgenera of that property. Only then can we try to show that the theory, even though incompletely described, is true, and therefore that the crucial fourth, Humean variety of skepticism in ethics, which denies that there is such a property as goodness, is false. We cannot show that we have knowledge of at least some ethical propositions unless we are clear about the content of those propositions and about the ways in which they hang together.

In effect, what we shall do in the present chapter is to take into account the application of the remaining undefined notions enumerated in chapter 2, namely, those of evil and of the degree and quantity of goodness or evil. All three of these notions are often expressed with the relational terms "better" and "worse," which for this reason must be regarded as ambiguous. For example, in no two of the following statements is "better" used in the same sense: "Pleasure is better than pain," "Happiness is better than pleasure," "Everything else being equal, it is better that two persons be happy rather than just one." The topic of egoism is the most prominent specific application of the general questions to be discussed in this chapter. For, the egoist in effect denies, in the most extreme manner, the ethical relevance of the most obvious quantitative measure of goodness: the number of persons who possess a certain kind of good. And his view is at all plausible only because ordinarily, at least implicitly, he is a hedonist and thus ignores the most important differences in degree of goodness by ignoring the plurality of intrinsic goods.

A characteristic theme of modern ethics is the sharp distinction between one's own good and the good of others, and a consequent preoccupation with the question,

Which, and to what extent, is one to promote? Hobbes held that "of all Voluntary Acts, the Object is to every man his own Good."[1] Bishop Butler responded by pointing out that often the object of our desires is the happiness of another person, and not, as is sometimes supposed, the pleasure *we* may derive from the satisfaction of these desires, even if such a pleasure does issue. Yet he felt compelled to say that "though virtue or moral rectitude does indeed consist in affection to and pursuit of what is right and good, as such; yet . . . when we sit down in a cool hour, we can neither justify to ourselves this or any other pursuit, till we are convinced that it will be for our happiness, or at least not contrary to it."[2] According to Kant, the only thing that is unconditionally good is a good will, that is, a will that acts out of respect for the moral law. Yet he also held that all human beings desire their own happiness, and that a necessary postulate of practical reason is that (very roughly) one's possession of a good will and one's happiness will coincide in afterlife. Sidgwick ended his *Methods of Ethics* by claiming that only a theological resolution is possible of the conflict between what he regarded as the rational demand that one promote the happiness of others and the no less rational demand that one promote one's own happiness. And in recent ethical theory we find John Rawls specifying that his rational contractors in the original position must be assumed to be mutually disinterested, motivated only by self-interest.[3] We also find Richard B. Brandt clearly believing that the question whether selfishness and benevolence are both fully rational, meaning by this not extinguishable under cognitive psychotherapy, is crucial to his program of basing ethics on the findings of cognitive psychology.[4] And Derek Parfit devotes much of his book *Reasons and Persons*, which is one of the most admirable achievements in contemporary ethics, to an examination of what he calls "self-interest theories."

If this theme is characteristic of modern ethics, what is characteristic of classical ethics, at least of Plato's and Aristotle's, is that in it neither the distinction between one's own good and the good of others, nor the question which is one to promote, looms very large. (Indeed, Plato's *Republic* is devoted to showing that justice and self-interest coincide; but for him self-interest was an incomparably richer notion than that employed by the egoist, and justice included far more than promoting the happiness of others. Indeed, to what extent and how it included this at all was left quite unclear, virtually ignored, except for the important observation, which shows that he cannot be interpreted as a rational egoist, that the philosopher-kings would prefer to pursue their purely intellectual interests but have the duty to engage in political activity in order to care for and be friends of the ruled.) Both Plato and Aristotle have therefore been accused of egoism and thus of moral blindness, but sometimes pardoned on the grounds that they lacked the benefit of Christian teaching. I suggest, however, that the reason they more or less ignored the distinction between one's own good and the good of others was very different in character.

How is this distinction to be understood? Contrary to the opinion of most modern moral philosophers, this question is far more complex and difficult than it appears to be at first glance. Clearly, the distinction involves two crucial notions: that of a good and that of the others. How we understand it depends therefore on how we understand these two notions. The moderns generally have had a rather simplistic understanding of both: the good is pleasure, often misnamed "happiness"; the others are all other human beings, perhaps all other sentient beings. Not so with Plato and Aristotle. They conceived of a whole hierarchy of goods, pleasure being only one of them and moreover itself falling into several very different, perhaps generically different, kinds.[5] And while their theories were explicitly concerned with man understood as a rational animal, they had no sympathy for the idea of the brotherhood of all men; indeed, they did not entertain it at all. On the contrary, they distinguished sharply between the Greeks and the barbarians, between the natural master and the natural slave, between the philosopher-rulers and the great majority of the population, who they supposed were capable only of manual labor, between gods and men, between adults and children, between men and women. It should not surprise us therefore that the simplistic modern problem of "rational" egoism did not really exist for them, and if Plato did confront it at all in the *Republic*, it was only to supplant it immediately with a much richer and much subtler problematic.

There are two extreme answers to the question of who the others are. The first is that there are no ethically relevant others. The second is that all things other than oneself are to be counted as the others. We may call the two positions, respectively, ethical solipsism and panethicism. By ethical solipsism I do not mean ethical egoism. The latter is the view that one ought to promote only one's own good, that it is not the case that one ought to promote anyone else's good (as an end). Indeed, it may seem that, given our definition of "ought" in chapter 2, egoism is self-contradictory. But to say this would be question begging, since the egoist in effect rejects just that definition. Perhaps this is why in *Ethics*[6] G. E. Moore rejected egoism simply by saying that it seemed to him self-evidently false, while in *Principia Ethica*[7] he had argued that it is self-contradictory. For in the latter work he in effect had adopted our definition of "ought," while in the former he seemed to allow that rightness is not identical with being optimizing, though he held that it is necessarily coextensive with it.[8]

Ethical solipsism, on the other hand, is the view that nothing is a good unless it is one's own good. And by panethicism I mean the view that one ought to promote the good of all things, including that of pebbles, rivers, forests, planets, and stars. As we have seen, today panethicism is most familiarly manifested in some conservationist and environmentalist movements, insofar as these are concerned with the preservation of the environment as something that is good in itself, rather than just as a means to the achievement of some of one's own ends, or the ends of human beings in general. And we have also seen that Augustine is a clear example of a philosopher who may be described as a panethicist, insofar as he held, on theological grounds, that everything that exists is good because it was created by God. But the thoughtful panethicist would not be an egalitarian, and Augustine was far from being one.[9] Although everything has its own good, the good of some things is far greater than the good of others, and the good of certain things may be so low in degree as to be irrelevant to our conduct. Many environmentalists seem not fully aware of this fact.

Ethical solipsism is manifested in the attitudes of people who not only see no reason to promote anyone else's good but fail to perceive anything that is someone else's state or condition as a good. I understand that such people are often encountered by psychiatrists in their practice. But there is no clear example in the history of philosophy of an ethical solipsist. The reason for this is not difficult to discern. An ethical solipsist can plausibly claim that no state or condition of anyone else is a good only if he believes that there is no one else at all, that is, only if he is a metaphysical solipsist. For example, if he regards his own pleasures as good, what possible grounds can he have for holding that only his pleasures are good except that there are no others capable of experiencing pleasure? But while I have no doubt that many philosophers have been metaphysical solipsists, I am unaware of anyone who has advocated the position (with the possible exception of Wittgenstein in the *Tractatus*). It is hardly surprising that no one has tried to convince us that only he or she exists or even just that he or she does not know that we exist. Whether metaphysical solipsism is true is a very difficult issue, which I shall not attempt to consider here. If true, then ethical solipsism is also true. But it should be clear that if the former is the only basis for the latter, then the philosophical interest of ethical solipsism reduces to that of metaphysical solipsism, which of course is not an ethical position at all.

The case of panethicism is quite different. It belongs strictly in ethics, even though, like all ethical theories, it requires a metaphysical and epistemological basis. What is the rationale for it? Clearly, as we have seen, it must include the view that all things have something in common with oneself, as well as the view that every thing can have something that may be counted as its good. But, just as clearly, the panethicist must also face the question of how to choose between one's own good and that of other things. For example, one could not reasonably hold that the goodness of one's own existence is equal to that of just any other thing, for example, a certain pebble. Why not? Because one has a nature far richer than that of a pebble and therefore, in addition to one's existence, one must take into account the goods corresponding to the aspects of one's nature that are additional to the mere occupancy of space, since one's existence is a necessary condition for the existence of those goods. When the required distinctions are made, panethicism is seen to coincide with the view developed in the previous chapter. And it leads to the following two theses regarding the question, My own good or the good of others?

First, that the question, Who are the others? has no simple answer. With respect to every abstract good there is, or at least there could be, a different set of relevant others, namely, all those who share the aspect of one's nature to which that good corresponds, and thus the general question, My own good or the good of others? has, or at least may have, a different answer, depending on which set and which good are at issue. The sets form a hierarchy ordered by the relation of set-inclusion. The set of social, intellectual, volitional beings (I assume that these three properties are coextensive) is a subset of the set of desiring beings, the latter is a subset of the set of sentient beings, this is a subset of the set of living beings, and this last is a subset of the set of beings occupying a place in space. The mere fact that the other is biologically a human being is no reason for special concern with his or her good. The imaginary race of human beings mentioned in the previous chapter, who irremediably lack sociality, intellect, and will, would deserve no greater concern from us than apes do. But the fact that the other is an intellectual being, even if a dolphin or an extraterrestrial creature, *is* such a reason. On the other hand, special concern is justified only with respect to those goods that are distinctive of such a being, namely, friendship, knowledge, and fortitude, and the goods that are necessary conditions for those, namely, existence and perhaps health. Intellectual beings have no special claim upon us with respect to goods such as bodily pleasure and the satisfaction of bodily desires, that is, no claim exceeding that of nonintellectual beings. The bodily pleasures and satisfactions of those we call human beings, even if they are intellectual animals, do not have greater intrinsic value, and thus a greater claim on us, than that of the bodily pleasures and satisfactions of cattle. One of the embarrassments of modern ethics has been the simultaneous embrace of both hedonism and what in recent years has been called speciesism. These two views are inherently incompatible.

My second thesis is that the question, My own good or the good of others? has a clear or at least ordinary application only to some goods, indeed to those corresponding to the lower levels of the hierarchy of being. One can and often does face a choice between one's own existence and that of another, whether a snake or a human, between one's own bodily pleasure and that of another, between the satisfaction of one's own bodily desires and the satisfaction of another's desires. And since modern ethics has been preoccupied with such goods, it has also, not surprisingly, been preoccupied with the question, My own good or the good of others? But this question has no clear or ordinary application to the other major goods I have identified, which is not to say that it never has *some* application. One does not usually face a choice between one's own health and that of another (though one might in special medical or financial contexts), and surely never between the firmness of one's own will and the firmness of another's will. One's possession of knowledge is usually not incompatible with another's possession of knowledge (though one's having special opportunities to acquire a certain knowledge may sometimes be incompatible with another's having those opportunities). The promotion of friendship within oneself toward others is hardly incompatible with the promotion of friendship in others, whether toward oneself or toward others, at least in the case of genuine friendship, not of what Aristotle called friendship based on pleasure or usefulness. And if there is a good of society *qua* society, the question, Whose individual good is it? does not even make sense. This is why philosophers who regarded knowledge or intellectual activity as the highest human good, as Plato and Aristotle did, could hardly take the question, My own good or the good of others? seriously. Nor could they take it seriously with respect to such goods as fortitude, temperance, and justice. This, I suggest, is Socrates' fundamental answer to Thrasymachus in *The Republic*.[10] And this is why Augustine, when he speaks of one's vision of God as the only end one should have, is not an egoist, as he might so easily be interpreted. For the vision of God is, for Augustine, the consummation of one's love of God and of all other beings made in the image of God. It is senseless to suppose that there can be competition between oneself and the others for the vision of God, that with respect to this, according to Augustine, highest good, the question, My own good or the good of others? could arise. The question whether Plato, Aristotle, or Augustine was an ethical egoist is simply not well defined.

But people do compete for money, office, fame, honor, power. An adequate ethical theory, however, is not likely to regard any of these as good in itself, though they all can be very good as means to other things that are good in themselves. And those other things for the sake of which they may be sought are usually, though not always, precisely the lower goods, namely, existence, health, pleasure, and desire-satisfaction, direct competition being not only possible but common with respect to at least the last two.

## 2. The Argument for Egoism

How should the question, My own good or the good of others? be answered with respect to such a good? Could ethical egoism, not to be confused with what I have called ethical solipsism, be true? The case of existence is complicated because, as we have seen, it is a good that is a necessary condition for all other goods. To some extent, this is probably true also of health. So let us ask our question with respect to pleasure. What I shall say about it will apply, mutatis mutandis, also to desire-satisfaction. I should emphasize that I am concerned here with ethical egoism, not with ethical speciesism. The latter is the view that even with respect to goods such as pleasure, which can be enjoyed by both intellectual and nonintellectual animals, intellectual animals, human beings, are to be accorded special concern. I have already denied this. With respect to pleasure, all animals are equal. I am concerned here with the view that it is not the case that one ought to promote anyone else's pleasure for its own sake, whether it be that of a man or a dog.

The egoist cannot simply assert that he ought to promote only his own pleasure, that it is not the case that he ought to promote anyone else's pleasure (as an end). To count as a philosopher he must offer some reasons for this assertion. And the only acceptable reason would be some relevant difference between his own pleasure and that of another. The mere fact that one is his own and the other another's, or that it has something to do with what Bernard Williams has called one's integrity as a person,[11] is not such a reason. We require a reason precisely for taking such facts as relevant. If there is no such reason, then egoism is not a philosophical theory but a personal decision about how to live. (It is not surprising therefore that in his major work in ethics, *Ethics and the Limits of Philosophy*, Bernard Williams questions the relevance of ethical theories; I am not suggesting, however, that his view is ethical egoism, to say nothing of its being hedonism.) Now what reason could there be?

Is there a relevant difference between one's own pleasures and those of others? The difference that has often been suggested is that one desires only one's own pleasures and never anyone else's. That this is so is the view ordinarily called hedonistic psychological egoism. But surely psychological egoism is not true, even if hedonism were true. And even if hedonistic psychological egoism were true, it would still not provide hedonistic ethical egoism with sufficient support.

It is not true because the desire that at least some others experience pleasure, for their own sake, is characteristic of almost all human beings,[12] and the fallacy of supposing that ultimately it is really a desire for the pleasure one derives from knowing that the other's pleasure is experienced was exposed long ago by Bishop Butler.[13] But suppose that psychological egoism were *in fact* true. Ethical egoism would still not follow. Why should we not regard the truth of psychological egoism as deplorable and embark on the task of reforming human desires (perhaps even through genetic engineering!), though initially our motive for doing this would still be egoistic, perhaps the desire for fame? And the probability of success is hardly relevant to the ethical question. It is no argument against an ethical theory that most or even all people would not share its ideals in their lives. The business of ethics is to tell us what is good and how we ought to act, and perhaps to try to modify our desires accordingly, but not to cater to our actual desires.

To serve as a foundation for hedonistic ethical egoism, psychological egoism would need therefore to be reformulated. It must hold that not only do all desiring beings in fact desire only their own pleasure but that this is necessarily so, either by logical or causal necessity, and therefore that they could not do otherwise. But what possible grounds can there be for such a strong claim? Moreover, the really substantive question remains unaffected. It could now be put as follows: Assuming that one *could* desire and thus promote another's pleasure (as an end), ought one to do so? The rejection of the assumption would merely render the question one of purely intellectual, philosophical, not practical, interest. We may agree that one *ought* to do x only if one *can* do x, and still ask whether if one *could* do x one ought to do x. As G. E. Moore remarked, "the direct object of Ethics is knowledge, and not practice."[14]

But the egoist has not been given his due. We have regarded the relevant difference between a certain pleasure of his own and a pleasure of someone else, and the more basic difference between him and another, as purely numerical. For, we have ignored, as we should have, possible qualitative differences, such as opportunity to promote some pleasure, or moral desert, as either irrelevant to the issue or incompatible with hedonism. And we have just argued that the qualitative difference on which hedonistic psychological egoism insists (that is, that one desires only one's own pleasures) either does not exist (since sometimes one does desire, as an end, that others experience pleasures) or is ethically irrelevant. Now, indeed, if the relevant difference between the egoist and another person, and therefore that between their pleasures, were purely numerical, there would be no more rationale for the egoist's position than there would be for a view that a certain physical law applies to one object and not to another, even though there are no relevant qualitative or relational differences between them. But is the relevant difference purely numerical? Is the difference between *me* and Dick the same as the difference between Dick and Bill, even if all three of us share the same relevant characteristics?

Let us compare the egoist's position with the not entirely dissimilar position of the epistemological solipsist. He denies that he can know that other minds exist, but not simply on the grounds that they are other. He appeals to what indeed is a relevant additional difference between him and others, an epistemic difference. And he finds this difference by relying on the epistemological view that no inference from bodily or behavioral states to a mental state satisfies any of the canons of validity, whether deductive or inductive. To know that another mind exists, he must perform such an inference. To know that his mind exists, that he himself is in a certain mental state, such as having a headache, he need not perform any inference; the proposition is self-evident to him. Even if he is wrong in believing that the inferences to the existence of other minds are fallacious, his case is a reasonable one, in virtue of the difference between his epistemic position with respect to his own mental states and his epistemic position with respect to the mental states of others. I am assuming, of course, that, contrary to the familiar Wittgensteinean view, one can know that, say, one is in pain. But Wittgenstein too insists on there being a fundamental epistemic difference; he only denies that one's epistemic position with respect to one's occurrent mental states is properly describable as one of knowing.

Is there an analogous reason in the case of the egoist? We can now appreciate his position as capable of a subtler formulation than we originally gave it. One is in a different epistemic position with respect to oneself than with respect to others not purely because of the numerical difference between oneself and the other. There is also another reason, which for want of a better term I shall call indexical difference. *I* am one of the persons in question, and the others are *you* or *they*. This difference is no more merely numerical difference, or reducible to any genuinely qualitative difference, than is the difference between past and present merely numerical or reducible to a difference between dates. And it is of course this indexical difference between me and you that puts me in a privileged epistemic position with respect to my own mental states, whether directly or by generating a qualitative difference on which the privileged position rests, namely, that I can be aware ("directly") only of my own mental states. The hedonistic egoist can now argue that it is the indexical difference between him and another person that puts him in a privileged ethical position, that constitutes his reason for believing that he ought to promote only his own pleasure. But to make his case, he must not only appeal to the fact that the difference between him and anyone else is indexical and not merely numerical, that the case is not like that of claiming a certain physical law to apply to one object but not to another even when there are no relevant qualitative or relational differences between them. He must also show how this indexical difference makes a difference to his ethical position with respect to himself and to others, as the epistemological solipsist can indeed show that the same indexical difference does make a difference to his epistemic position with respect to his own mental states. (The epistemological solipsist in fact need not *show* this: the difference in epistemic position is unquestionable, whatever epistemological implications we take it to have; but the difference in ethical position that the egoist claims to exist is far from unquestionable and must be argued for.) Whether the egoist can do this is an open question. I doubt that he can. And, unless he does, his "theory" can only be described as groundless, unreasoned discrimination against all others—worse than, say, political discrimination on the basis of race or sex, since the latter at least appeals to qualitative differences (race, sex), irrelevant though they are. It could not be described as *rational* egoism. The mere fact that we all have selfish inclinations is not a reason for regarding it as true. The presence of an inclination, whether selfish or not, is not *evidence* for the truth of the proposition that one ought to act in accordance with it, though it is a *motive* for so acting. The ambiguity of the word "reason," to which I drew attention in chapter 2, section 7, is seductive and often leads to philosophical disaster.

Derek Parfit has correctly argued that ordinary egoism, or the principle of self-interest, rests on a metaphysically inadequate understanding of selfhood and of personal identity.[15] I have much sympathy with his view,[16] but to discuss it here would take us too far from the concerns of this book. We may think of my arguments in this section as directed at the "egoist of the present moment." If adequate they would of course hold also against the egoist with respect to what is ordinarily regarded as a whole lifetime, the prudent egoist.

## 3. The Degrees of Goodness

I have remarked that the panethicist, though acknowledging the intrinsic value even of a pebble, could not reasonably hold this value to be equal to that of himself. For he has a nature far richer than that of any mere pebble, indeed than that of any inanimate object. Similar remarks may be made regarding comparisons of the values of other entities in the hierarchy of being. The comparison of the value of a pebble with that of a blade of grass may prompt no clear decision, but this is not so when we compare the value of a pebble with that of a fully grown, healthy oak tree. On the other hand, it is unclear that a decaying, virtually dead oak tree has greater intrinsic value than a pebble. But it is not unclear that the panethicist could not reasonably hold that his value is equal to that of any plant, even of a magnificent oak tree. Only perverse moral thinking would advocate the sacrifice of a human being for the preservation of an oak tree. And only perverse moral thinking would advocate that a human being's value is not greater than that of any mere animal, that a human being may be sacrificed for the preservation, for example, of a fish.

In all these comparisons the decisive consideration is the nonnormative conception of the richness or perfection of the entities being compared, their place in the hierarchy of being. This conception leads us then to the normative conception of the intrinsic goodness the entities have or can have. In each case we are required to consider whether, everything else being equal, the sacrifice of one being for the sake of another being that is lower in the hierarchy would be acceptable, and in each case the answer seems to be unequivocally negative. And the reason behind this is that to sacrifice a being is to sacrifice its existence and therewith all the other goods it enjoys or can enjoy. The sacrifice of a human being is the sacrifice of a social, intellectual, volitional, desiring, sentient, living, existing being, and thus of its friendships, knowledge, fortitude, satisfaction, pleasures, and health, or at least of its capacity for these; that of a pebble (presumably the breaking it up) is just the sacrifice of a spatial being, just the sacrifice of its existence. As we saw in the last chapter, this is how the ideas of the dignity of humanity, of the respect we owe a human being *qua* a rational creature, of each rational creature's being an end, of the special intrinsic value of human life, of man's having been made in the image of God, receive the sort of grounding that otherwise they seem to lack.

But it is one thing to have a hierarchy of the values of certain beings, another to have a hierarchy of the abstract goods the presence of which determines those values. For it may seem that the great value of a human being is purely *quantitative*, that it is simply its possessing (at least potentially or to some degree) all seven of our abstract goods, and the very small value of a pebble is simply the fact that it possesses only one of these seven goods. There is much truth in this. We have here a third legitimate application of the notion of quantity of goodness, additional to and quite unlike those I have mentioned earlier, those involving numbers of persons and time periods. But we may now raise the further question, which no longer concerns comparative judgments regarding the goodness or badness of the *existence* or *destruction* of a being, whether the abstract goods themselves form a hierarchy in respect to *degree* of goodness. If they do, then judgments about the preferability of *certain ways of being* would also be capable of being grounded.

I suggest that the answer to this question should be affirmative, though my defense of it here must remain woefully sketchy. Surely mere existence is the lowest abstract good, so low that it often is not recognized at all. This is quite evident in the case of a human being. Strictly speaking, for a human being to merely exist is for it to be dead, to be a corpse, and this strikes us as of so small significance that we are even inclined to deny that a corpse is a human being (though sometimes inclined to affirm this—as we can easily see from even a casual observation of some funerals). We immediately recognize that bodily health (at least to the extent of being alive) is incomparably better than existence as a mere corpse. But it is not even remotely as valuable in itself as pleasure. A person in a deep coma, even if healthy enough to be unquestionably alive, and perhaps in some respects healthier than a noncomatose human being (for example, in respect of not having heart disease), is an object of pity, and if later he or she exhibits symptoms of pleasure, this is a cause of joy. But while the parents, siblings, and friends of such a person may be satisfied with these symptoms, what they hope for are also symptoms of cognition, will, and love.

Indeed, one cannot have health without existence, and thus the question, Which is a greater good? may seem to have an almost trivial answer in favor of health. But to say this is to confuse the intrinsic goodness of existence with its extrinsic goodness as a logically necessary condition for health. And a similar dependence does not seem to obtain in every case involving the other abstract goods. (But it does obtain between most of the characteristics to which they correspond: genuine sociality is impossible without intellect and will, will is impossible without intellect, *perhaps* intellect is possible without sentience, but sentience is impossible without life, and life is impossible without existence.) Pleasure is possible without health, satisfaction of desire is possible without pleasure, knowledge is possible without satisfaction of desire, though fortitude is perhaps not possible without at least some knowledge, some cognitive achievement of the intellect, and friendship is certainly not possible without knowledge but perhaps is possible without fortitude. Are comparative questions regarding them unanswerable, except on the basis of essentially quantitative considerations about which is a necessary condition for which? Surely they are not. For example, as long as they are considered solely in themselves and not as means to, or necessary conditions for, other goods, pleasure is obviously a greater good than health. Hedonism is a familiar and extremely persuasive view, false though it is.

It is not less clear that satisfaction of the desires is a greater good than pleasure. Epicurus's ethics may be defective but only because it is not the whole truth, not because it is false. Its ideal seems to be mainly a life of satisfied desire, not of pleasure, though pleasure is undoubtedly also held to be good. Imprudence, which presumably is deplored by all, often consists in succumbing to the pursuit of pleasures at the expense of the satisfaction of at least some of one's desires.

Is knowledge a higher good than satisfaction? The question seldom requires an answer, since seldom must one choose between the two goods. But what parent would not prefer to have an intellectually developed even if not particularly happy child rather than a happy imbecile? And of course what is wrong with an imbecile is not the supposed neurological or mental defect we call low intelligence but the absence of intellectual accomplishments, of knowledge, in the sense of information and especially understanding.

That fortitude, firmness of will, what we often call character, is regarded as a higher good than knowledge seems commonplace, at least among nonacademic people. The disorganized genius, incapable of sustained effort at anything and a plaything to his inclinations and whims, is, whatever his intellectual accomplishments, obviously not preferable (except perhaps as a means) to the person of moderate intelligence but in firm control of himself. It is the latter, not the former, who arouses our unqualified admiration. And this is especially true in the case of the sort of fortitude in which virtue or good will consists.

That friendship, the good corresponding to sociality, is the highest good would be taken by most thinking people to be too obvious to require discussion. A life as a Robinson Crusoe is almost not worth living. As Aristotle observed, the loss of one's friends is often regarded as the worst evil that can befall one. A person with a loving personality, but without erudition or much fortitude, is regarded as far preferable to one who is brilliant and courageous but entirely self-centered.

That the good (if there is one) of society *qua* society is greater than any individual good has of course been a central theme in much of common moral thought, even if usually unacknowledged by philosophers. (It must not be confused with the good acknowledged by classical utilitarianism, which is reducible to goods of individuals.) That the glory of one's country justifies great suffering, or that the building of a communist society, or the conquest of space, does so, are common beliefs, which even if not defensible in their specific forms, are surely defensible in their general form of regarding the good of a society as superior to any individual good or the aggregate of any individual goods, even if in some cases the optimizing action may involve the sacrifice of the former and the promotion of the latter. It is these common beliefs that have often been taken to express the highest human ideals and to justify sacrificing even one's life. Unwillingness to fight for one's country or for the communist ideal has often been the object of the severest moral censure.

As I have warned that they would be, the above remarks are very sketchy, and it is easy to think of counterexamples. Is the memorization of the contents of a telephone book (a case of knowledge, though not of understanding but of mere information) a greater good than the pleasures of a normal sexual life? Is a life of fortitude preferable to a life of great pain? Is a loving, friendly moron preferable to a cold, selfish genius? Could any societal goal justify slavery? I believe that these are not genuine counterexamples to the hierarchical order of the *abstract* goods outlined earlier but rather examples of the difficulty of rendering the account of that order precise and detailed enough to provide answers to specific questions.

The chief reason for the difficulty is that, as I remarked in the previous chapter, the abstract goods seem to have a hierarchical order mainly in the sense that their highest or ideal species have that order. This allows *with respect to degree of goodness* for overlap and even reverse order between some of the other species of one good and some of the species of another good. (If the reader wonders how this could be so, he or she may recall what I said in chapter 5, section 8, about the possibility of equally adequate classifications and of cross-classifications, a possibility due to the transcendental nature of the concept of identity.) The good of knowledge provides perhaps the most obvious example. In the previous chapter I argued that what is clearly an intrinsic good is theoretical knowledge, the entertainment and acceptance on grounds of evidence of universal and especially of abstract singular propositions, and primarily knowledge in the sense of understanding, not information. But the memorization of the contents of a telephone book is still an example of knowledge, and even if we suppose that it is an intrinsic good, it would be one of so low a degree that many pleasures would be greater goods. On the other hand, that even some mere information is regarded as an intrinsic good is evident from the fact that so many devote most of their lives to inherently undesirable work only in order to be able to spend their evenings reading mysteries, watching television, gossiping with neighbors, or to spend two or three weeks a year in travel, especially to foreign lands. What are all these if not examples of curiosity, of aiming at knowledge for its own sake, even if the knowledge has as its content merely the identity of the murderer in the novel or the motion picture, or a neighbor's sexual escapades, or the physical features of a street in a foreign city? We are seldom aware of the fact that most of what we seek for its own sake is precisely knowledge, that usually our controlling interest in life is curiosity. But the sort of knowledge so sought is far inferior to that sought by the physicist at the frontier of his discipline. Yet few can grasp that this is so, simply because few have any conception of the sort of knowledge the physicist seeks.

When it comes to comparisons of other goods with the good of society *qua* society, our uncertainty has an obvious explanation: we do not know what that good is, indeed whether there is such a good at all, the proposals that it is national glory, or the building of communism, or space exploration, or even the flourishing of the arts and the sciences, being open to the objections mentioned in the previous chapter.

Comparison of *concrete* goods with respect to intrinsic goodness are of course even more difficult. The fact that each abstract good is itself a genus under which many species, indeed subgenera, fall, and that while one abstract good as such may be better than another abstract good, a species or subgenus of the former might not be better than some species or subgenus of the latter, is part of the explanation of the difficulty of applying the hierarchy of the seven abstract goods to concrete cases. But another part of the explanation is that a concrete good may involve also much that is bad, it may exemplify abstract evils. For example, although knowledge in general is a far greater good than satisfaction in general, and perhaps extraordinary intellectual achievement more than compensates for great dissatisfaction, the memorization of a telephone book has so little intrinsic value, if any, and probably no extrinsic value, that it can never compensate for the evil of the great dissatisfaction, perhaps pain, it would presumably involve, and for the omission it would require of far better cognitive alternatives. Even the knowledge acquired as a result of a good college education, perhaps a great good that justifies much sacrifice of pleasure and satisfaction, may not be so great as to compensate for the evil of the profound dissatisfaction in some people it sometimes involves.

Comparisons of concrete goods are rendered even more difficult when *quantitative* considerations other than those involved in the issue of egoism, with which we have already dealt, are also taken into account. Such considerations are familiar when a choice between the good of one individual (not oneself) and the good of several other individuals must be made. The axiom of classical utilitarianism that the pleasure (pain) of two or more individuals is a greater good (evil) than the pleasure (pain) of one individual, assuming that they are in all other respects the same, is also an axiom of any adequate ethical theory. But its application to particular cases is difficult, especially when the choice is between the pleasure of two or more individuals and the pain of one. How much misery for one person is justified by how much joy for a thousand persons? But quantitative considerations are also relevant to intrapersonal comparisons. A lifetime of satisfaction is obviously a (quantitatively) much greater good than a month of satisfaction, if they are of equal degree. But could the degree of the latter be so great as to justify the sacrifice of the former? And how great must be the pain and dissatisfaction one expects for the rest of one's life in order that suicide be a lesser evil?

These are familiar questions, and while in the abstract they are hardly answerable, in concrete situations we all know that a plausible answer can often be given. Perhaps this is the most that can be expected of an ethical *theory*. What such a theory lacks, namely clear application to concrete situations, requires an examination of the details of each concrete situation and thus the services not of a philosopher but of a person with a rich experience with life, though also with a philosophical education. Of all the major moral philosophers, Aristotle showed the greatest awareness of this fact.

Were it possible to regard the goodnesses of goods as arithmetically additive, taking into account the differences between them *both* in respect of degree and in respect of quantity, the theoretical difficulties we have discussed might be somewhat mitigated, though, as we shall see in chapter 8, by no means eliminated. But, as I pointed out in chapter 2, section 2, this might not be possible. The reason is that while quantities of goodness are arithmetically additive, degrees of goodness perhaps are not. Does it make sense to say that, for example, understanding is twice, or three times, etc., better than pleasure, even if we are quite confident that it is better? We shall return to this topic in chapter 8, where we shall be concerned not with the comparison of intrinsic goods, whether abstract or concrete, as we have been in the present chapter, but with the comparison of actions with respect to the totality of goodness they may contribute, with respect to the property of being right or wrong.

# CHAPTER SEVEN

# Our Knowledge of Good

## 1. Intuition and Self-Evidence

Even if the phenomenological plausibility and metaphysical intelligibility of our ethical theory have been demonstrated, the epistemological question remains. In the previous chapters I largely ignored it and, for the sake of succinct exposition, have often written as if we already had an answer to it, but all I have said so far could be a description of a massive ethical hallucination. Metaphysics has told us what sort of property goodness would be, and since it would be generic, what at least some of its subgenera and species would be, *if* there is such a property as goodness. But that this condition is satisfied is not the business of metaphysics to determine. Phenomenology may convince us that goodness and the derivative ethical properties of rightness and virtue are objects of consciousness, not themselves acts of consciousness or mysterious inhabitants of consciousness, nor reducible to any such acts or inhabitants. But could not that consciousness be illusory, just as perceptual consciousness can be illusory? Indeed, Sartre himself thought that it was illusory. The objective status of goodness must not be confused with a status in reality. Colors too are objects of consciousness (it is senseless to suppose that they are properties of acts of consciousness or of any inhabitants of consciousness—if there are sense-data, they are peculiar *objects* of consciousness, not *in* consciousness), but whether colors are parts of reality, whether they are real properties of material objects, is by no means settled by that phenomenological fact. And even if we supposed that they are, it does not follow that the questions whether we know, and if we do, how do we know, the real color of any given particular object, have been answered. The same point can be made, of course, also regarding the so-called primary qualities, for example, shapes.

In this and in the following chapter I shall be using the word "knowledge" in the sense of information, not understanding. The understanding we may have achieved in this book of at least some of the fundamental ethical propositions was the result, indeed the sole purpose, of our phenomenological and metaphysical investigations. The task we face now is to determine whether, given that we understand them, we know, or at least can know, that they are true. It should also be noted that in this chapter we are primarily concerned with the conception of knowledge that would illuminate our knowledge of the *fundamental* ethical propositions, those about the goodness of abstract goods. Such knowledge can only be noninferential; indeed it is the sort of knowledge the objects of which have usually been described as self-evident. It is primarily in the next chapter that we shall consider the nature of inferential knowledge, insofar as it may have ethical propositions as its objects. For knowledge of what actions are or would be right (or wrong) can only be inferential, given our definitions of right action and of wrong action in chapter 2.

The epistemological problem before us has three parts. First, do we, or at least can we, know that there really is such a property as goodness? Second, do we, or at least can we, know that it is exemplified by any given abstract entities, that is, do we, or at least can we, actually know of any abstract entities, for example, pleasure and friendship, that they are good? Third, do we, or at least can we, know of any concrete entities, e.g, my friendship with Peter, that they are (unqualifiedly) good? The third question presupposes an affirmative answer to the first and second. But the first question may be answered affirmatively and the other two negatively, and the first and the second can be answered affirmatively and the third still negatively.

With respect to the first question, what I have already said may seem to suffice for an affirmative answer. The possibility of what can be called ethical illusion with respect to it may seem forestalled by our phenomenology. Such illusion can mislead us, it may be said, in our attribution of goodness to something, but not in our recognition of goodness as a real property, just as perceptual illusion may mislead us regarding the real shape or color of an object, or even regarding the existence of the object, but not regarding the existence of such a property as that shape or that color. Even if all experiences of circular things were illusory, there could be no doubt that there is such a shape as the circle, which is rather extensively studied by geometry. Indeed, one may be the victim of what I have called conceptual illusion with respect to goodness, a failure of understanding. A familiar example of such an illusion would be the confusion of goodness with one of its species, an example of something like what Moore called the naturalistic fallacy. But whatever other results our discussion of the metaphysical nature of goodness may have had, it should at least have prevented the occurrence of such a conceptual illusion, of such a failure of understanding. Yet, further defense of an affirmative answer to the first question may be needed, and it will be provided if we can answer affirmatively the second question. For if we do know that certain abstract entities, for example, pleasure and friendship, are good, then there must be such a property as goodness. So, we turn now to the second question.

The reasons for being unwilling to answer it affirmatively are familiar. That pleasure or friendship is good is hardly a proposition that can be established by observation or by scientific investigation, except through radical and therefore for us irrelevant redefinitions of the terms in it, such as some of those we discussed in the last section of chapter 2. Nor can it be established by logic except again through irrelevant redefinitions. Nor can it be established by appeal to "conceptual connections" that are not reducible to formal logical connections. The idea of such conceptual connections is too unclear, perhaps incoherent, to support so much weight. (The fate of such appeals in trying to solve the standard problems of epistemology, for example, in trying to solve the problem of our knowledge of other

minds by appealing to Wittgenstein's notion of a nondefining criterion, is instructive.) One might find these alternatives exhaustive and conclude that, whatever the
phenomenological and metaphysical facts may be, we simply do not and cannot
have knowledge of such propositions. I should remark that the view that a proposition
may be established only on the basis of logic and the sorts of fact scientific investigation may disclose, though it may seem to be a rather uninteresting leftover from
the positivism of the thirties, still dominates the thinking of many contemporary
moral philosophers, including, as we have seen, Richard B. Brandt. We may
describe it as the basis of yet another, very common, *fifth* variety of skepticism in
ethics, namely, the view that ethical knowledge is impossible because it can be
obtained neither by science nor by logic. I agree with its premise but will devote
this chapter to showing that its conclusion is false. No other discussion of this very
simple and very familiar variety of ethical skepticism will then be needed.

Could we have knowledge of ethical propositions that is quite different from
any of those mentioned in the previous paragraph? W. D. Ross explicitly argued
for the existence of an objective property goodness from the fact that "we are directly
aware ['our reason informs us'] that conscientious action, for example, has a value
of its own, not identical with or even dependent upon our or anyone else's taking
an interest in it."[1] By "direct awareness" Ross meant knowledge in the strictest
sense, as the addition later of the phrase "our reason informs us" confirms. Indeed,
elsewhere he used the terms "knowledge" and "direct apprehension" interchange-
ably. For example: "we apprehend that conscientiousness or benevolence is good
with as complete certainty, directness, and self-evidence as we ever apprehend
anything."[2] And: "That an act, *qua* fulfilling a promise . . . is *prima facie* right,
is self-evident. . . . It is self-evident just as a mathematical axiom, or the validity
of a form of inference, is evident."[3] Much earlier, H. A. Prichard had written:
"We recognize, for instance, that [the] performance of a service to X, who has
done us a service, just in virtue of its being the performance of a service to one
who has rendered a service to the would-be agent, ought to be done by us. The
apprehension is immediate, in precisely the sense in which a mathematical apprehension is immediate."[4]

But, even earlier, G. E. Moore had been subtler. He agreed that truths about
"what kind of things ought to exist for their own sakes," that is, are good in themselves, are self-evident[5] and allowed that goodness is an "object of thought,"[6] that
"we are all aware of" it,[7] and even called the propositions stating what kinds of
things are good in themselves intuitions.[8] But he also insisted that by so calling
them he meant "*merely* . . . that they are incapable of proof,"[9] and that the self-
evidence of such a proposition consisted merely in the fact that the proposition is
"evident or true, *by itself* alone; that it is not an inference from some proposition
other than *itself*."[10] He denied that there is any special faculty or special way of
cognizing such propositions. "In every way in which it is possible to cognize a true
proposition, it is also possible to cognize a false one."[11] Yet such a proposition may
be "evident to me, and I hold that that is a sufficient reason for my assertion,"
though it is not a logical reason, or evidence, for the truth of the proposition.[12]
Obviously, Moore was not an intuitionist, in the sense in which this term has been

commonly used in twentieth-century ethics, namely, of one claiming that there is a special and infallible faculty of cognizing ethical propositions. In the next section I shall return to these important passages.

All three philosophers appealed to our having a certain knowledge of ethical truths, of the sort familiar to, readily recognizable in, ordinary ethical thought. All three satisfied the epistemological requirement I stated at the beginning of this book (pp. 4–5). It is an essential part of the ordinary conception of knowledge that certain truths are regarded as obvious, self-evident, not in need of defense, and that our knowledge of them is regarded as immediate. It is no part of this conception that there must be special causal connections between our beliefs in those truths and the facts that make them true, or that we should have arrived at those beliefs through any special "mechanisms," reliable or not, or that they should cohere appropriately with the rest of our beliefs. The ordinary conception of knowledge is unqualifiedly foundationalist, in at least one familiar sense of this much-abused, recently invented term.

But what Moore saw, that Ross and Prichard did not see, is that our knowledge of self-evident truths, such as the fundamental propositions of ethics, but also those of mathematics and logic, must not be supposed to consist in, or rest upon, some special mode of awareness, or of apprehension, or of consciousness, even if there are such modes of consciousness. (Such a supposition also is not a part of the ordinary conception of knowledge.) The reason is simple. If such awareness could be nonveridical, then its occurrence would not be a sufficient condition for the truth of the proposition. But if it could not be nonveridical, then the epistemological question would immediately shift from the truth of the original, say ethical, proposition to the truth of the proposition that we are indeed aware of what it asserts in this infallible way, rather than in one of the many familiar fallible ways. To merely call the awareness intuition, or apprehension, or, with Russell, acquaintance, answers no question.[13] More fundamentally, to make an appeal to our awareness of what we claim to know, in defending our claim, would be to confuse the phenomenological question regarding the subject matter of the claim with the quite distinct, even though intimately related, epistemological question. And, especially if that subject matter is ethical, it would be to weaken the ethical theory, since, notoriously, one could simply deny that one is in fact engaged in the appropriate mode of awareness, that one does see, presumably with the light of reason, the goodness of certain things.

On the other hand, in *Principia Ethica* Moore offered no clear substitute for Ross's or Prichard's view. He did describe the propositions in question as *evident* but did not explain clearly what he meant by this. However, in *Some Main Problems of Philosophy* (the 1910–11 lectures), he attempted to offer an explanation, though only incidentally and without going into detail. There he described a self-evident proposition as one such that we can "by merely considering [its] terms . . . —by getting a perfectly clear and distinct idea of what it means—see at once that it must be true; in the way in which you can see, by merely considering what the proposition means, that things which are equal to the same thing are equal to one another,"[14] and earlier he had suggested, in connection with Hume, that to say that a proposition is known intuitively is to say that it is self-evident in the sense just explained.[15] We may recall that Hume defined knowledge as "the assurance arising from the comparison of ideas,"[16] and held that "the objects of knowledge and certainty" are the relations of resemblance, contrariety, degrees in quality, and proportions in quantity or number, "which depend solely upon ideas."[17] He explained that what he meant by such dependence is that the "relations are unalterable, so long as the ideas continue the same."[18] I suggest that we may express the same thought by saying that it is inconceivable that the relations in question should not hold between the "ideas" they relate. Obviously, Hume's view involves no appeal to anything like intellectual intuition. Such an appeal would have been not only totally foreign but in direct contradiction to the fundamental principles of his philosophy.

Although in his later work Moore would not have agreed that the sort of knowledge just described is the only genuine knowledge (in his articles "A Defense of Common Sense" and "A Proof of the External World," for example, he argued that we have genuine knowledge that obviously is not of that sort), in *Principia Ethica* he clearly believed that it is the sort of knowledge we can have of the fundamental ethical propositions. The account of it that he gave in *Some Main Problems of Philosophy*, like Hume's account, seems to apply only to our knowledge of necessarily true propositions. But for our purposes this is not a defect, since the ethical propositions with which we are concerned in this chapter are all necessarily true, if true at all. They all assert a relation between universals, namely, the genus-species relation. But what *in general* could knowledge, as described by Moore and Hume, be? It is, I suggest, what may be called knowledge in the strict, Cartesian sense. This is why Moore distinguished sharply our epistemic position with respect to good from our epistemic position with respect to right. We can know, even in the strictest sense, that certain things are good in themselves, but we cannot know which of our actions are right. For to know the latter we must know both the immediate and the remote consequences of our actions, and this we cannot do.[19]

But what is knowledge in the Cartesian sense? (I am not asking this as an exegetic question. The label "Cartesian" is a familiar and natural one for the view I shall try to describe, and I believe it is also exegetically defensible, but my purposes in this book certainly do not include such a defense.) And, more specifically, since in this chapter we are concerned only with knowledge of abstract goods, which would generally be noninferential, what is noninferential knowledge, in the Cartesian sense? To be sure, we can and must say that it consists in the self-evidence of the propositions known, but what does this mean? What could be meant by self-evidence when we describe certain propositions as self-evident? We need detailed answers to these questions if we are to understand what knowledge of ethical propositions is possible. For it is clear that the basic propositions ascribing goodness to abstract entities (I am not concerned in this chapter with any other ethical propositions) may be accepted only on the grounds that they are self-evident. They are hardly inductive generalizations or deductive consequences of other propositions. And, as I noted in chapter 1 and will argue further in this chapter, it would be idle to try to defend them by appealing to their coherence with other accepted propositions, or to any explanatory power they might have. I shall now attempt to provide the needed answers.


## 2. The Cartesian Alternative

In the *Meditations* Descartes did not argue for his fundamental proposition that he exists (or that he thinks) by simply appealing to his acquaintance with, or awareness of, himself (or his thinking). He could not have done so consistently, for if God could deceive him regarding the truth of propositions such as "Two and three is five," why could God not deceive him regarding the truth of propositions such as "I feel pain" and thus even of "I am aware of myself" and "I am aware that I am thinking"? In fact, Descartes argued for the proposition that he exists by arguing that not even God could deceive him regarding its truth, because he must exist, indeed think (think that it is true), if he is to be deceived. What is the significance of this argument? Certainly not that it provides what Moore called logical reasons from which the proposition could be inferred. If it did, that he exists or thinks would not be the first truth Descartes could not doubt, and he was committed to its having this priority. In any case, the fact that the proposition that God deceives him presupposes, entails, his existence does not itself entail that he exists. *P* may entail *Q* even if *Q* is false. Nor, I suggest, is Descartes merely saying that nothing, not even the existence of a deceiving God, could be a ground for doubting that he exists. For he would have to assume that he has considered *all* possible grounds for doubt—hardly an assumption he has a right to make at that austere stage of his meditations. Moreover, why should the absence of grounds for doubting a proposition, the absence of possible or actual evidence for its falsity, be itself a ground for accepting the proposition, evidence for its truth? There may be propositions such that nothing actual or possible is evidence for their truth or for their falsehood.

Descartes's argument, I suggest, is best understood (I do not make the exegetic claim that he so understood it) as simply an appeal to Descartes's finding it inconceivable, unthinkable, that he should be mistaken ("deceived") in believing the proposition that he exists (or that he thinks). This unthinkability is a brute psychological fact. It does not entail the proposition formally or in some "synthetic a priori" way. But this does not render the psychological fact in question unrelated to the truth of the proposition. For this fact consists precisely in Descartes's finding himself incapable of making sense of what it would be for him to be mistaken in believing that the proposition is *true*. (Not: of what it would be for it to be false, for the proposition might be contingent, as "I exist," when asserted by Descartes, certainly was.)

Indeed, as I hinted in the previous section, what I have called the Cartesian conception of (noninferential) knowledge seems to be that adopted, almost explicitly and with great subtlety, but little clarity, by G. E. Moore in *Principia Ethica* in passages seldom read or at least discussed by those who accuse him of appealing to "mysterious intuitions." He asserts that

> the fundamental principles of Ethics must be self-evident. But I am anxious that this expression should not be misunderstood. The expression "self-evident" means properly that the proposition so called is evident or true, *by itself* alone; that it is not an inference from some proposition other than *itself*. The expression does *not* mean that the proposition is true, because it is evident to you or me or all mankind, because in other words it appears to us to be true. . . . It would not be a self-evident proposition if we could say of it: I cannot think otherwise and therefore it is true. For then its evidence or proof would not lie in itself, but in something else, namely our conviction of it. That it appears true to us may indeed be the *cause* of our asserting it, or the reason why we think and say that it is true: but a reason in this sense is utterly different from a logical reason, or reason why something is true. . . . That a proposition is evident to us . . . may even be a *reason* why we ought to think it or affirm it. But a reason in this sense too, is not a logical reason for the truth of the proposition, though it is a logical reason for the rightness of holding the proposition. . . . We must not therefore look on Intuition as if it were an alternative to reasoning. Nothing whatever can take the place of *reasons* for the truth of any proposition: intuition can only furnish a reason for *holding* any proposition to be true: this however it must do when any proposition is self-evident, when, in fact, there are no reasons which prove its truth.

Moore adds that his intuition of its falsehood is "the only valid reason" for his holding that the proposition "Pleasure is the only good" is false.[20] I understand Moore to be saying the following.

A self-evident proposition is one that is evident but not in virtue of its being inferred from another proposition. Its being evident consists in its appearing to be true, and this, more precisely, consists in our being unable to think that we are mistaken. (As we have seen, he has already denied that it consists in our having some infallible sort of awareness of the truth of the proposition.) But this fact does not entail its being true. What it does entail is at most the essentially ethical proposition that we are right in *holding* the proposition to be true, that we are right in *claiming* to know it. The foundation of knowledge is self-evidence understood as our finding mistake unthinkable. I have substituted "finding mistake unthinkable" for Moore's "I cannot think otherwise," in order to make the view applicable also to self-evident contingent propositions. I have no doubt that Moore would have accepted the substitution. The difference between the two phrases was irrelevant to him in the passages quoted because there he was concerned with the self-evidence of necessary propositions, with respect to which unthinkability of falsehood entails unthinkability of mistake.

The *general* Cartesian conception of knowledge is, put briefly and somewhat inaccurately, the conception of knowledge as the unthinkability of mistake, both in inferential and in noninferential cases, though it is with the latter that we shall be primarily concerned in this chapter. (In inferential cases mistake would be unthinkable because the only inference that could lead to knowledge would be *demonstration*, whether deductive or "synthetic a priori," from propositions that are self-evident in Moore's sense.) It is the traditional philosophical conception of knowledge, though in the history of philosophy it has been more familiar as the conception of knowledge as the *impossibility* of mistake. When so described it also fits well, as we shall see, the ordinary conception of knowledge, the likely response that the thoughtful layman would give to the question, What is knowledge? The classical view that knowledge has as its object the universal, the unchangeable, the necessarily true, while of the particular, the changeable, the contingently true, we can have only opinion, was surely motivated at least in part by the fact that there is a clear sense in which one cannot be mistaken regarding a necessary truth. (But, of course, there is also a clear sense in which one can be mistaken.) And the common view, both classical and modern, that knowledge is a kind of direct awareness or apprehension was surely motivated in part by the belief that one cannot be mistaken about what one apprehends or is aware of directly.

Nevertheless, to describe knowledge as the *impossibility* of mistake would be wrong, for the same reasons, as we have seen, that it would be wrong to describe it as infallible apprehension. For, like the latter, impossibility is something that requires determination; it is itself a prime candidate for being an *object* of knowledge. And what would we say about the nature of one's knowledge of *it*? The traditional answer, which seems to me correct, is that it consists, in the epistemologically crucial case of primary, noninferential knowledge, in one's finding unthinkable, inconceivable, unimaginable, incomprehensible the state of affairs one judges to be impossible and so, *eo ipso*, the state of affairs that one is *mistaken in believing* that it does not obtain. The answer applies also, though with an important modification, to one's knowledge of contingent truths, such as that one has a headache or that one exists. One who has a headache at *t* finds at *t* unthinkable, inconceivable, the state of affairs that one is *mistaken in believing that one has a headache at* t, though (and this is why the truth is contingent) one finds perfectly thinkable, conceivable, the state of affairs that one does not have a headache at *t*. And one finds unthinkable, inconceivable, the state of affairs that one is *mistaken in believing* that one exists, though one finds thinkable, conceivable, the state of affairs that one does not exist. What is distinctive of one's knowledge of a necessary truth is that one not only finds the state of affairs that one is *mistaken in believing* it to be unthinkable but also finds the state of affairs expressed by the negation of the necessary truth to be unthinkable. Let me explain further.

The unthinkability of falsehood is not the same as the unthinkability of mistake. The former entails the latter, but the converse is not the case. Descartes found *mistake* in believing that he exists unthinkable, but he could not have found the *falsehood* of the proposition that he exists unthinkable. To have done the latter would have been to find that he is a necessary existent. And, of course, in both cases unthinkability should not be confused with failing to *understand* the proposition it concerns. To find it unthinkable that the proposition "This page is both rectangular and not rectangular at the same time" is true, one must of course understand the proposition, one must know which proposition it is the truth of which one finds unthinkable. Similarly, one must understand the proposition "I do not exist" if one is to find it unthinkable that one should be mistaken in believing that it is false. The difference between the two cases consists in the fact that in the former case one cannot think or conceive of, or envisage, not only the state of affairs of one's being mistaken, but also the state of affairs the proposition purports to describe, while in the latter case one cannot think or conceive of, or envisage, the state of affairs of one's being mistaken but *can* think or conceive of, or envisage, the state of affairs the proposition purports to describe. In both cases, one's understanding of the proposition is presupposed, not denied.[21]

I have spoken of the Cartesian conception of knowledge as the unthinkability of mistake. The contemporary reader would inevitably ask whether truth and belief are not also necessary conditions of knowledge. For my purposes, it would suffice merely to add these to the unthinkability of mistake and say that the three together are what constitutes knowledge. But the artificiality of such an addition should be obvious. In general, we should be skeptical about accounts of fundamental concepts in terms of conjunctions of several logically independent necessary conditions. But we don't need the addition. Doesn't *finding* mistake in believing *p* unthinkable include believing *p*? As to truth, indeed finding mistake in believing *p* unthinkable does not entail that *p* is true. Yet what we find *unthinkable* is precisely that *p* is not *true*. I shall come back to this point.

Although in this section I am defending the Cartesian conception of knowledge in general, it should be clear that it suffices for my purposes to show that it explicates and justifies claims to the self-evidence of certain necessary propositions. For it is such claims that are made regarding the goodness of abstract goods, and they alone are of concern to us in this chapter. Claims about the rightness or wrongness of particular actions are never self-evident or necessarily true, if understood according to the conceptual scheme offered in chapter 2, nor are they demonstrable (whether deductively or in some "synthetic a priori" manner) on the basis of self-evident propositions. But while this more modest goal would be justified, I shall proceed to argue in favor of the Cartesian conception of knowledge in general, partly for the sake of simplicity of exposition but mainly because the competing conceptions of knowledge often deny the very applicability of the notion of self-evidence, whether to necessary or contingent truths.

Though extremely austere, the Cartesian conception of knowledge is by no means purely philosophical, or of no application. If freed from Descartes's metaphysical doubt, from the possibility of divine (or demonic) deception, it has a clear and natural direct application not only to our knowledge of our own existence but also to our knowledge of elementary logical and mathematical propositions, and, as we have seen, to our knowledge of our own present occurrent states of consciousness, which of course have been the paradigms of what we know "with certainty." I have already remarked that, contrary to the common opinion today, it is the Cartesian conception that was the traditional conception of knowledge, espoused, for example, also by Plato, Aristotle, Locke, and Hume, at least insofar as knowledge was taken to require the *impossibility* of mistake, or *infallible* apprehension, or *indubitability*.

Its advantages over recent, rival conceptions are noteworthy. Unlike the various current "internalist" definitions of knowledge as a kind of justified true belief, which do not limit justification to (infallible) self-evidence and demonstration, it has a firm phenomenological grounding. Finding mistake unthinkable is a brute psychological fact, discernible by the person as directly as any psychological fact could be. The notions of nondemonstrative justification, or nondemonstrative evidence, or epistemic preferability, or epistemic probability, etc., have, I suggest, no phenomenological grounding at all. What is this relation between two beliefs that consists in one of them justifying or rendering evident, but not entailing, the other? What is this relation between two propositions that consists in one of them being epistemically preferable to, or more reasonable to accept than, the other? What is this property, whether relational or monadic, that constitutes the epistemic justifiedness or probability of a belief or proposition? If it is supposed to be monadic, what could be meant by saying that a belief is justified, even though fallible, yet not in virtue of its relation to another belief or anything else? I suggest that we have no idea because no such relation or property seems to be given phenomenologically. We need not be Humeans in order to insist that such primitive notions should correspond to *something* that is phenomenologically discernible. It is significant that the question I have just raised is simply ignored in recent discussions of knowledge as justified true belief. Some of the notions I have mentioned are defined in terms of others, but invariably a primitive epistemic notion remains. Of course, what I object to is not that this primitive notion is left undefined, but that it is not provided with any phenomenological grounding. Indeed, ordinarily it receives no elucidation at all. Roderick M. Chisholm's otherwise admirable epistemological works[22] provide us with a familiar example of the target of my objection in this paragraph. What do I mean by elucidation and phenomenological grounding of a primitive notion? An example, however imperfect, of what I mean is what I have attempted to do in this book for the primitive notion of goodness. I shall return to this point and discuss it in detail in chapter 8.

And, unlike the various recent "externalist" causal and reliabilist theories of knowledge, the Cartesian conception of knowledge has obvious and direct relevance to the epistemologically central case, that of the appraisal of first-person, present-tense epistemic judgments. For epistemology, which *ex officio* is concerned with the truth of the most important propositions, for example, that there is an external world, the crucial question can only be, How can *I* determine that a certain belief I now have constitutes knowledge? (for to determine this is to determine that the belief is true). The Cartesian view offers a clear answer; indeed, it is intended precisely as an answer to this question, as the dialectic of Descartes's first two meditations shows. A causal theory, on the other hand, provides no answer at all. My belief constitutes knowledge, it tells us in its simplest version, only if it enters in an appropriate causal relationship to the fact that is its object. It is curious to find philosophers attempting to elucidate the concept of knowledge in terms of one of the most obscure and controversial concepts, that of causality. And that the elucidation does not fit the paradigm of knowledge, namely logic and mathematics, is generally recognized. Such an epistemology seems to be a case of *obscurum per obscurissimum*. But I shall not pursue this point. Rather, it suffices to ask, How can I determine now with respect to any belief I hold that it does enter in such a causal relationship? Causal relationships are notoriously difficult to determine. But even if they were not, the fact remains that any such determinations can only be highly derivative; they must be based on a rich store of knowledge one already has. And, finally, surely if I am to determine that there is such a causal relationship, I must determine that its relata exist. But one of these relata is precisely the fact that I try to determine that I know. In attempting to determine whether one's present belief constitutes knowledge, one is therefore either begging the question or embarking on a vicious regress, or one simply stops soon with causal beliefs the cognitive status of which one cannot determine.

Similar, indeed even more telling, remarks may be made about more complicated causal conceptions of knowledge and about conceptions of it in terms of the nomological or probabilistic reliability of one's cognitive states. For example, Alvin I. Goldman summarizes his reliabilist account of justification as follows: "beliefs are deemed justified when (roughly) they are caused by processes that are reliable in the world as it is presumed to be. Justification-conferring processes are ones that would be reliable in worlds like the presumptively actual world, that is, in normal worlds."[23] Imagine the person asking himself the question, "Am I justified in believing that there is an external world?" finding an answer by investigating his belief-causing processes! And how is their reliability itself to be determined? Wouldn't the determination be obviously circular or viciously regressive?[24] My argument in this paragraph is in effect an argument for the view that the concept of knowledge needed for serious first-person, present-tense epistemic judgments, in particular those concerning the fundamental problems of ethics but also those of epistemology, must be such that if one knows then one *can* by mere reflection (assuming the possession of the concept of knowledge) know that one knows; it must not be "externalist."[25]

This requirement is due not to a confusion of levels of knowledge, as has been argued by William P. Alston,[26] but to a clear awareness of the centrality of first-person, present-tense epistemic judgments, especially when these are concerned with propositions the truth of which matters a great deal (as they are in the standard epistemological problems, with which Descartes wrestled, for example, whether I might be dreaming now, whether it is true that there is an external world), to a clear awareness of what such concerns of epistemology are about. Thomas Nagel has put all this nicely: "The central problem of epistemology is the first-person problem of what to believe and how to justify one's beliefs—not the impersonal problem of whether, given my beliefs together with some assumptions about their relation to what is actually the case, I can be said to have knowledge."[27] I shall return to this point. Incidentally, the Cartesian would appeal to the same principle, the unthinkability of mistake, in determining the truth of the proposition that one knows that one knows a given proposition.

It is easy to argue against reliabilist theories on grounds less fundamental than those to which I have appealed. Surely sometimes I am justified in believing, indeed I know, that, say, I am in pain. What is the reliable "process" that causes the belief? Introspection? But I don't regard it as reliable regarding other beliefs it causes, for example, that I am in love. Surely, the justifiedness of my belief that I have a headache has nothing to do with the reliability of any process or mechanism. Similar remarks can be made about the justifiedness of our beliefs in elementary logical and mathematical propositions. Indeed, there we have only something like intellectual apprehension to offer as the reliable "process," hardly what the reliabilist has in mind. The fact is that the idea of a reliable belief-producing process is quite unclear. Roderick Chisholm has recently pointed out that "it is difficult if not impossible to formulate a definition of 'reliability' which will not require us to say, of every true belief, that it is arrived at by means of a reliable procedure."[28] I take his point to be that if the procedure is described sufficiently specifically, it could not issue in a false belief, for if it did, we would not count it as the same procedure. But then how general must the description be?

The advantages of the Cartesian conception over so-called coherence theories of knowledge and justification (not to be confused with coherence theories of truth) are also evident. It makes clear the connection between the psychological state that is the basis of a claim to knowledge (or "justified" belief) and the truth of the proposition one claims to know (or to be justified in believing); a coherence theory does not do this, because for it the psychological state may only be a belief that the proposition coheres appropriately with other propositions one believes—a fact the connection of which with the truth of the proposition is at best mysterious.[29] When Keith Lehrer, echoing Thomas Reid, tries to explain "the truth connection" between justification as coherence and "truth about reality" by appealing to "our conception of ourselves as trustworthy with respect to some matters in some circumstances and untrustworthy about other matters in other circumstances,"[30] he is engaging not in philosophical reasoning but in avowing epistemic faith. And, as Ernest Sosa has remarked,[31] it is hardly plausible to suppose that the justifiedness of, say, my belief that I have a headache depends on its coherence with my other beliefs.

It is worth noting that while the Cartesian conception appeals to a certain familiar brute psychological fact, a coherence theory appeals to relations between statements or between beliefs. But not all knowledge is adequately expressible in a statement (consider describing a facial expression or a taste), nor need the acquisition and employment of knowledge that is so expressible involve the making or even the thinking of statements. As to beliefs, they are almost entirely dispositions, manifested chiefly in behavior and only seldom in occurrent beliefs or thoughts or feelings. And relations, whether logical or explanatory or whatever, among such dispositions are at best a most obscure matter, presumably because of the obscurity of the notion of the propositional content of a *dispositional* belief, hardly something that could serve as the basis of a first-person, present-tense epistemic judgment. In fact, in any particular case concerning the justification of a first-person, present-tense belief, the coherentist can only appeal to his occurrent beliefs at that time. But such beliefs can only be very few, and their coherence would hardly be significant even from the coherentist's point of view. Did the reader have, a minute ago, an occurrent belief that there was a wall behind her? Did she detect the belief introspectively? How many occurrent beliefs does she so detect now? Is she aware of logical or causal or explanatory relationships (if any) among them? Much of current epistemology rests on an uncritical acceptance of the new way of beliefs, somewhat as seventeenth- and eighteenth-century philosophy rested on the new way of ideas. Both seem to me to be largely, though not wholly, philosophical mythologies.

Of course there are other, well-known traditional reasons for rejecting coherentism, which I shall not canvass here. As Alvin Goldman has recently argued, coherentism would seem to justify "belief systems concocted out of thin air, fabricated by paranoia or neurotic defense mechanisms, or otherwise generated by sheer fantasy," whether coherence is understood as mere logical consistency or in some stronger sense.[32]

I can be brief about proposed elucidations of knowledge and justification in terms of explanatory power. We have in them an even more obvious case of *obscurum per obscurissimum*. The nature of explanation, and the criteria for something's being the *best* explanation (of certain facts), are familiar topics in the philosophy of science, and it is also familiar how difficult they are. Their difficulty, of course, is due to the generally admitted obscurity of the notions of explanation and of best explanation. Even if this were not so, there are obvious reasons for not accepting such explanationist elucidations. Alvin Goldman writes: "The truth that I now have an itch in my thigh does not explain anything else I believe; nor, perhaps, is it explained by any of my other beliefs. Still, it is justified."[33] He also points out, in those same pages, that the theoretical propositions of physics have presumably highest explanatory power but are hardly as justified, as worthy of credence, as ordinary beliefs based on perception and introspection, which have at best minimal explanatory power.

Descartes began his *Meditations* with questions about why he should trust his senses and regarded the most fundamental of these questions to be: Do I, and if I do how do I, know that I am not dreaming now? The reader may consider how the conceptions of knowledge against which I have argued might answer this question, indeed, more fundamentally, whether they are even relevant to it. For it is a question that most intuitively expresses the sort of concern that defines epistemology as a distinct branch of philosophy. If one thinks the question is silly, then one should also think that most of the history of modern philosophy is silly. And to scoff at it is not to answer it. The truth is that it is a question we all understand, its importance we all acknowledge, and if an epistemological theory is not even relevant to it, then, even though we may continue to call it epistemological, we must distinguish it sharply from those theories, like Descartes's, which *are* relevant even if perhaps unsuccessful.

But, understood in the way I have explained, Cartesian epistemology is not foundationalist, if by foundationalism we mean theories according to which the self-evident beliefs on which all other knowledge and rational belief are based are self-evident in the sense that they are made evident by directly apprehended facts. It has been objected to such theories that a belief can be made evident by a fact only if the latter is itself understood as having propositional content that is also evident, and so on ad infinitum.[34] Whatever the merits of this argument may be, it does not affect the Cartesian conception of self-evidence outlined here. As I have repeatedly remarked, the Cartesian need not, indeed ought not to, appeal to apprehension or any mode of awareness in grounding his fundamental beliefs. The latter are fundamental in the sense that he finds it unthinkable that they should be mistaken, not in the sense that they are instances of direct apprehension of reality, even though the Cartesian need not deny that they are, or at least involve, such apprehension. Of course, if by foundationalism we mean the general view that there are self-evidently true beliefs, by which alone other beliefs can ultimately be justified, then what I have called the Cartesian conception of knowledge is foundationalist. Any adequate conception of knowledge ought to be foundationalist in this sense. There are self-evidently true beliefs. Sometimes it is self-evident to me that I have a headache, and whenever I think about it, it is self-evident to me that two and two is four. As to the additional thesis of foundationalism that self-evident beliefs are the foundation of the justifiedness of all other justified beliefs, perhaps the following should suffice. If what I have said about the merits of the non-Cartesian theories is true, then how else could those other beliefs be justified?

The standard objection to appeals to unthinkability of mistake is that the fact that one finds mistake unthinkable does not entail that there is no mistake, that, with respect to any given proposition $p$, the conditional proposition "If I find mistake in believing that $p$ unthinkable, then I am not mistaken in believing that $p$" does not express an entailment, that it need not be true. (The objection may be even that the antecedent provides no reason at all for accepting the conclusion.[35] We shall see that it fails in its first version for reasons that also make it fail in this second version.) But how do we show ultimately that a certain conditional could be false, that it does not express an entailment? By showing that it is possible for the antecedent to be true and the consequent false. And, ultimately, how do we in fact show *this*? By finding it thinkable that both the antecedent is true and the consequent false, which I assume requires that we find it thinkable that the antecedent is true *and also* that we find it thinkable that the consequent is false. But the consequent in the above conditional is precisely "I am not mistaken in believing that $p$." If I find thinkable that it is false, then *I find thinkable that I am mistaken in believing that* p. But this, the italicized clause, contradicts the antecedent. Put briefly, to show that unthinkability of mistake does not entail that there is no mistake, I must be able to think that there is no mistake, and this would be so only if mistake after all was not unthinkable, only if the antecedent of the conditional is false.

I do not suggest, however, that this shows that the conditional proposition we have considered does express an entailment. It certainly does not express formal or any kind of synthetic a priori entailment. Indeed, if it did, it could not serve as the fundamental epistemic principle, for we should be able to ask then whether we know, and if we do, how do we know, the logical (e.g., the law of noncontradiction) or synthetic a priori principles that ground such entailment. And the argument applies only to the first-person, present-tense case, as it should for the reasons I have already given. My argument has been that I cannot show that the conditional proposition does *not* express an entailment, that I cannot show that it need not be true, in the only ultimate way I can show this about any conditional proposition, namely, by finding it thinkable that the antecedent is true and the consequent false. (And if this cannot be shown, then it follows that it also cannot be shown that the antecedent does not provide even a reason for accepting the conclusion.) From this it does not follow that it *does* express an entailment. What it expresses is *sui generis*, as it must be if it is to serve as the fundamental epistemic principle.

This argument suggests the answer we would give to another familiar objection: that what one person finds unthinkable another may find thinkable. That another really finds thinkable what I find unthinkable is itself something I find unthinkable. I can only understand his or her report as due to a misunderstanding, either of the proposition in question or of what is meant by "thinkable." A similar response would be made to the suggestion that another may find unthinkable what I find thinkable. It would also be the response to any purported ground for doubting the proposition regarding which I find mistake unthinkable, for example, the possibility of demonic deception. It cannot be a genuine ground, I would say, for I find mistake in judging that the proposition is true unthinkable, and therefore I find such demonic deception to be itself unthinkable.

Of course, in my argument I have relied on the assumption that unthinkability (or inconceivability) of *falsehood* (and thus also of mistake) is our only ultimate *ground* for judgments of *logical impossibility* in the broad sense of "logical," in which it is applicable to any absolute impossibility, including what are sometimes called synthetic a priori impossibilities. But is not this assumption true, whatever the merits of the general Cartesian conception of *knowledge* may be? To suggest that the ground for such judgments is, say, the law of noncontradiction, would be an *ignoratio elenchi*. For what is the ground for accepting the law of noncontradiction? Surely the unthinkability of its being false (and thus also of our being mistaken in believing it). Let the reader consider why he or she is certain that this page cannot be both rectangular and not rectangular at the same time. Surely the reason is not some abstruse theory about language or logic.

But can the Cartesian conception of knowledge be freed from metaphysical doubts, whether from the possibility of divine or demonic deception or essentially similar sorts of doubt entertained by recent epistemologists in the form of science fiction? Could God have made me intellectually so defective that I could be mistaken in believing even when I find mistake unthinkable? I shall not consider this question here beyond remarking (1) that when raised *generally* it applies to any conception of knowledge, for it demands that we give intellectual reasons for believing that our intellectual faculties are not massively, irremediably, through-and-through defective; (2) that, obviously, when raised with respect to any *particular* proposition regarding which I find mistake unthinkable, it would be sufficiently answered by me with the tautological remark that I find it unthinkable that I should be mistaken in believing this proposition when I find it unthinkable that I should be mistaken in believing it; and (3) that any purported ground for doubting the *particular* proposition cannot be a genuine ground for me since I find it unthinkable that I should be mistaken in believing the proposition. H. A. Prichard gave essentially the same answer, as follows: "When we know something, we either do or can directly know that we are knowing it, and when we believe something we know or can know that we are believing and not knowing it, and in view of the former fact, we *know* that in certain instances of its use our intelligence is not defective, so that Descartes's difficulties fall to the ground."[36]

That the Cartesian conception of *inferential* knowledge (that is, its insistence that the inference must be demonstrative) does not fit the vast majority of our everyday inferential *uses* of the word "know"—with respect to propositions about material objects, the past, the future, other persons' occurrent mental states, etc.— is familiar and occasions the standard philosophical problems that constitute traditional epistemology. I shall consider this fact more fully in the next chapter, where it belongs, since our knowledge of right and wrong, unlike our knowledge of abstract goods and evils, can only be inferential. But it is not the case that these everyday uses involve some other concept of knowledge, one that is "weaker" than Descartes's. For we have a genuine concept only if we have criteria for its application. And regarding these ordinary uses we have no criteria. Usually, this is unimportant and our everyday use of "know" is similar to our everyday uses of words such as "circle," "white," "love," which are often, indeed usually, applied to things to which on reflection we should not have thought their application really correct. (How many surfaces that we describe as circular satisfy the definition of the circle? And those that do not, do they satisfy some other genuine, but "weaker" notion of circle? What is the definition of that weaker notion?) But when we use the word "know" with respect to propositions the truth of which is of great concern to us, we find ourselves guided, however implicitly, by a notion of knowledge such as Descartes's, at least insofar as it is the notion of knowledge as indubitability, or as the impossibility of mistake. I would say I know that I will be in my office tomorrow, if the issue was whether I will be able to keep a routine appointment with a student. But I would not say that I know that I will be alive tomorrow, even though if I will not, then I will not be able to keep the appointment. Should I buy life insurance today? If I know that I will be alive tomorrow, then I know that I will not need life insurance today. Therefore, I could save a little money by not buying it today, and presumably tomorrow I will be able to repeat this reasoning. If most people thought they knew they would be alive the next day, there would be little opportunity for success in the life insurance business.[37] H. A. Prichard wrote: "If you were asked in a law court, 'Are you certain of the truth of what you have just said?', you would probably answer, 'Well, if it comes to that, there is precious little I am certain of.' It is no use to object, 'Well, if you are going to restrict what we know to what we are certain of, you are going to reduce what we know to very little.' For nothing is gained by trying to make out that we know when we do not. . . . "[38] Everyday thought, whether about ethical matters or any others, would readily assent to all this and thus would allow that the Cartesian conception of knowledge is very much its own, the ordinary, conception of knowledge, though philosophically clarified and made explicit.

In the next chapter (section 2) I shall return to the above epistemological considerations, but with a different purpose: to explore in detail their relevance to the question of the nature of rational, or probable, or justified belief, belief that everyone would admit falls short of being knowledge but some would claim is more than mere belief. For, with respect to right and wrong, as these were defined in chapter 2, it is at most rational belief we can hope for, and not knowledge, even of the weakest variety, if there were such a variety. The argument of the present section will not be complete until the argument of section 2 of chapter 8 has been given, and the reader may wish to postpone final judgment until then.

## 3. Our Knowledge of Abstract Goods

I have defended what I called the Cartesian conception of knowledge for two reasons that are crucial to the thesis of this chapter. The first is that the Cartesian conception of knowledge seems to provide the only plausible account of our knowledge of abstract goods. For it seems to provide the only substantive, positive account of what it is for a proposition to be self-evident. As we have seen, the usual defense of the fundamental ethical propositions has been to say that they are self-evident, and this accords with ordinary ethical thought. But it is not enough to say this. It is necessary also to elucidate it, and to elucidate it in such a way that the propositions in question are indeed seen to be self-evident. The Cartesian conception of knowledge, I believe, alone provides the required elucidation.

I have argued that the traditional appeal to privileged modes of awareness, to "intuition," is quite inadequate. The somewhat analogous appeal to conceptual relationships that are not reducible to formal entailments has not even been made coherently; for we have no coherent, detailed account of what such a relationship might be, especially in the case of ethical propositions. But if such an account were provided, it would almost certainly itself hold that unthinkability of mistake is the ultimate criterion for determining in any particular case that the conceptual relationship does hold. And I have agreed that propositions such as "Pleasure is a good" are neither empirical generalizations or hypotheses, nor reducible to logical truths. Indeed, this fact was the basis of the fifth and perhaps most common variety of skepticism in ethics. (See above, p. 139.) That basis would be destroyed if it were shown that empirical generalizations or hypotheses, and logically true propositions, themselves express knowledge only if they satisfy the Cartesian conception of knowledge, and that at least some ethical propositions do satisfy that conception, indeed far more obviously so than any empirical generalization or hypothesis. Our knowledge of at least some ethical propositions would be of the same nature as our knowledge of the basic propositions of logic and pure mathematics and thus far superior to any scientific, empirical knowledge we may have.

I have suggested that the Cartesian conception of knowledge can show that we do have knowledge of (some) fundamental ethical propositions. Perhaps in other respects a reliabilist conception of knowledge is preferable. But surely we have no idea of what reliable mechanisms might be productive of true beliefs in such propositions. A coherentist conception of knowledge may also in other respects be preferable. But, notoriously, in the case of ethical judgments, coherence is especially suspect as a criterion of justification. The possibility of equally coherent but fundamentally different and incompatible systems of ethical beliefs is evident in a way in which it is not evident in the case of scientific beliefs, to say nothing of ordinary beliefs about the objects we perceive. And we have no clear idea of any coherence of ethical beliefs with nonethical beliefs, to which we might appeal, since, again notoriously, we have no clear idea of logical (deductive, inductive, explanatory, probabilistic) relations between unquestionably ethical and unquestionably non-ethical propositions. (The correspondence between the levels of the hierarchy of being and the seven abstract goods, to which I appealed in the previous two chapters, is hardly the sort of coherence that coherentists have in mind.)

As to non-Cartesian but foundationalist accounts, for example, Roderick M. Chisholm's, which appeal to primitive notions such as more-reasonable-to-believe-than, they too may in other respects be preferable to the Cartesian conception (for example, in allowing us to have knowledge in most cases in which we *say* that we have knowledge). But they fail to account for our knowledge of abstract goods by failing to be *specific* about the epistemic status of such knowledge. That the highest epistemic status must be ascribed to propositions such as "Pleasure is good" by a cognitivist in ethics is clear. Surely it makes no sense to say that it is only probable that pleasure is good. Probable in relation to what? Or intrinsically? Now the highest epistemic status is called by Chisholm certainty and defined roughly as follows: a proposition $p$ is certain if and only if there is no other proposition that it is more reasonable to believe than $p$ is.[39] But even if we did understand what it is for a proposition to be more reasonable to believe than another, surely we have at most "knowledge by description" of what it is for it to be such that there is no other proposition that is more reasonable to believe than it. The Cartesian conception of knowledge provides us with "knowledge by acquaintance" of what *it* regards as the highest epistemic status a proposition can achieve. And this is important. For Chisholm's non-Cartesian account leaves it open, indeed indeterminable, whether a given proposition is certain, that is, such that no other proposition is more reasonable to believe than it. Have we considered *all* propositions? The Cartesian account merely asks us to try to think that we are mistaken in believing the proposition, and to say yes to it if we find ourselves unable to do so.

So my lengthy defense of the Cartesian conception of knowledge can be understood as having a more modest goal than the reader perhaps thought: to show not so much that that conception is the correct one but rather that there is a conception of knowledge (in fact the standard, traditional conception) that, if correct, can make clear that we do have knowledge of abstract goods, of the fundamental propositions of ethics, and moreover that the rival conceptions fail to do so. This is my first reason for appealing to it.

My second reason for appealing to the Cartesian conception of knowledge is that this conception allows us to show the irrelevance of the skeptic's most familiar argument. I have in mind his simply denying that he *intellectually apprehends*, or *intuits*, what ethical statements assert, even if he were to admit, under the pressure of our earlier phenomenological considerations, that in some sense he is *conscious* of properties such as goodness. This is his usual response to Moore, Prichard, and Ross, indeed to Plato. As we have seen, it is not applicable to Moore, though it does seem to be applicable to Prichard and Ross, as well as to Plato. And on this the skeptic can hardly be refuted by mere phenomenological appeals, for it may well be that (as Moore in effect held) there is no such privileged mode of consciousness as intellectual apprehension or intuition. This is why I went to some lengths to show that the concept of such a mode of consciousness is no part of what I called the Cartesian conception of knowledge. Finding mistake in a certain belief unthinkable is not a mode of consciousness, though it is an occurrence in consciousness and presupposes consciousness of that regarding which mistake is found to be unthinkable. In what way we are conscious of what we assert by saying that two and three is five is a difficult and extremely important question. But how we answer it does not affect the fact that we find it unthinkable that we should be mistaken in making the assertion; it does not affect the fact that we do know that two and three is five. Similarly, as we saw in chapter 4, it is a difficult though necessary task to elucidate the way we are conscious of the goodness of abstract goods. But what ultimately matters would be the brute fact that, at least with respect to some of these abstract entities, we find it unthinkable that we should be mistaken in believing that they are good, that they are abstract goods. I should make clear that my point is not that there are no infallible modes of consciousness. My point is that epistemology cannot rest on appeals to what such a consciousness discloses because in any particular case it is an open question whether one is indeed engaged in a consciousness *of such a mode*.

Moreover, we find it also unthinkable that the abstract entities that are good might not have been good, and in this respect our knowledge of abstract goods is like our knowledge of logic and mathematics, and unlike our knowledge of our own existence and of our own present occurrent mental states. Both rest on the unthinkability of mistake, but while in the case of the latter the falsehood of the proposition known is thinkable, in the case of the former even that is not thinkable. Not only do I find it unthinkable that I am mistaken in judging that two and three is five, I find it unthinkable even that two and three might not have been five. But although on a certain occasion I find it unthinkable that I am mistaken in judging that I have a headache, I find it quite thinkable that I might not have had a headache on that occasion. The propositions about abstract goods, which may be described as the axioms of ethics, are thus not only knowable but necessary. This is as it should be, if they assert a relation between universals, between nontemporal entities, namely the genus-species relation. As Moore argued, "all judgments of intrinsic value are . . . universal," in the sense that "a judgment which asserts that a thing is good in itself . . . if true of one instance of the thing in question, is necessarily true of all."[40]

Well, after all this has been said, do we really know with respect to some abstract entities that they are good? If we mean by "know" what the Cartesian means, it seems to me the answer is clear and requires little defense. It is unthinkable that we should be mistaken in judging that existence, health, pleasure, satisfaction, knowledge, fortitude, and friendship are good, if we understand them in the manner explained in some detail in chapters 5 and 6. Indeed, much of that explanation consisted precisely in rendering those judgments self-evident, though only in the present chapter can we claim to have provided a theoretical grasp of the nature of their self-evidence. But, needless to say, there is no room for genuine *arguments* that would show that they are indeed self-evident!

Meinong held that "Anyone who considers the facts . . . cannot well deny that justice, gratitude, and benevolence carry the guarantee of their worth in themselves."[41] And, more recently, Philippa Foot has written that "It is not obvious what someone would mean if he said that temperance or courage were not good qualities, and this not because of the 'praising' sense of these *words*, but because of the things that courage and temperance are."[42] Neither Meinong nor Foot holds what I have called the Cartesian conception of knowledge, and their ethical theories differ importantly from mine, but what they say accords well with this conception. Can we conceive of what it would be for us to be mistaken in our beliefs (which surely are at the core of everyday ethical thought) that Meinong's and Foot's examples are examples of goods? Or that life is good (and death bad), that pleasure is good (and pain bad), that knowledge is good (and ignorance bad), that friendship is good (and friendlessness bad)? Usually, one who would deny such attributions of goodness would be, I suggest, no more comprehensible to us than someone who denied that yellow is a color. We do not *usually* disagree about these most fundamental attributions of goodness, about the axioms of ethics, except through misunderstanding, mainly by confusing them with attributions of goodness to some concrete entities exemplifying the abstract goods in question (for example, a certain particular act of gratitude or a certain particular occurrence of pleasure), when these concrete entities are considered as causes of something else, or as contributing to the character of organic unities to which they belong.

Indeed, major moral philosophers seem to have been guilty of this confusion and have rested fundamental theses of their theories on it. For example, in arguing that the only thing that is good without qualification is a good will, Kant dismisses other obvious candidates, such as intelligence, courage, health, and even happiness, on the grounds that "they can . . . be extremely bad and hurtful" if used wrongly or if they have bad consequences.[43] A similar, though less clear, argument seems to lie behind Sidgwick's view that the notions of the virtues which "Common Sense . . . may seem to regard as intrinsically desirable" contain reference to good or well-being as an ultimate standard, and at least some are regarded as "virtues only when they are directed to good ends."[44] His argument seems to be that "our experience includes rare and exceptional cases in which the concentration of effort on the cultivation of virtue has seemed to have effects adverse to general happiness, through being intensified to the point of moral fanaticism, and so involving neglect of other conditions of happiness."[45] Even Plato was guilty of this confusion when he rejected the definition of justice as telling the truth and paying one's debts on the grounds that sometimes these have undesirable effects.[46] Some concrete instances of abstract goods may indeed be bad, but not *qua* such instances, but *qua* contributory factors, whether causal or noncausal, to something else. That this is so is quite irrelevant to the question whether the abstract entities of which they are instances are goods. Moore's method of isolation was a lasting contribution to clear thinking about these matters, precisely because it allows us to make this distinction sharply.

If the attribution of goodness to certain abstract entities, such as pleasure, is self-evidently true, then we have an answer not only to the second but also to the first epistemological question we identified at the beginning of this chapter. We have a demonstration of the existence of the property goodness itself, a demonstration of the best sort available to us: our finding it unthinkable, inconceivable, that we should be mistaken in judging that certain entities exemplify it. This demonstration does not replace the phenomenological reasons we gave much earlier for admitting that we are conscious of this property. We could hardly find mistake in some of our attributions of it unthinkable if the property were not phenomenologically accessible, if it were not an object of consciousness. Yet, the demonstration sharpens, focuses, and enlightens the relevance of the phenomenological reasons. And it renders more plausible (at least from the point of view of ethics) the existence of modes of consciousness that we may reasonably describe as intellectual intuition, namely, the several general modes of consciousness we have of universals *qua* universals, which we distinguished in chapter 4, since we need not insist that such modes of consciousness are by their very nature infallible. The mere fact that their objects are universal, abstract, nontemporal, unchangeable, necessary, etc., does not entail that we cannot be mistaken in our judgments about them, though it does entail that if true these judgments are necessarily true. Thus we are free from the chief burden that what is generally called intuitionism has been forced to bear. The demonstration also makes unnecessary the appeal we made earlier to the perhaps questionable thesis that illusion, whether perceptual or generally phenomenological, is possible only with respect to the existence of concrete entities and to the exemplification by them of certain properties, not with respect to the existence of those properties themselves.

If we consider the abstract goods whose goodness we do find self-evident, it should be clear that we are directly motivated by our finding their goodness self-evident to tend to seek them, though, since they are abstract, only in general and not necessarily in any particular concrete instance; that at least in their case "reason" is directly productive of "desire." It should require no argument that we do "desire," or, better, tend to seek, existence (at least in the sense of preserving or prolonging human existence, life), health, pleasure, satisfaction, knowledge, fortitude, friendship. Any one who did not, who professed indifference to any of these in general (not just in certain particular cases) would leave us speechless, just as would any one who denied their goodness. (I have already dealt with the issue of psychological egoism, whether one tends to seek them only for oneself or also for others.) The directly motivating power of the cognition of good is an empirical fact, especially obvious with respect to the goods I have mentioned. How it would be explained by the psychology of the future (present-day psychology is conceptually too impoverished to even attempt such an explanation) is a question that must be left open. Perhaps it is not merely an empirical fact; perhaps it is metaphysically necessary. Whether this is so will have to be left to a future metaphysics of the person to decide.

But our (unqualified) attributions of goodness to concrete entities, even to whole classes of concrete entities, are hardly self-evident. We often disagree about them and certainly find mistake in our beliefs about them quite thinkable. The gap there between belief and motivation can be great, and understandably so. For example, we may disagree regarding the rightness (not to be confused with the virtue, the "morality") of some military action or some economic decision. I suggest, however, that the disagreement ultimately concerns the nonethical properties and especially the consequences of such concrete entities, which properties and consequences are extraordinarily numerous, often of great complexity, and largely unknown, and yet must be known if a defensible ethical judgment is to be made. Indeed, it is a familiar fact that in discussions of such cases we quickly find ourselves disagreeing about nonethical matters, such as the long-range effects of the action. We have very little, if any, knowledge about these matters and therefore skepticism regarding them may be justified. And it is hardly surprising therefore that the uncertain ethical judgments we make about them may well fail to be motivating. But the nature of such skepticism must not be misunderstood. To use an analogy, we do not know, presumably *cannot* know, the exact number of grains of sand on our planet, but we do know that this number, whatever it is, is either even or odd. Skepticism concerning a certain bit of geology is no reason for skepticism concerning mathematics.

On the other hand, only seldom are we concerned with unqualified predications of goodness with respect to concrete entities, or with the rightness of actions in the sense of being optimizing. Ordinarily, we are concerned with just one or two of the good (or bad) qualities of a concrete thing, and with just the more or less immediate consequences of an action. The realism and cognitivism generally presupposed by such concerns are fully explained by our theory. Those qualities and consequences are (or can be) really good (or bad), and ordinarily we believe that we do (or at least can) know that this is so.

Yet, obviously, it would be an exaggeration to say that we *never* disagree in our attributions of goodness to abstract entities. For example, I quoted with approval a statement by Meinong in which he implies that the goodness of justice is self-evident. But, in chapter 5, I myself argued that justice is not a distinct abstract good, and not good at all if understood in some familiar ways, for example, as the proportionality of pleasure to virtue, and of pain to vice. I do not know exactly what Meinong meant by justice in the statement I quoted, and it is just possible that he meant something that I do not regard as good. I also quoted with approval a statement by Philippa Foot implying that the goodness (as understood by her) of the qualities of temperance and courage is self-evident, at least in the sense that it would be unclear what would be meant by someone who denied it. And I do not know exactly what Foot would include in the concepts of temperance and courage or exactly what she meant by "good" there, and therefore it is possible that I should disagree with her. Other examples of possible disagreement with respect to abstract goods can easily be given. How would such a disagreement be explained?

Part of the explanation would be what I have just suggested, that abstract singular terms such as "justice," "temperance," and "courage," to say nothing of "goodness," have a variety of meanings, and the disagreement may be due simply to our speaking of different things. But a more interesting part of the explanation is to be found, I suggest, in the occurrence of what I have called conceptual illusion (see above, pp. 55–56, 138). Justice is an obvious example of something with respect to which such an illusion may occur. What exactly a person is thinking when he or she thinks of justice is not at all a simple and easy question even for that person to answer. And even if in a sense answered, for example, by a more or less stipulative definition, in another, deeper sense it may remain unanswered. The person may be confused about the place that justice so defined occupies in conceptual space, about its similarities to and differences from other abstract entities and about the degrees of these similarities and differences, about the genera under which it falls. (For example, the person may be confused as to whether it is a good of individuals or a good of societies, whether he or she is thinking of justice in the soul or of justice in the state). No wonder, then, that we may disagree about the intrinsic goodness of justice. The level of generality of most of the abstract goods and therefore of the property of goodness itself is so high that to achieve genuine knowledge of them we must first engage in difficult conceptual work, in establishing an adequate classificatory scheme, in seeking genuine understanding of the two contradictory propositions between which we must choose, indeed perhaps in trying to discover, to formulate two such propositions that would deserve our attention, the sort of work in which we engaged in chapters 4 and 5. But this fact is not a ground for skepticism. It is a ground only for admitting that ethics is not the easy branch of philosophy that sometimes it is believed to be.

In addition to conceptual illusion, sheer ignorance may often explain disagreement. David B. Wong reports that in Confucian morality there is no emphasis on intellectualist ideals such as Aristotle's life of contemplation (*theoria*).[47] But what did Aristotle mean by *theoria*? Suppose that he meant (I do not suggest that he did) the sort of intellectual activity exemplified in his *Metaphysics*. Do we have reason to believe that Confucius ever engaged in such an activity, that he even had a conception of metaphysical thought of the Aristotelian sort? To take a more general example, whole cultures have been ignorant of what we regard as philosophy and are therefore incapable of knowing whether or not it has intrinsic value. The same can be said of most forms and levels of scientific, mathematical, literary, and artistic achievement.

Another part of the explanation of disagreements with respect to abstract goods is that unlike, say, mathematical judgments, ethical judgments, even those about abstract goods, by their very nature concern conduct, whether directly or indirectly, our own or that of others, and usually conduct *affecting* ourselves as well as others. We have a stake in ethics that we do not have in mathematics and therefore are subject to the temptation to deceive others and to the illusions of self-deception. One's knowing what one ought to do, even if by its very nature it consists in one's wanting to do it, is quite compatible with one's wanting more to do the opposite, and the conflict, when public, is often resolved with disingenuous denials that one ought to do the thing in question, and, when private, with one's convincing oneself, perhaps through what Sartre called distraction, that it is not really something one ought to do. And one's knowing what one ought to do depends ultimately on one's knowing what abstract entities are good and what abstract entities are bad. (The unsuccessful student may sincerely deny the value of knowledge.) The moral life is largely a battle against inclination, as Kant held, and thus a fertile source of bad faith. To say this is not to retract my earlier claim that ethical knowledge is naturally motivating. It is to acknowledge that nevertheless it may fail to be decisive. Even though to "desire" the good is to be aware of its goodness, there are other kinds of desire, at least the bodily desires, whose objects need have nothing to do with goodness, and sometimes, indeed often, these desires win the battle.

What I have said in the last few pages constitutes my response to a *sixth*, very familiar variety of skepticism in ethics, namely, the view that disagreement about ethical matters is so widespread that either such matters are not subject to genuine cognitive appraisal or, if they are, we lack the means of such appraisal. Notoriously, there is only a most tenuous connection between the premise and the conclusion of this argument, and it is hardly evident to what extent the premise is even true. If it is to be made plausible yet still remain relevant, the premise would need to be developed through a whole system of distinctions among the great variety of "ethical matters," then meticulously tested empirically with respect to each, and finally a judicious and detailed philosophical argument would need to be given for the relevance of *each* identified disagreement to the issue of skepticism in ethics; to my knowledge no one has done this. In any case, the view has been subjected to severe criticism by others, criticism with which I generally agree.[48] Therefore, I shall not discuss it further.

But I have made an admission in this section that now opens the door to a *seventh*, far more serious variety of skepticism in ethics: skepticism with respect to the possibility of an affirmative answer to the third epistemological question I distinguished at the beginning of this chapter, namely, whether we can know the *unqualified* goodness of any concrete entities, and in particular the rightness of any actions.

# CHAPTER EIGHT

# Our Knowledge of Right

## 1. Philosophical Skepticism Regarding Right and Wrong

The skeptic may accept, at least for the sake of the argument, the realist and cognitivist position I have so far defended. He may agree that there is such a property as goodness and that we do have knowledge of some abstract goods. We may know that friendship, fortitude, knowledge, satisfaction, pleasure, health, and existence are good. But actions are concrete entities, and unqualified judgments about their goodness, that is, rightness, are therefore judgments about concrete goods. As Aristotle pointed out, "it is with particulars that conduct is concerned." And a concrete entity, such as an action, has many properties and enters in many relations, both causal and noncausal, with respect to which it may be judged to be good or bad, and to describe it as good without qualification can only mean, as I argued in chapter 2, that it is optimizing, that on the whole it contributes at least as much goodness or as little badness as any of its alternatives would. Perhaps we can know all of its *intrinsic* properties and even its more or less immediate consequences, as well as its relevant noncausal relations to other things. And everyday ethical thought is mostly concerned, however unjustifiably, with the goodness or badness of just these properties, consequences, and relations. But its *unqualified* goodness, its being a *right* action, perhaps *the* right action, the action the agent *ought* to perform, is largely, even if not solely, a function of the goodness of *all* of its consequences. Even Rawls writes: "All ethical doctrines worth our attention take consequences into account in judging rightness. One which did not would simply be irrational, crazy."[1]

It would be absurd to say that one ought to perform an act of charity on the grounds that charity as such is good or even on the grounds that the immediate consequence of the action, say the pleasure of a certain person, is good, if one knows, for example, that the pleasure produced will be of brief duration and that the action will cause great misery for the rest of the person's life. But, for all practical purposes, the totality of the consequences of any action is infinite. For these consequences are all the events that would not have occurred if the action had not been performed, not just those that would ordinarily be described as caused by the action or as the events for which the agent is responsible. The latter, narrower notion of consequence may be appropriate in the theory of virtue and vice, of praise and blame, of reward and punishment. But it is the former, wider notion of consequence that is appropriate in the theory of right and wrong. As an ethical agent I want to perform the action that would make the most difference for the better, not just an action for which I might be praised. And the skeptic now points out that as a matter of empirical fact we know virtually nothing about the totality of the consequences, broadly understood, of any action, and certainly do not know whether on the whole it is good or bad. He plausibly adds that this ignorance of ours is not just temporary, that, on the contrary, it is an inevitable consequence of the inherent limitations of the human cognitive capacities. And his conclusion is that while we may know abstract ethical truths, we cannot know concrete ethical truths. But it is knowledge of concrete ethical truths that conduct requires. I shall call this sort of skeptic empirical. His appeal is to what he takes to be empirical facts about the human condition. But there can also be philosophical skepticism regarding our knowledge of right and wrong, and I shall consider it first. It appeals to the obvious inapplicability of the strict Cartesian conception of knowledge I have defended to the sort of judgments knowledge of right and wrong would require.

Indeed, it should be evident that on the Cartesian conception of knowledge we could not possibly know anything about even the immediate consequences of our actions before they have taken place.[2] Mistake in any judgment about consequences is quite thinkable. But the philosophical skeptic need not rest his case on this obvious fact. He can go on to argue that the familiar attempts to avoid Cartesian epistemology and to short-circuit the discussion of skepticism by defining knowledge in terms of some other epistemic notion, such as epistemic justification, or epistemic preferability, or epistemic probability, are deeply unsatisfactory. It is characteristic of such attempts that they regard knowledge as compatible with the possibility of mistake, not of course in the sense that they deny that "If S knows that $p$ then $p$" is necessarily true but in the sense that they deny that the evidence one has for the proposition that $p$ need entail $p$. Now what is wrong with this view, the skeptic would point out, is not so much that it violates the use of "know" in the strict sense, in the sense in which I would deny that I know that I will be alive tomorrow, however "probable" this may be and however "justified" I may be in believing it. What is wrong is that it fails to make clear the *epistemic* notion of justification or of probability to which it appeals by failing to make clear its *connection* with the notion of *truth*. This is obvious if, as usual, this epistemic notion is undefined, not even elucidated, and as I have argued, it should also be obvious if it is given a coherentist definition. (The skeptic would ignore reliabilist definitions because they presuppose the sort of knowledge that is at issue, that is, that certain beliefs produced by a certain process *are* true.) Another way of putting the skeptic's case is to say that the view in question fails to elucidate a notion of a kind of evidence that is other than, weaker than, demonstrative evidence (that is, evidence entailing the proposition for which it is evidence), and yet one that has a connection with the (possible) truth of what it is evidence for. By contrast, in the logically basic cases the connection of demonstrative evidence, say, that $p$, to the truth of the proposition for which it is evidence, say, that $q$, is quite transparent. *P entails q.* It is absolutely impossible that $p$ should be true and $q$ false. We find it unthinkable, inconceivable, unimaginable that $p$ is true and $q$ false.

This is why the sort of skepticism we are considering now questions not only that we have knowledge but that we have any sort of "justified," or "rational," or "probable" belief in the cases to which the Cartesian conception of knowledge is inapplicable. This is why it is directly relevant to the topic of the present chapter: the serious noncognitivist regarding the totality of the consequences of our actions would claim that we cannot have even rational, or probable, or justified beliefs about them, not just, as most persons would agree, that we cannot have knowledge of them, even in the laxest sense of "knowledge."

To argue, whether by way of a definition, or by an "epistemic principle" obtained from one knows not where, or by listing reminders of the ordinary uses of epistemic terms, that in such cases, to which the Cartesian conception of knowledge is inapplicable, we do at least have evidence, is at best to begin an epistemological inquiry, not to terminate it. Even if it were correct to say that the fact that $p$ constitutes evidence that $q$, and even if anyone who denied that it does would be taken to violate the use of the word "evidence," this would be significant only if the word "evidence" is not equivocal. (What I say here would hold also if we substituted "justification" for "evidence." I shall use the latter term because the former is notoriously ambiguous: there is also moral justification, prudential justification, legal justification, aesthetic justification, etc., not just "epistemic" justification.) In the epistemologically problematic cases it must mean either the same as it does in the epistemologically unproblematic case of demonstrative evidence (in which $p$ entails $q$) or its meaning must be related to the latter as a species to another species of the same genus. Otherwise, it would be equivocal and the fact that it is used correctly would have no epistemological significance. (There need not be any financial institutions in a city on a river just because the river has banks.) Now the first alternative is, *ex hypothesi*, ruled out. The task then is to discover, make intelligible, intellectually visible, the genus under which both senses of "evidence" might fall. What approach should we take in embarking on this task? I suggest that it should be the same as our approach to the topic of goodness. Epistemology must show that Evidence is a genus under which are subsumed several, equally legitimate species, demonstrative evidence being only one of them; just as in this book I have tried to show that Goodness is a genus with a variety of species. But I believe that the thesis of this paragraph deserves more extensive and independent explanation. The philosophical skeptic would hold that his opponents can learn something from him even if they do not agree with him.

## 2. The Account of Evidence Required to Rebut the Philosophical Skeptic

Many philosophers have held that there is an important connection between epistemic and ethical concepts. Plato regarded the Form of the Good, i.e., Goodness itself, as the ground not only of all goodness, but also of all being and knowability. The medievals, as we have seen, regarded goodness and truth as two of the transcendentals, ranging across all the categories and coextensive. If we say that something is true if and only if, at least as a matter of logical possibility, it is knowable, then we can call truth an epistemic concept, in an etymologically proper sense of "epistemic." But I have already said what I have to say about these classical and medieval views.

In contemporary philosophy the connection has also been discussed. For example, in the 1950s, Roderick M. Chisholm based his epistemology explicitly on what he called "the ethics of belief,"[3] and A. J. Ayer defined knowledge as including "the right to be sure."[4] More recently, Chisholm has suggested that the "normative" epistemic concepts, such as that of justification, can be understood in terms of the general concept of intrinsic value, which in turn can be understood in terms of the deontological concept of "requirement."[5] Ernest Sosa[6] and Alvin Goldman[7] have held that at least in part epistemology should be thought of as an account of the intellectual virtues, and that there are important similarities between epistemic and moral evaluation. And Richard Foley has proposed that the notion of epistemic rationality is a species of the general notion of rationality, which he assumes is concerned with means-ends relationships. If one's goal is believing true propositions (now) and not believing false propositions (now), and if on reflection one believes that one can accomplish this best by believing Y, then it would be epistemically rational for one to believe Y.[8] Just as Philippa Foot held (at least at one time) that morality is a system of hypothetical imperatives, so Foley in effect holds that cognition is such a system. I shall return to some of these views. My chief purpose in this section, however, is to sketch a very different approach to the issue.

I shall assume the core of the ethical theory defended in this book, namely, that the central notion in ethics is that of goodness. I shall also assume that the central notion in epistemology is that of evidence (including self-evidence), that this notion contains more clearly and unambiguously whatever epistemological relevance is contained in the recently invented and quite amorphous notion of "epistemic justification" (I shall return to this point), and that the notion of knowledge can be understood in terms of the notions of belief, truth, and a certain sort of evidence (including self-evidence).

Now I do not believe that any reduction of either of the two notions of goodness and evidence to the other is plausible, nor do I believe that much is achieved by trying to understand them both in terms of some third, more general notion, but will not attempt to defend this belief here, except for some remarks to be made at the end of this section. I shall be concerned rather with the striking structural *analogy* between the philosophical problems raised by the notion of goodness and the philosophical problems raised by the notion of evidence, and wish to draw attention to the question whether this analogy is due to the two notions themselves having analogous *formal structures*. If they do, I believe we would have the sort of understanding of evidence that a solution of the standard epistemological questions, including that raised by the skeptic regarding our knowledge of right and wrong, seems to require. My chief topic in this section is the nature of evidence, and I appeal to what I have argued in this book to be the facts about goodness only insofar as they may cast light on the former. The reader who disagrees with me about goodness may nevertheless be interested in what would follow if I *were* right about it. It may seem perverse to attempt to understand one problematic notion by comparing it with another problematic notion. But there are no nonproblematic notions in philosophy, and, as I have argued before, it is through comparisons, analogies, that philosophical understanding is most likely to be achieved.

The fundamental question in ethics has been, What sorts of things are intrinsically good? As I have repeatedly remarked, the truth is that mature ordinary ethical thought regards a great variety of things as intrinsically good and thus recommends a great variety of actions as likely to realize a good. Now, if there is a plurality of intrinsic goods, and since calling all of them good is surely not mere equivocation (nor can it be a matter of mere "family resemblances"), then they must have a common property, namely, goodness. I have argued that the only plausible account of that property is as generic. This is not the place to defend further this account of goodness. Here I am concerned with the possibility of an analogous account of the notion of evidence. If such an analogous account can be given, the epistemological consequences would be far-reaching, whether or not my account of goodness is adequate.

So let us turn to the notion of evidence. Analogously to the case with ethics, the fundamental epistemological question has been, What counts as (genuine) evidence? The traditional epistemological problems, which define and justify the existence of epistemology as a branch of philosophy, are merely applications of this question. Do sense experiences constitute evidence for the existence of material objects? Do observed past and present conjunctions constitute evidence for the occurrence of similar conjunctions in the unobserved past and present, and in the future? Do ostensible memories constitute evidence for the occurrence in the past of the ostensibly remembered events? Does the behavior of others constitute evidence for their having certain particular, or indeed any, feelings and thoughts? Do the predictive success, explanatory power, simplicity, elegance, and so on, of a theory of physics constitute (together or severally) evidence for the existence of the unobservable entities the theory asserts? Does the coherence of a set of beliefs constitute evidence for the truth of those beliefs? (I ignore the question whether the fact that a belief has issued from a reliable belief-forming process is evidence for its truth, since it is merely a special application of one of the questions I have already mentioned, namely that of induction: Does the fact that a certain process has produced a sufficiently high ratio of true beliefs in the past constitute evidence that the beliefs it produces now or will produce in the future are also true?) Of course, we often assume that all these do constitute evidence and disagree only about how high, how good, is their evidential status. But, clearly, the fundamental question is whether they constitute genuine evidence at all. The serious skeptic with respect to any one of them gives a negative answer.

For all those to count as evidence, they must have something in common. Presumably, something's being evidence is a relational property, the relation involved holding between that which we call evidence and that for which it is evidence. (I shall ignore here, as irrelevant for our present purposes, the question of how to understand self-evidence, which was the topic of the previous chapter.) And now we face very much the same sort of question that we faced with respect to goodness.

There seems to be nothing discernible in the cases of alleged evidence mentioned above that they all have in common. And the similarity can be quickly seen to extend further. Since here it is also implausible to suppose that we have mere equivocation or mere family resemblances, we have systematic reasons to try to reduce the apparently different kinds of evidence to just one, but our chief reason is the natural desire to legitimize our common beliefs about what we know or at least have evidence for believing, that is, to avoid skepticism. (I am not concerned with the possibility of reducing what we seem to have evidence for to what we take to constitute our evidence for it, for example, of material objects to sense experience. This kind of reduction is attempted when the sort of question I *am* concerned with here, for example, whether there is a genuine evidential relation between sense experience and the existence of material objects, as these are ordinarily understood, has been answered negatively.) Inductive evidence may be the one proposed, though the prospects of reducing any of the others to it seem very dim today. Explanatory power is another candidate, but, as Richard Fumerton has argued persuasively,[9] its evidential status presupposes that of inductive evidence, which itself presupposes the evidential status of ostensible memories. Coherence, insofar as it is plausible at all to accord it evidential status, seems to presuppose the evidential status of explanatory power, and thus again of induction and of memory.

But I shall not discuss the details of these or other such proposed reductions. I am concerned here with exploring further the analogy between goodness and evidence and the possibility that what I have said about goodness may cast light on the nature of evidence. And the obvious next question in this exploration is whether we should not understand the evidential relation as *generic*, and the kinds of alleged evidence I have mentioned and assumed to be mutually irreducible as involving different species of the same generic relation. If so, the legitimacy of none would be threatened by its irreducibility to another. Nor would it be threatened by our failure to discern anything *specific* ("supervenient" or not) that it has in common with the others. And the standard epistemological questions I mentioned earlier would receive a nonskeptical solution. But at this point a serious breakdown of the analogy between goodness and evidence seems to threaten.

In both cases there is a species that has seemed especially secure. In the case of goodness, that is pleasure. In the case of evidence, that is demonstrative evidence, evidence that entails (whether deductively or in a "synthetic a priori" manner) that for which it is evidence, a sort of evidence I purposely did not add to my list in order to present the case for the analogy between goodness and evidence in the most persuasive way. That pleasure has occupied this special place in both ordinary ethical thought and in the history of ethics can be explained easily. It is familiar to everyone, and its goodness can be grasped by everyone, perhaps even by infants.

Not so in the case of demonstrative evidence. Its secure status as a sort of evidence has quite a different explanation. It seems to be unique in that the evidence, for example, the truth of the premises of a valid deductive argument, directly involves the truth of that for which it is evidence, the conclusion of the argument. It's not just that the truth of the premises guarantees the truth of the conclusion. We also understand *why* this is so, we can, so to speak, see (in the simple cases) the *connection* between the truth of the premises and the truth of the conclusion. This, of course, is exactly what seems missing in all the other kinds of ostensible evidence. And it is not an accidental characteristic of demonstrative evidence. Clearly, it is what *constitutes* its being evidence. How, then, can the other kinds of ostensible evidence have anything in common with demonstrative evidence that would render intelligible the subsumption of them with it under the same genus? Whatever kind of evidence we consider, it is clear that what is essential to our concern with it is our belief that there is a connection between the truth of (the propositions describing) what constitutes the evidence and the truth of that for which it is evidence, even if the connection is not such that the former necessitates the latter. In the case of demonstrative evidence, we can discern, almost feel, the connection. In all other cases we don't even have an idea of what connection there might be, even though we believe that there is one. (It would be useless to suggest that the connection is that between truth and probable truth, for by "probability" here we must mean epistemic, not, say, statistical, probability, and, in inferential cases, this is nothing but the alleged *nondemonstrative* truth-connection with which we are concerned. For example, if 70% of all A's are B's, we can say that the probability that this A is a B is .7, but the issue is whether this fact has epistemic significance. As Hume and Russell remarked, even if the sun has risen every day in the past, the issue is whether this fact gives us any reason for believing that it will rise tomorrow.) It is this radical difference between demonstrative evidence, which is unquestionably genuine evidence, and all other kinds of evidence, that, I suggest, is the deep ground of skepticism with respect to the existence of material objects, the validity of induction, the existence of other minds, and so on, not any picturesque possibilities of deception by evil demons or of our being brains in a vat.

Perhaps we merely don't discern *now* the evidential connections in the cases of nondemonstrative evidence; perhaps they are there nevertheless and will be discerned after proper inquiry, as we discern a demonstrative connection sometimes only after considerable reflection. Perhaps with respect to evidence we are somewhat in the position of small children with respect to goodness. They are aware of the goodness of the paradigm of pleasure, namely bodily pleasure, and often unable to perceive anything else as intrinsically good. But they grow up and most of them become capable of such perception. Yet, in the case of evidence, the beliefs in truth connections that are not entailments are, of course, generally not a result of growing up. Indeed, just the opposite seems to be the case. We form such beliefs early in life and it is the understanding of demonstrative evidence that generally is a result of growing up, indeed of formal education. So the disanalogy between goodness and evidence seems even greater. But at least it is clear now what the task of epistemology is. It is to uncover, to elucidate, to make it possible for us to discern, truth connections in the cases of nondemonstrative evidence, *if* there are such truth connections. Only then can we see them as cases of genuine evidence. For what is not in question is that demonstrative evidence *is* genuine evidence. And if nondemonstrative evidence is not sufficiently like it, if it is not a set of species in the same genus as it, then it is not genuine evidence.

There are further considerations casting doubt on there being a significant analogy between goodness and evidence. The identification of the species of goodness and their systematization have usually rested on a correspondence between them and the characteristic aspects of human nature. We explored this correspondence in detail in chapter 5. Pleasure (in the paradigmatic sense of bodily pleasure) corresponds to sentience, knowledge to the intellect, friendship to our being social beings, and so on. No reduction or any sort of "naturalism" is implied by this. It is simply that we can see (at least sometimes) that a certain good is the good corresponding to a certain aspect of human nature. This fact raises our confidence in our identification and systematization of the various kinds of goods and suggests that they are genuine goods, since the corresponding aspects of human nature are genuine aspects of human nature. At least this was the approach characteristic of Platonic and Aristotelian ethics. It has also been our approach in this book.

Now, if we consider the matter superficially, it may seem that very much the same is true of the various alleged kinds of evidence. Demonstrative evidence, presumably, corresponds to the intellect, perceptual evidence to perceptual experience, memorial evidence to memorial experience, inductive evidence to habitual expectation, evidence for the existence of other minds to our observation of others' behavior. But the appearance of similarity is deceptive. In the case of goodness, the identification and systematization of its species, even if facilitated and rendered more plausible by their correspondence to aspects of human nature, are not logically dependent on our finding such a correspondence. The good we call (bodily) pleasure can be recognized, and its goodness appreciated, directly and independently. The same can be said about knowledge and friendship. Of course, we may conceive of them as having to do with, respectively, sentience, intellect, and sociality, but we can know them, to use Russell's distinction which here, even if not elsewhere, is useful, by acquaintance, not only by description. Now this is also true of demonstrative evidence. Of course we acknowledge its special correspondence to the intellect. But we are also directly acquainted with it. We do not know it merely as the sort of evidence, whatever it may be, that corresponds to the intellect. In some people this may be all they know about it. But at least the readers of this book know it also by acquaintance.

The case with the alleged other kinds of evidence, however, seems quite different. Were this not so, there would not be the corresponding standard epistemological problems. It seems clear that, for example, we have no acquaintance at all with any evidential relation, any truth connection, between (propositions about) sense experience and (propositions about) the existence of material objects. At most we have knowledge of it by description: the evidential relation, whatever it may be, that holds between sense experience and the existence of material objects, for example, between my seeming to see a desk before me now and there being a desk before me now. We may believe that the definite description is satisfied, but we are not acquainted with what is described. Of course, we must allow for the logical possibility of inferential knowledge that it is satisfied, but if the inference is supposed to be nondemonstrative, then we would be begging the question raised in this section, and if it is supposed to be demonstrative, then it is difficult to imagine how it could be both valid and also based on premises that are self-evident or of which we have demonstrative knowledge. A similar claim can be made about all other alleged kinds of nondemonstrative evidence.

Contrast this again with the case of the species of goodness. We (or many of us) know directly, by acquaintance, the goodness of pleasure, of knowledge, of friendship. Anyone who knows pleasure only as the good corresponding to sentience, knowledge only as the good corresponding to the intellect, and friendship only as the good corresponding to sociality, deserves our pity. For, in a rather obvious sense, he doesn't know pleasure, knowledge, or friendship, even if he does know *that* the definite descriptions are satisfied. Yet, I suggest that with respect to the ostensible kinds of nondemonstrative evidence we all are very much like such a person. Whether we are to be pitied would depend, of course, on whether these kinds of evidence are genuine or merely ostensible.

It is often said today that the crucial question in epistemology is the nature of epistemic justification (evidence), not of knowledge, the latter being considered to be merely a kind of justified true belief. But if we follow the tradition and count as inferential knowledge only beliefs based on demonstrative evidence, and if our reflections in this section have been adequate, then we can say that our (so far) only clear understanding of inferential justification (evidence) is of that present in inferential demonstrative knowledge, and that the challenge is whether there are any other kinds of inferential justification (evidence). It is the notion of (demonstrative) *knowledge*, not that of justification (evidence) in general, that is clear and distinct, and the notion of justification (evidence) must earn its rights to application in other cases, and thus its independence, by allowing us to discern in these cases something they have in common with those to which the notion of demonstrative evidence applies. If the notion of justification (evidence) fails to do so, then epistemology has little need of it.

Even if what I have said so far is true, we need not accept skepticism. I have not argued that there is no nondemonstrative evidence, but only that so far none has been made intellectually visible. Yet the reader may say that my argument at least suggests a skeptical conclusion, and then claim that this suggestion depends on my tying the notion of evidence too closely to the notion of truth, on my assumption that the evidential relation is a kind of truth connection. But this may be denied. One may argue that "justification" (notice how much easier it is to state this argument by using the term "justification" rather than the term "evidence") is an irreducibly normative term, either irreducibly deontic or irreducibly aretaic. My mistake, one may argue, is analogous to that of the utilitarian: the attempt to explicate the notion of ought in terms of the notion of (nonmoral) good. But in fact, the argument would proceed, in ethics there are at least two other alternatives. One is to regard the notion of ought as irreducible (as, for example, Prichard and Ross did); the other is either to explicate it or to replace it with the notion of what a virtuous person would do (as Aristotle in effect held). Similarly, it may be argued, in epistemology, instead of looking for truth connections, we should rely on the irreducible deontic fact that in certain circumstances one belief justifies another, or even is self-justified; or on the equally irreducible fact that the belief is justified if it is held in appropriate circumstances by an intellectually virtuous person, for example, by one who is consistent, intelligent, original, and in possession of properly functioning doxastic mechanisms (we can see how both coherentism and reliabilism fit in a virtue epistemology). The attraction of these alternatives explains the otherwise strange phenomenon of the almost obsessive use in recent epistemology of the broad, largely ethical, and clearly normative notion of justification, instead of the traditional notion of evidence. For the latter indeed is inseparable from the notion of truth and has no special connection with ethics. But what motivates the adoption of either of these alternatives? I think that, at least in the case of the pure deontologist in epistemology, it is the belief that only thus can skepticism be avoided. In the case of the virtue epistemologist (whether or not he is also a coherentist or a reliabilist or both), I believe the main motive is still the same, though there is an additional, perfectly legitimate motive, namely (as is clear in Alvin Goldman's work), to examine what would make one an intellectually good person.

Now deontological epistemology and virtue epistemology are open to immediate objections analogous to those to which deontological ethics and virtue ethics are open. The chief objection to the latter two is that neither takes seriously enough the consequences of our actions, if it takes them into account at all. And the goodness or badness of their consequences is surely very much relevant to the question whether they ought to be performed, even if one is not a pure consequentialist, for example, even if one allows that certain kinds of action have intrinsic value (whether goodness or rightness) that must also be taken into account. How serious this objection is, I shall not discuss here; much of chapter 2 and of the rest of this chapter is devoted to such a discussion. But it seems to me that the analogous objection to deontological and virtue epistemologies is devastating. It is that they do not take seriously enough the question of the truth-value of the beliefs they count as justified, the connection, if any, between their being justified and their being true. (The objection does not apply to Sosa's and Goldman's views. It does seem to apply to Chisholm's, and most clearly to views such as Hilary Putnam's, who indeed rejects any independent notion of truth.) In ethics we have independent reasons for believing that certain actions (for example, lying) ought not to be performed, even if they would be beneficent, and that certain traits of character, for example, compassion, are good in themselves, even if sometimes they result in maleficent actions. Nothing analogous is present in epistemology. There, any concern we have with a belief is inherently tied to the truth-value of the belief. Although, as Roderick Firth pointed out long ago, there are nonepistemic, perhaps moral or religious, reasons why we ought to, or at least are permitted to, hold certain beliefs,[10] such reasons are not what we are concerned with in epistemology. Epistemology exists as a branch of philosophy chiefly to investigate how we may tell which beliefs are true and which are false. It is only when faced with the skeptic that we look for deontic properties of beliefs, such as "being justified," that are not to be understood in terms of conduciveness to truth, though even if we found such properties, it would be unclear why they should be of epistemological interest. And whatever epistemological interest a virtue epistemology may have, it seems to be exhausted by the light it throws on what intellectual traits would be conducive to the holding of (a sufficient ratio of) true beliefs.

Of course the deontological epistemologist may follow Brentano in adopting what Chisholm has recently called (without endorsement) his epistemic definition of truth, roughly, that a true judgment is one that is evident in the sense of being correct.[11] And the virtue epistemologist may define a true judgment as one that the intellectually virtuous, at least rational, person would accept, though perhaps, as in Putnam's view, in epistemically ideal conditions.[12] Or a third sort of epistemologist may adopt a coherentist theory of justification and answer the question about the evidential status of coherence by adopting also a coherence theory of truth. It remains true, however, that the only plausible motivation behind such definitions of truth is that they create the illusion that we need not take skepticism seriously, in other words, that we need not take the traditional epistemological questions seriously.

But perhaps Foley's conception of cognition as a system of hypothetical imperatives (this is not his phrase) offers an alternative to ours that is not subject to the above objections. It tells us that if our goal is believing (now) true propositions and not believing (now) false propositions, then we should believe what we believe, on careful reflection, to be a means to this goal. The connection with truth is explicitly preserved here. But of course Foley's is not a deontological epistemology at all. For that we need categorical deontic statements, in the sense corresponding to Kant's notion of a categorical imperative. In fact, a view such as Foley's (I go considerably beyond what he says) is a version of the traditional conception of epistemology. What is this conception? The same as the one I have taken for granted: the inquiry into whether hypothetical propositions such as the following are true: If your goal is to believe true propositions and avoid believing false propositions, then generally believe what, on careful reflection, is suggested by your sense experiences, by your ostensible memories, by your observation of other persons' behavior, and so on. On this conception, epistemic statements are normative only in the unexciting, though genuine (see above, pp. 38–39), sense in which Kantian hypothetical imperatives may be said to be normative. But obviously it also faces the chief problem of traditional epistemology, with which we have dealt in this section, and which in our present terminology can be stated as follows: In general, for a hypothetical imperative to be true, there must be a connection, whether causal or logical or of some other kind, between the means mentioned in the consequent and the goal mentioned in the antecedent. For an *epistemic* hypothetical imperative to be true, the connection that there must be is precisely what I have called the evidential, the truth connection. In the case of demonstration, there is such a connection. The general epistemological problem is that no evidential connections are discernible in the nondemonstrative cases.

What do I mean by "discernible"? Is it not disingenuous, the reader may ask, to describe the task of epistemology as the discernment of nondemonstrative evidential connections when it is obvious that nothing I would call such discernment is possible? But this is not obvious. A comparison with ethics may again be instructive. Contrary to the usual opinion, the history of ethics can be viewed as exhibiting progress, though by no means a continuous one. Progress in what respect? In identifying, in allowing us to discern, great goods that otherwise might have remained concealed, at least from philosophers. Examples would be Plato's account of justice in the soul, the Christian conception of universal love, Kant's notion of a good will, Moore's accounts of aesthetic appreciation and personal affection. Why can't we expect similar progress from epistemology?

An important part of H. A. Prichard's ethical theories was the claim that there are no probabilities in nature. His somewhat quaint example was that of considering whether to try to revive someone who seems to have fainted, by shouting. But I do not *know* that he has fainted. (The man might be having a heart attack, and shouting would be the worst thing I could do.) Well, why not say that I know that he has *probably* fainted and that shouting would *probably* revive him? Prichard writes: "It needs, however, but little reflection to realize that there are no such things as probabilities in nature. There cannot, e.g., be such a thing as the probability that someone has fainted, since either he has fainted or he has not." Prichard proceeds to suggest that what is expressed by the probability statement "must consist in our mind's being in a certain state or condition."[13] Prichard's point, of course, was not that we could not express the fact that, for example, the person's symptoms characterize the members of a set 70 percent of whom have fainted, by saying that the probability that he has fainted is .7. In this sense there are probabilities in nature. But there could be that fact regardless of whether the man has fainted or has not. What, then, is its relevance to the question whether the man has fainted? Prichard's point, I suggest, was that it has no such relevance. Perhaps he was mistaken, but, I believe, in the sixty years since he wrote this, epistemology, despite the more than hundredfold growth of its literature, has not shown that he was.


## 3. The Philosophical Skeptic Returns

The philosophical skeptic could now easily appeal to what I have said in the previous section as supporting his skepticism. Indeed, to call such a position skepticism would be inaccurate. For my claim has been only that we do not have a clear, genuine concept of nondemonstrative evidence, not that such a concept is impossible, or that though possible it lacks application. It is the task of epistemology to provide us with such a concept or to show that it is impossible, a task it has not yet fulfilled. So the skeptic may state his position not by denying that *there could be* such a concept (which of course is the concept of evidence needed for any knowledge or even merely rational belief about the consequences of our actions), but by denying that *we in fact have it*, that we employ the concept of evidence in cases other than demonstration with genuine understanding, in accordance with clear criteria that connect the alleged evidence with the truth of what it is supposed to be evidence for.

This is why the skeptic cannot be answered in the manner proposed by A. C. Ewing (and many others), namely, that

> by saying that the right act in a given situation is not the act which would in fact produce the best possible consequences, but the act which it would be rational to choose taking into account only the goodness or badness of the likely consequences and the degree of probability of these consequences . . . we could know with certainty what we ought to do in very many cases despite the uncertainty of predictions, because we can know at least that it is probable that the results will be better if we do A than if we abstain from doing it or vice versa.[14]

The point of the skeptic, however, is not merely that we cannot know what consequences our actions will have but also that we cannot know what consequences our actions will *probably* have. And his reason for the latter claim is that the required notion of epistemic probability either is unintelligible or at least has not yet been made intelligible.

Indeed, the sort of skepticism we are considering was not unfamiliar in traditional ethics, even though it was seldom mentioned, and perhaps the recognition of its power explains why utilitarianism is a rather recent ethical theory, the flourishing of which has coincided with the flourishing of the epistemic optimism stimulated by the advances of the natural sciences. That the proper object of ethical inquiry is, as for Plato and Aristotle, the identification of what is good in itself, or of the human excellences and thus of the actions that manifest them, or, as for Kant, the identification of the actions that are duties, in his sense, are the major preutilitarian secular positions. This can hardly have been a historical accident. After all, utilitarianism is not an ethical theory unlikely to occur to one who is at all concerned with the subject matter of ethics; it is probably the simplest and, at least initially, the most plausible ethical theory. Perhaps the explanation of this historical fact is that the standards of knowledge as understood in traditional philosophy were generally so high, and the absence of appeals to any vague notion such as "epistemic probability" or "epistemic justification" so notable, that it would have been taken to be a matter of course that the kind of knowledge the application of utilitarianism requires is not humanly possible, perhaps, as for Plato, not even logically possible because it has to do with the world of becoming, not with the world of being. In the *Groundwork of the Metaphysics of Morals* Kant argued that had nature endowed us with reason as a means of achieving happiness, it would have made a very poor choice: for reason, "with its feeble vision," can hardly "think out for itself a plan for happiness and for the means to its attainment."[15] Kant's argument concerned the knowledge needed by the egoistic hedonist, that is, by one whose principle of action is to maximize one's pleasure or happiness in a complete life, but has even more obvious application to any form of utilitarianism.

But once this has been said, we must not make the mistake of thinking that the moral of our story is to go back to Plato or to Aristotle or to Kant, either by simply ignoring what I have called the theory of right and wrong or by identifying right actions with virtuous actions, whether in the Platonic or Aristotelian or Kantian sense, or with duties, in the sense defined in chapter 2. The truth in utilitarianism is that the consequences of our actions do matter, even if not always as greatly as utilitarians have thought, and therefore our inability to know these consequences would be a fact of crucial importance for ethics, one that cannot just be ignored. Whether we describe this fact as our inability to know right from wrong, or merely acknowledge it and then reserve these terms for what we have called virtuous and vicious actions, or for what we have called duties and offenses, is a purely verbal question. What matters is that we distinguish the concepts of right action, virtuous action, and duty, and their contraries, as I defined them in chapter 2, not what words we use to express them.

The power of the sort of skepticism we have considered so far in this chapter perhaps also explains the special attraction of some varieties of theological ethics. Of course, the consequences of our actions do matter. They can affect the total goodness of the world, and it is for the sake of this goodness that God created the world. But at least some of the most general classes of the actions we ought to perform, and of the actions we ought not to perform, are determined for us by divine revelation, even if we think that we could discover them also by our unaided reason. How can we know that the former actions would lead to good overall and not to evil? The answer is not that it does not matter whether they would or would not but that we can be sure that, to put it crudely, God "will see to it" that they would. Just as Descartes found in God a guarantee of the existence of an external world, so such a theological ethics can find in God a guarantee that certain actions would not fail to be optimizing. Aquinas made a sharp distinction between our knowledge of the universal and necessary propositions of natural law, accessible to unaided reason, and our knowledge of "the operable matters, which are singular and contingent," with which practical reason is concerned.[16] The latter is not inerrant, indeed "different people form different judgments on human acts," and "in order, therefore, that man may know without any doubt what he ought to do and what he ought to avoid, it was necessary for man to be directed in his proper acts by a law given by God, for it is certain that such a law cannot err."[17] Bishop Butler wrote: "The happiness of the world is the concern of him who is the lord and the proprietor of it; nor do we know what we are about when we endeavour to promote the good of mankind in any ways but those which he has directed; that is, indeed, in all ways not contrary to veracity and justice."[18] The good is what ought to be promoted, but we can know how to do so only by following the ways God has directed. And Hastings Rashdall, an avowed utilitarian (albeit an "ideal" one), argued that the existence of God and the immortality of the soul are necessary postulates of ethics, on the grounds that "The course of events must itself be governed by the same Mind which is the source of our moral ideas, and be ultimately directed toward the ends which the moral ideal . . . sets as the goal and canon of human conduct."[19] However, again, the moral of this paragraph is not that we should adopt a theological ethics. For such an ethics rests at least in part on faith, and faith is not something one decides to have.

Of course, an open-minded philosopher must consider the possibility of a theological ethics that rests solely on reason. I have in mind a theory in which the existence, omniscience, omnibenevolence, and omnipotence of God are demonstrated, as well as the proposition that the existence of God entails that certain actions would be optimizing. What might these actions be? They might include those possessing intrinsic goodness, what I called duties in chapter 2. They might include virtuous actions, that is, actions the agent *believes* would be optimizing and performs because of that belief. Such a resolution of the problem of our knowledge of right and wrong would indeed be analogous to Descartes's attempted resolution of the problem of our knowledge of the external world. But do we have the required theory? Nothing is more familiar to philosophers than that the standard arguments for the existence of God are open to serious objections. (And the theory would need to include much more than arguments for the existence of God.) But what substantive philosophical argument is not open to serious objections? I know of none. Indeed, notoriously, no argument for the existence even of the external world is immune to serious objections, perhaps even more serious than those directed to the standard arguments for the existence of God. Yet this does not suffice to establish the possibility, to say nothing of the reality, of the required theological theory.

## 4. Empirical Skepticism Regarding Right and Wrong

While skepticism regarding our knowledge of right and wrong may quite justifiably base itself on the Cartesian conception of knowledge described in the previous chapter and on the essentially Humean doubts about the notion of nondemonstrative evidence to which I have drawn attention in the present chapter, it may also simply appeal to the empirical fact that not even the loose everyday employment of the notions of knowledge and evidence would support the claim that we know, or even have evidence worth having, with respect to any of our actions that it is right (or that it is wrong). Our skeptic may adopt not so much a philosophical as a purely empirical position.

This is the appropriate place to note that the seventh skeptic's case need not include any particular position on controversial issues such as whether every action has endless consequences, or exactly how the notion of a consequence is to be defined, or whether the notion of the totality of the consequences of an action is sufficiently determinate, or how actions are to be individuated and what is to count as an alternative to an action.[20] Indeed, this is evident in the case of the philosophical skeptic, who would not allow for knowledge of, or even rational belief about, any consequences of any action, however these are understood. But it is evident also in the case of the empirical skeptic. This is why I did not consider it necessary in chapter 2 to engage in a detailed discussion of these issues. It is sufficient for the philosophical and the empirical skeptic's case that we agree with common sense that an action can have a wide variety of consequences, whether intended or not, that most of these can be quite distant in the future, and that we do understand, even if not very clearly, what is meant by saying that the consequences of a certain action are (or were, or would have been, or would be, or will be) better on the whole than the consequences of another action open to the agent. And the empirical skeptic now just endorses what common sense says about our ability to know, or even have rational belief about, the totality of the consequences of our actions, and thus about the goodness or badness of that totality.

Examples from public policy supporting the empirical skeptic's case abound and are familiar. The massive rescue package approved by Congress in 1983 to keep the Social Security System from bankruptcy in the next 75 years rested on the assumption that the average fertility rate during those years would be 2.0, and that the life expectancy for women would rise to 84.4 years by 2060, and for men to 76.3. It was understood that even slight deviations from these figures might have major social, economic, and political consequences. But of course no one placed any confidence in their accuracy. Another example: It would seem obvious that the enormous quantity of dairy products that the federal government has stored as a result of its dairy price support policies can best be used to feed the millions of persons in Africa who live on less than what the United Nations considers a survival diet. Not only is no better use for it in sight; there seems to be nothing else that can be done with it. Yet a major consideration (however motivated) seems to be that a long-term effect of such charity may be the hopeless depression of the African farm economy and even greater starvation in later years. A third example is the tax reform law of 1986. It was generally agreed, even by its writers, that not even its short-term consequences for the economy were predictable. Yet its consequences are crucial for its justifiability, even though it may have been motivated also by considerations of justice and simplicity.

Examples from our personal lives also abound, even though we seldom like to dwell upon them. A certain person's years of unhappiness may be largely due to an unfortunate choice of a spouse. A woman in her early twenties confidently chooses to have an abortion on the grounds that bearing a child would interfere with her career and therefore lead to unhappiness. But will she bitterly regret her decision when she is in her fifties, when she no longer can bear children? Or when she is retired? A person seeking his first position accepts what seems to him the best offer. This involves a move to another part of the country, and the intertwining of his life with the lives of a number of people (coworkers, subordinates, superiors) with whom he has had no previous connection. What would be the long-term effects of this decision? The fact is that the person has no knowledge to support a defensible answer.

And what about the consequences of any one of these actions in the *twenty-sixth* century? They may then be quite diffuse, each may be quite insignificant by itself, but surely their totality will be enormous and its goodness or badness possibly much greater than the goodness or badness of the immediate consequences. But we have no knowledge whatever of any relevant events in the twenty-sixth century, nor anything even resembling rational opinion. J. J. C. Smart has argued that the remote effects of an action "tend rigidly to zero, like the ripples on a pond after a stone has been thrown into it,"[21] though he does not explain how he knows that this is so. Peter Geach has replied that the consequences of Brutus's murder of Caesar "include the play Shakespeare was going to write, the heroism and villainy of the French revolutionaries inspired by his act, and so on indefinitely."[22]

The skeptic is likely to point out that the consequences of one's actions usually depend also on what actions others are performing or will perform, and indeed also on what actions one oneself will perform in the future. There has been much discussion in the recent literature over the question whether a utilitarian theory can provide one with guidance as to how to act in cases involving other agents' actions, or even one's own future actions. The theory I have defended is not purely consequentialist and avoids some difficulties by drawing attention to the intrinsic value of certain actions, to their being duties. An example would be the difficulty posed by the question, Why should one vote in a national election if it is virtually certain that one's vote would not make a difference? Our answer would simply be that voting is a duty, an action of intrinsic worth that it possesses in virtue of our station as citizens of a democratic state. But other difficulties cannot be avoided in this way.

The United States ought to develop a new nuclear weapon, let us suppose, if the Soviet Union will develop one, and ought not to do so if the Soviet Union will not. And, again let us suppose, the Soviet Union ought to develop a new nuclear weapon if the United States will do so, and ought not to if the United States will not. Neither knows what the other will do. The best outcome, let us suppose, is that neither develop the weapon, and the second best is that both do. What does utilitarianism or, for that matter, our theory advise? I am not convinced that such cases constitute an insuperable *logical* difficulty for utilitarianism or for our theory but will not consider whether they do. What is relevant to our topic is that, whether or not they do, at least they suggest extraordinary *epistemological* difficulties for both utilitarianism and any theory like ours that takes the consequences of actions seriously, difficulties to which the empirical skeptic would be certain to appeal.

After arguing in a recent book that neither act-utilitarianism, nor rule-utilitarianism, nor utilitarian generalization can deal adequately with such cases, Donald Regan urges that the correct solution is provided by what he calls cooperative utilitarianism, that, roughly, what the United States and the Soviet Union ought to do is to cooperate in the production of the best outcome. (This is not his example.) But, as he realizes, this is easier said than done. So he proceeds to write: "[If two persons are to co-operate] each must be attempting to produce a jointly valued outcome by co-ordinated behaviour; each must be correctly informed about the consequences of various patterns of joint behaviour; each must be aware that the other is properly motivated and well informed; each must be aware that the other is aware that he (the first of the pair) is properly motivated and well informed; and so on . . . What is true for a group of two is true for larger groups as well."[23] Later in the book, after an even more detailed and demanding statement of what cooperative utilitarianism prescribes, and a defense of it against the charge that it is either circular or involved in an infinite regress, Regan writes: " 'Can it possibly be the case,' the reader has no doubt been saying to himself, 'that every agent attempting to make a moral decision is required to go through a process as intricate as the fully spelled-out [cooperative utilitarianism]?' The answer, I suggest, is: 'Theoretically, yes. Practically, of course not!' " He remarks that, "in practice, agents . . . should take some shortcuts, just as agents following other theories use rules of thumb."[24]

For Regan's purposes, which are logical, not epistemological, this may be an adequate answer. But it would not be an answer to the empirical skeptic, who, unimpressed by talk about shortcuts or rules of thumb, would simply point out that the kind of knowledge of other persons' awareness, information, and motivation, to say nothing of one's knowledge of *their* knowledge of *one's own* awareness, information, and motivation, or one's knowledge of the consequences of various patterns of joint behavior, is simply unavailable. If my example of the United States and the Soviet Union has not already made this evident, let me add that in any decision that the leader of either country ought to make, he would need to take into account the remote consequences of their joint behavior, and to do that he would need to take into account the awareness, information, and motivations of future leaders of the two countries, indeed also his own future awareness, information, and motivation, which of course are very much subject to change. On some views of human agency, the required knowledge of future decisions and actions is metaphysically impossible. But it is sufficient for the skeptic's claim that, whether possible or not, we do not have it and, moreover, do not have the slightest idea of how even to begin acquiring it.

Moore argued that "our utter ignorance of the far future gives us no justification for saying that it is even probably right to choose the greater good within the region over which a probable forecast may extend."[25] John Maynard Keynes responded by saying that "if good is additive, if we have reason to think that of two actions one produces more good than the other in the near future, and if we have no means of discriminating between their results in the distant future, then by what seems a legitimate application of the Principle of Indifference we may suppose that there is a probability in favour of the former action. . . . We assume that the goodness of a part is *favourably* relevant to the goodness of the whole."[26] The philosophical skeptic will deny, of course, both that we can know that it is probable that the action will have better consequences in the near future and the assumption (Keynes's principle of indifference, or of insufficient reason) that, very roughly, if we *have no* reason for believing of two contradictory propositions that one is more probable than the other, then we *do have reason* for believing that they are equally probable, indeed that each has a probability of one-half.[27] But will the empirical skeptic accept Keynes's response? He would hardly find the highly controversial principle of indifference acceptable; it would be too philosophical for him, being neither justified empirically nor evident to common sense. (The fact that we often appeal to it in gambling tells us something about the nature of gambling, not about the justifiability of the principle.) In any case, if we are fully aware of what is involved in the idea of *all* the consequences of an action, he would say, then even if the fact that it is more probable that the action would have better consequences in the near future increases the probability that the action would have a better *totality* of consequences, it does so by such a minute, perhaps infinitesimal, degree as to be irrelevant to serious ethical concern with the question whether one ought to perform the action. (It does provide one with a decision procedure, but so would the principle that decisions are to be made by flipping a coin.) An example may help to make this clear.

The president of the United States contemplates a certain military action. It is probable, let us suppose, that during the first twenty-four hours it would have better consequences than refraining from the action would. But there is no reason to believe with respect to either alternative that beyond this period it is more likely to have better consequences. The empirical skeptic would say that the president, if acting solely out of concern for the goodness or badness of the totality of consequences, might as well make his decision by flipping a coin. In fact, adopting this decision procedure might be better, since it would avoid the virtually certain badness (boredom, unpleasant work for many) of performing the calculations of what consequences the action would have even in the first twenty-four hours. The invasion of the Soviet Union by Germany in 1941, and of Iran by Iraq in 1980, might well be examples of the folly of the probabilistic reasoning Keynes seems to endorse.

What I have called empirical skepticism regarding our knowledge of, or even probable opinion about, right and wrong is by no means unfamiliar to writers in ethics. Indeed, virtually everyone who has considered utilitarianism has noted, if not the impossibility, at least the extraordinary difficulty a utilitarian agent faces in trying to determine how to act. But few have acknowledged the overwhelming importance of this fact. (Alan Donagan is one of those few.)[28] What could the reason be? One reason might be the vague belief, which we have been examining, that "at least we can know probabilities." A second reason, perhaps, is that empirical skepticism is not a philosophical theory at all. It is merely straightforward and hard-nosed common sense. It requires no abstruse, highly technical explanation and discussion, which are so dear to the hearts of professional philosophers. A third reason is that the empirical skeptic has nothing to say that is of relevance to the theory of virtue and vice, of praise and blame, of morality, and moral philosophers have often been concerned with just that branch of ethics. But a fourth, perhaps the main, reason is that what the empirical skeptic says is too painful and yet seems virtually unanswerable. It has tended to be ignored, very much as most, not all, contemporary epistemologists and philosophers of science have tended to ignore Hume's challenge to induction yet have presupposed in their theories that somehow or other this challenge can be met, even though they have no idea of how this might be done.

But empirical skepticism was not ignored by Sidgwick, who provided an extensive discussion of the epistemic difficulties that even the egoistic quantitative hedonist (whose concerns are far narrower in scope than those of the utilitarian) faces in trying to maximize his pleasures by following what Sidgwick called the "empirical-reflective method." Sidgwick clearly understood the importance of the painful conclusion to which his discussion led. He acknowledged that the calculation the hedonic calculus demands "is too complex for practice; since any complete forecast of the future would involve a vast number of contingencies of varying degrees of probabilities, and to calculate the Hedonistic value of each of these chances of feeling would be interminable." Indeed, he immediately followed this observation by saying: "Still we may perhaps reduce the calculation within manageable limits, without serious loss of accuracy, by discarding all manifestly imprudent conduct, and neglecting the less probable and less important contingencies."[29] However, Sidgwick noted what he called "deeper" objections to the practicability of the calculus. We must assume that verifiable comparative judgments regarding the intensities of pleasures—past, present, and especially future—can be made, as well as that the intensity and the duration of a pleasure are commensurable (so that a determinate value of a quantity of pleasure may be obtained). Past experiences of pleasures are of little value in estimating future pleasures. All we can go on are the representations of them in the imagination, and these can hardly be trusted. And the judgment often depends on the circumstances in which it is made. (A satiated person, we know, is unwilling even to go to the food store, a hungry person "raids" the food store.) Moreover, of many future pleasures we may have no present conception at all. Even "the most careful estimate of a girl's pleasures . . . would not much profit a young woman: and the hedonistic calculations of youth require modification as we advance in years."[30] Other persons' advice is unreliable, often conflicting, and in any case we may not be sufficiently like those persons with respect to the kinds, intensities, and durations of the pleasures we can experience. Common sense provides us with a list of sources of pleasure, for example, health, wealth, social position, family affections, congenial occupation, but not with a clear answer regarding their relative value.

If these are difficulties for the egoistic hedonist, the corresponding difficulties for the universalistic hedonist, i.e., the classical utilitarian, Sidgwick himself, are enormously greater. In the concluding paragraph of his discussion of egoism Sidgwick says: "I have no wish to exaggerate these uncertainties, feeling that we must all continue to seek happiness for ourselves and for others, in whatever obscurity we may have to grope after it: but there is nothing gained by underrating them, and it is idle to argue as if they did not exist."[31] (Clearly, a theory like ours that acknowledges many goods, not just pleasure or happiness, faces even greater "uncertainties.") In the final book of *The Methods of Ethics* Sidgwick considers specifically the epistemic difficulties of universalistic hedonism. He suggests that "current morality expresses, partly consciously but to a larger extent unconsciously, the results of human experience as to the effects of actions,"[32] and earlier has argued that the morality of common sense coincides to a great extent with that of universalistic hedonism. But he is fully aware of how uncertain reliance on current morality would be. We must suppose that the average member of the community has represented in his consciousness with some accuracy "the whole sum of pleasurable and painful consequences, resulting from any course of action." But "in all ages ordinary men have had a very inadequate knowledge of natural sequences." They also have been influenced by "false religions."[33]

And there still are the deeper objections, as Keynes was to point out,[34] though he aimed them at Moore's theory. First, to perform the needed calculations we must assume that "degrees of goodness are numerically measurable and arithmetically additive." But can we attach sense to saying that the degree of a certain pleasure or good is, say, twice as great as that of some other pleasure or good, even if we do know that it is greater? I enjoyed my dinner yesterday more than I enjoyed my dinner the day before, but what could it mean to say that I enjoyed it twice as much?[35] I have argued that friendship is better than knowledge and that at least some species of knowledge is better than some species of pleasure. But what could it mean to say that the first is, say, twice better than the second, and the second, say, three times better than the third? Second, we must assume that degrees of probability are themselves subject to the laws of arithmetic. [36] But, given the *ordinary* information we possess, can we attach sense to saying that, for example, in relation to such information the election of presidential candidate A is twice as probable as the election of presidential candidate B, even if we know the former is more probable than the latter? Bookmakers may offer odds, because it is their business to do so, but this does not mean that their odds, or anyone's odds, are based on a genuine arithmetical ratio of the probabilities; and it would be the height of epistemological perversity to hold that the odds offered *define* that ratio. Third, how do we take into account the element of risk? Should we assume that "an even chance of heaven or hell is precisely as much to be desired as the certain attainment of a state of mediocrity"? Recent theories of "rational choice" have helped us little in meeting Keynes's challenge.

Keynes's objections may tempt us to suppose that all these difficulties, which affect not only Sidgwick's and Moore's but also our theory, support not skepticism regarding our knowledge of right and wrong but rather the conclusion that the notion of an optimizing action is defective and therefore that we should seek a definition of right action quite different from that proposed in chapter 2. (I shall devote the next section to a consideration of specific such definitions that have been proposed.) Additional support for this conclusion might be found in the difficulties, to which I have already alluded, of making clear the criteria for the individuation of actions, and the notions of an alternative action, of a consequence of an action, and of the totality of the consequences of an action. But the chief difficulty remains that of making clear the notion of *the* goodness contributed by an action, as determined by both degree and quantity of goodness—the third sense of "better" distinguished in chapter 2, in which we may say that the consequences of a certain action are better on the whole than those of any alternative action.

Could it be that the notion of an optimizing action is logically defective? I believe that how this question should be answered would depend on what kind of logical defect is imputed. Vague and rather indeterminate the notion certainly is, but this is hardly sufficient for the radical conclusion that it be abandoned. Self-contradictory it does not seem to be. But perhaps, not for the epistemological reasons the skeptic has given, but for logical reasons such as those I have mentioned, there are no truth-conditions for its application. I doubt that this is so (though there may be no harm in admitting that there are no *clear* truth-conditions for some of its applications), but to show that it is not would require a separate, perhaps even lengthier investigation. If it is, then the skeptic would have won, so to speak, by default. It would be *logically* impossible to know of any action that it is optimizing.

But this conclusion would hardly justify abandoning the notion of optimizing action and proposing some other definition of right action. The truth is that, as the continuing attraction of utilitarianism shows, it is a notion central to ethical thought and is naturally expressed with words such as "right" and "ought." (I shall return to this point in the next section.) If its application should indeed be faced with insuperable logical difficulties, especially our inability to state clear truth-conditions for describing the total goodness contributed by one action as "greater" than the total goodness contributed by any of its alternatives, this would be a tragic fact about ethical thought, not a reason for gerrymandering its conceptual territory. And though it would have different roots, the tragedy would not differ from that insisted on by the empirical skeptic. That we cannot know what is right would be the tragedy, whether this be due to our insufficient epistemic powers or to the logical indeterminateness of the notion of right action.

It would be useful to compare in this respect skepticism about our knowledge of right and wrong with skepticism about our knowledge of external objects existing independently of our awareness of them. Berkeley argued that we cannot have such knowledge. One of his arguments was, in effect, that it would need to be inferential, and that no suitable inference would be valid. But another of his arguments was that the very supposition of the existence of such objects is incoherent, because such objects are inconceivable, or self-contradictory, since to be is to be perceived. Despite his protestations to the contrary, we may take both arguments to support a skeptical position, in the broad sense of skepticism, employed in this book, that includes both noncognitivism and irrealism. For, his view that ordinary objects are ideas and therefore exist is an example in epistemology of just the kind of move that we must not make in ethics, namely, to save the appearances by defining "right action" in some other way.

However, I am concerned in this section with the straightforward claim of the empirical skeptic, who, as I noted earlier, makes no controversial philosophical assumptions, raises no technical logical questions, but rests his case simply on what he thinks common sense would readily acknowledge: that we cannot know what actions are right because we cannot know what would naturally be described as their long-range consequences, although, like common sense, he finds no difficulty in understanding the idea that the totality of the consequences of one action may be better than the totality of the consequences of an alternative action. If he wins, then the logical difficulties of the notion of optimizing action would be, at most, of logical, not ethical, interest. If he does not, then perhaps we would need to face a third version of skepticism regarding right and wrong, which we may label logical skepticism.

The power of the empirical (though not of the philosophical) version of skepticism regarding right and wrong might be somewhat mitigated by the observation that at least in part it rests on a rather pessimistic view of the capabilities of psychology, sociology, political science, and economics. Indeed, these disciplines are still in their infancy. But what exactly are the skeptic's reasons for doubting that their development will lead to well-confirmed theories, similar in scope and reliability to the theories, say, of present-day biology? And would not such theories allow for rational judgments, even if not genuine knowledge, regarding the goodness or badness of the totality of the consequences of our actions? But surely, the skeptic would say, to indulge in such a speculation is to grasp at straws. And there are theoretical reasons for regarding human affairs as partially but necessarily unpredictable. [37]

It has also been argued, even by Moore (though on p. 149 of *Principia Ethica*
he says, "we never have any reason to suppose that an action is our duty," meaning
by "duty" what one ought to do; see also p. 152), that certain practices, such as
the keeping of promises or telling the truth, are necessary for the preservation of
civilized society, which surely itself is necessary for the achievement of most of
what we regard as good (*Principia Ethica*, pp. 157–58). But, *pace* Moore, even if
this is true, it provides us with no guidance as to how to act. Is it really true that
*stringent* observance of the practice, say, of keeping promises or telling the truth
has at least so far contributed to the preservation of civilized society? Could it be
that what have done so are rather the widespread violations of it? How many
disastrous wars have been avoided by breaking promises and even formal treaties,
and by judicious diplomatic lies? Has the alleged massive tax-cheating we are told
is characteristic of Italy had effects worse than moderate tax-cheating, such as that
characteristic of the United States, would have had? What would major changes
in either practice have implied, respectively, for Italian and American civilization
and national character? The fact is that we do not know. [38] But the crucial, generally
acknowledged, empirical fact is that seldom if ever do we have reason to believe
of any *particular* action, say, the breaking of a particular promise, that it would at
all affect the relevant practice. And it is with respect to particular actions that we
need guidance. Finally, what reasons do we have for believing that the collapse
now of civilized society, which allegedly would result from abandoning the practices
Moore writes about, will not lead to the emergence of a far better society six centuries
from now? What was, indeed will be, the ultimate effect of the collapse of Roman
civilization? Moore might reply that the practices in question are essential for the
preservation of all civilized societies, including those of the future. But even if we
could know that they are, this would not provide us with guidance as to how to
act. For it may be that, for all we know, the breakdown, resulting from the cessation
of such a practice, of our present civilized society would lead to the emergence of
future societies in which the practice is far more firmly entrenched and the benefits
of civilization are much greater.

It has often been suggested by utilitarians that the agent may rely on rules of
thumb, the reliability of which has been shown by past experience. But this suggestion just fails to take the skeptic seriously; it does not meet his challenge. *What*
past experience, he will ask, shows that even one act that has accorded with the
rule will have had a totality of consequences better than that which would have
resulted if the act had not been performed? After all, only a tiny fraction of these
consequences have already occurred, and an even tinier one is known to us. One's
keeping most of one's promises in the past may *seem* to have led so far to nothing
very bad and perhaps to some good. But only so far! One's keeping one's promise
to marry S may have had so far mostly good consequences. But they still have many
more years to live together. And they have had children most of whose lives are
still ahead of them, and who have or will have their own children. Think of all
that the keeping of one promise has started! In any case, it is just false that one
even knows that most of one's actions of keeping a promise have had mostly good
consequences in the past. One knows very little about what consequences most of

them have had. One knows even less about the past consequences of other people's acts of keeping a promise. And, surely, one knows virtually nothing of the consequences that the alternative acts, whether one's own or that of others, would have had if those acts had been performed. The skeptic is certain to remind us that to know whether a certain contemplated action would be right, one must know not only what consequences it would have but also what consequences each of its alternatives would have. These are not epistemological, philosophical claims. They are truths that common sense readily acknowledges.

Nevertheless, the empirical skeptic might be persuaded that there are extreme cases in which we do know or at least have rational opinion (using "know" and "rational" without epistemological scruples, which of course is what distinguishes the empirical from the philosophical skeptic) about the totality of the relevant consequences of the decisions we face. Perhaps we do know that certain extreme military actions would be likely to lead to the annihilation of humankind, and perhaps we have no conception of any consequences this might have that would make it desirable. But even if this is so, it is difficult to think of another example.

The empirical skeptic may be persuaded also that we can know that certain imaginary extreme *practices* would have unmitigatedly disastrous consequences, e.g., the practice of everyone's trying to kill every human being he or she sees, which presumably would lead to the extinction of humankind. Other imaginary practices, e.g., everyone's lying on every occasion, can be known to lead at least to the temporary destruction of everything that is valuable about humankind, including its language and civilization in general. But, for the reasons given earlier in connection with Moore's view, the skeptic would say we cannot know that this would not be only temporary and that in the long run it would not result in the cessation of the practice and the emergence of humans and a civilization far better than the present ones. But even if we could know this about the practice of universal lying, and even if we could know it about other imaginary practices, including milder variations of the two I have mentioned (e.g., the practice of killing whenever angry), it does not follow that we can know of any individual action that would conform to one or more of them that *it* would even probably have a bad totality of consequences.

J. J. C. Smart has proposed[39] that we call an action "which is, on the evidence available to the agent, *likely* to produce the best results," rational and "reserve the word 'right' as a term of commendation for the action which does in fact produce the best results." Here, as elsewhere in this book, I try to avoid the much-abused term "rational," for the reasons given in chapter 2, section 7. But it is clear that the skeptic would be quite unmoved by Smart's use of it. He need not deny that there is an innocuous sense in which we could say that a person who performs an action because he *believes*, on the basis of what he *believes* to be evidence available to him, that it is likely to produce the best results, is (to that extent) rational, and that the action itself is rational. But he would deny that the person can *know* or even *justifiably* believe that the action is likely to produce the best results. All of the examples we have considered support empirical skepticism not only with respect to knowledge but also with respect to probable opinion. Of course, Smart is not unaware of this. He writes: "until we have an adequate theory of *objective* probability, utilitarianism is not on a secure theoretical basis."[40]

## 5. Redefining Right Action

The most familiar recent attempts to avoid empirical skepticism regarding right and wrong have consisted in tampering with the notion of right action defined in chapter 2. But my definition of it was not idiosyncratic. Not only did it agree with the spirit, if not the letter, of the classical utilitarian, as well as Moore's and Rashdall's "ideal utilitarian," notion of right action; it was also the result of an argument. An action can be said to be *unqualifiedly* good, I argued, only in the sense of being optimizing. There is nothing else that could be meant by its unqualified goodness. It is this, obviously central, sense that I chose to express with the phrase "right action." Indeed, it constitutes a regimentation of the most common ordinary notion of right action, namely, that of Aquinas's first principle of natural law, "Good is to be done and promoted and evil is to be avoided," but a regimentation already implicitly approved by ordinary ethical thought, not one imposed upon it by philosophers. That a right action is one that leads to good is a proposition central to ordinary ethical thought, and its obviously justified revision into the proposition that the right action is one that leads to the *most* good would readily occur to and be accepted by any nonphilosopher. And I identified two other, but *qualified*, senses in which an action can be said to be good, namely, those I expressed by the words "virtuous" and "duty." What words we use to express these very different senses is unimportant. What is important is that we keep them distinct, and that if we introduce some other sense, there be a genuine rationale for doing so.

I have already considered one familiar alternative definition of right action, namely Ewing's (and others') view that a right action is one that is most probably optimizing, not one that is actually optimizing. As I remarked then, such a view begs the question against the philosophical skeptic. But we have seen that it also fails to take seriously the empirical skeptic, who, on grounds of common sense, simply remarks that we cannot have even the needed knowledge of significant probabilities. At least, however, such a definition of right action keeps faith with the fundamental conviction that the guiding principle of conduct must be that good be done and promoted and evil avoided. This is not true of some other proposed alternative definitions.

For example, so-called rule-utilitarians *define* (or at least "explicate") a right action as one that conforms to a rule the general practice (or acceptance) of which is or would be optimific, that is, has or would have better consequences than those there would be if the practice did not exist, or than the consequences that the general practice of any alternative rule would have. They seldom consider the question how we may know of any practice that it is optimific, that *no* alternative to it would have better consequences, the question we asked earlier in connection with Moore. They seldom consider even the question whether we know that it has generally good consequences.[41] (I have already remarked that the skeptic may allow that certain imaginary practices can be known to have irremediably *disastrous* consequences; allowing this would give the rule-utilitarian no comfort.) But even if we could know about a given practice that it is optimific, the skeptic would say, the definition has no real rationale behind it. Look, he would say to the rule-utilitarian, I'll give you a present; you can *have* that precious word "right" and use it as you wish. But I would still ask my question, though now using another word, namely, how can we know about any action that it is optimizing? Anyone who thinks that this question is unimportant can hardly be interested in ethics. For let me remind you that an optimizing action is one that contributes most goodness. (Sidgwick wrote: "a truly moral man cannot say to himself, 'This is the best thing on the whole for me to do, but yet it is not my duty to do it though it is in my power.' ")[42]

The skeptic in effect would ask the rule-utilitarian, How would the ethically relevant fact (assuming, recklessly, that we can know it to be a fact) that a certain practice has generally good consequences or is even optimific, render the fact that a certain action (which may or may not have good consequences) conforms to the practice also ethically relevant? To say that if the practice is optimific then any action that conforms to the practice is optimific would be to commit the fallacy of division, and in any case would be obviously false. To say that because the practice is optimific the action is *likely* to be optimific would beg the question against the skeptic. Of course, neither answer is genuinely rule-utilitarian. What would be a rule-utilitarian answer is to say either that such conformity is what is meant by saying that the action is *right*, or at least that it is what should be meant.

Let us consider the first alternative. Appeals to meanings, or to "the logic of our moral concepts," or to "the moral point of view," would leave the skeptic quite unmoved. His question could be reformulated as follows: Even if we assume that there is a sufficiently clear such concept of right action, how would this be relevant to my conduct? Why should I do the right action, if it is so understood? This is not the egoist's question. Nor is it the question that lay behind the third variety of skepticism, which we considered in chapter 3, section 4. It is a question about the rationale for performing an action describable as right, independently of considerations about the goodness or badness of its consequences. That the action is describable as right does not constitute such a rationale. No doubt, if we rummage sufficiently through ordinary usage, we would discover that "right action" has a variety of more or less determinate uses, only one of which is its use in the sense of optimizing. For example, the phrase is standardly used for actions I have called duties, as well as for actions expected to have good, and no outweighing bad, more or less immediate consequences. But none of this casts doubt on the independence and overwhelming importance of our defined notion of right action. What I have said should suffice as an objection also to the second alternative, namely, that the rule-utilitarian definition of "right action" is offered as stipulative or revisionary, and not as expressive of what is actually meant by "right action." There is not even the appearance of a rationale for any such stipulation or revision, unless it is the ultimately question-begging assumption that the motivating force of the very word "right" should be used as a tool in the sort of moral education that would be optimific.

My argument against rule-utilitarianism applies to all the many versions of it, since it is directed at the very idea on which rule-utilitarianism rests as a distinctive ethical position. It applies also to the closely related theory of utilitarian generalization, which rests on the same idea but defines a right action as being such that everyone's doing that *sort* of action in relevantly similar circumstances would be optimific, or at least defines a wrong action as being such that everyone's doing that sort of action in relevantly similar circumstances would have unacceptably bad consequences. Even if the rules the rule-utilitarian has in mind, and the sorts of action and relevant similarity the defender of utilitarian generalization has in mind, are understood so narrowly, so specifically, that what they recommend is exactly what the act-utilitarian recommends, the idea on which their theories rest remains defective, for the reasons I have given.

Another redefinition of right action, characteristic of some theories of "virtue ethics," is that a right action is one that is virtuous, whether in the strict sense of "virtuous" defined in chapter 2 or in one of the broader senses also noted there. And it is appropriate here to remind the reader that empirical skepticism does not apply to judgments of virtue. Only philosophical skepticism might include the claim that we cannot know the motives behind an action or the character of an agent. Thus, the third part of ethics we distinguished in chapter 2, the theory of virtue and vice, of praise and blame, of morality, is not affected by the variety of skepticism now under consideration, just as the first part, the theory of good and evil, is not affected. This fact is not unimportant. Many of our ethical judgments concern virtue and vice, motivation, character. And whether or not agents are ever justified in believing of any action that it would be right or that it would be wrong, the fact is that all agents do hold such beliefs and therefore their moral character can be evaluated on the basis of the role the beliefs play in their decisions about how to act. Not uncommonly, therefore, we apply the terms "right" and "wrong" to actions on the basis of what we know about the motivation and moral character behind the actions; they are terms of praise and blame and it is natural to find ourselves sometimes praising or blaming actions while what we really intend to do is to praise or blame motives and character. But to point this out would be irrelevant as an answer to the skeptic regarding right and wrong. Of course, a virtuous person, one who acts because of what he or she believes is right, or because of some other good motive or disposition, deserves our praise. But we would hardly say that the person ought to perform the action if we knew that it would lead to great evil. Indeed, we sometimes say that a person ought to do what he or she believes is right, and that the person would be justified in doing what he or she believes is right, but we say this when we ourselves claim no knowledge whether what the person believes is right is really right, and our permissiveness finds sufficient justification in the fact that if one does what one believes is right because of that belief, at least one is virtuous.

A similar response may be made to the suggestion that the skeptic be answered by applying the word "right" not to actions that are optimizing but to actions that the agent believes to be optimizing (whether or not the agent performs them because of this belief, that is, whether or not they are virtuous). Such a terminological change would be just that: terminological. It would not meet the seventh skeptical challenge. To do so it would need to be supplemented with the nonterminological claim that the question whether a certain action would be optimizing is irrelevant to, or at least of secondary importance to, the agent's chief ethical concern in deciding whether or not to perform the action, or to our chief ethical concern in appraising his or her action. And clearly this claim would be false in the case of the agent, and in our case true only in an irrelevant sense. It would be false to suppose that the agent is concerned not with the question whether the action would be optimizing, but rather with the question whether he or she believes that it would be optimizing. And if *we* are concerned with the agent's belief that it would be optimizing, this would be either a purely psychological concern, that is, we may be interested in the quite nonethical question whether the agent does have that belief, or an ethically important but to the present issue irrelevant concern about whether he or she would be acting because of that belief, that is, whether the action would be virtuous. Insofar as both the agent and we are concerned with the question whether he or she is *to perform* the action, which is the crucial ethical question about conduct, it would be false to suppose that we are concerned with the question whether the agent *believes* that the action would be optimizing, rather than with the question whether the action would *be* optimizing.

Of course, we could revise our conceptual scheme (outlined in chapter 2) and define a right action as an action the agent believes is optimizing. (It would be circular to define it as an action the agent believes is right.) But as soon as we did this, it would be evident that what matters to us (I ignore here the importance of virtue) is whether the action is *optimizing*, not whether it is *right* in that defined sense of "right." The skeptic's target would now become the possibility of our knowledge that some actions are optimizing, not the possibility of our knowledge that they are right, and his argument would be ethically just as disturbing as it was in its original formulation. Indeed, it would be the same argument stated in different words. And he will again remind us that to say that an action would be optimizing is to say that it would contribute most *good*. Anyone who says, therefore, that he or she does not care whether a certain action would be optimizing could not care about the subject matter of ethics.

Brand Blanshard reports that in a conversation he had with G. E. Moore about utilitarianism (no date is given, but it must have taken place in the 1940s or 1950s), Moore said: "It seems to me self-evident that we should try in every case to make the world as much better as we can."[43] Indeed, Moore's assertion may strike us as unrealistic, since we seldom believe that there is anything we can do to make the world better. But this is not (or ought not to be) the case with statesmen, and it is significant that utilitarianism was proposed by Bentham as a guide to legislation. The really great statesman *is* motivated by the desire to make the world, or at least his own country, as much better as he can, and often believes that he knows how this may be done. If *we* lack this motive, the reason is not that we do not share the statesman's goal but that, not being in a position of power, we seldom believe that we can make the world or even just our country better.

In one of several recent challenging articles, Marcus G. Singer writes: "A moral theory is for the guidance of human beings, who are not omniscient beings. A moral theory that implies that whether an action is right or wrong is something that 'only God knows' is in so far forth incoherent."[44] He claims that even when "it *would have been better, all things considered,* if the act had not been performed," the act might not have been wrong, meaning by this presumably (he is not explicit) that the agent might have believed either that it would be better, all things considered, to perform it, or at least that this is probable. But, again, the issue seems to me only terminological. If we agree with Singer, we would merely need a new term for what he calls the act that it would have been better, all things considered, to perform. The sense this new term would express is essential for any moral theory that recommends that an agent perform the right act, in what I have taken to be Singer's sense of "right," and is logically prior to the latter. The notion of an act the agent *believes* it would be better, all things considered, that it be performed, and the notion of an act the agent believes is probably such that it would be better, all things considered, that it be performed, presuppose but are not presupposed by the notion of an act such that it would be better, all things considered, that it be performed. Of course, Singer would not question this. He only questions the coherence of a moral theory that cannot offer guidance to human beings, who are not omniscient. But the skeptic is not proposing a moral theory. In a way, he is making precisely the point Singer is making, but he is free from the illusion that if a moral theory prescribes that an agent do what he or she believes would be best, or even what he or she believes would probably be best, then it provides the agent with guidance worth having. In any case, Singer's view faces serious conceptual difficulties. As Moore remarked, if an action does not turn out to have good consequences, even though at the time it was performed it was probable that it would, "we should naturally say . . . not that the action was right, but rather that [*the agent*] *is not to blame.*"[45] Is the sense of "right" when used with respect to past actions different from that in which it is used with respect to present and future actions? Does the word "right" express correspondingly different concepts?

A. C. Ewing distinguishes between the sense in which " 'The action we ought to do' may mean that action which is really preferable, taking everything into account" and "the most common sense," in which it may mean "the action which it is, humanly speaking, preferable to choose, though it may not in fact necessarily turn out best." He argues that we could not know of any action that it ought to be done in the former sense, and therefore that we should not choose that sense. Yet he admits that this sense is "still highly relevant for ethics. For it is only because, if I find out what is right in [the latter] sense and act accordingly, I am more likely to approximate to what is right in my [former] sense, that I ought to do what is right in my [latter] sense at all. We only consider what we ought to do in the [latter] sense as a means to this approximation."[46] I shall not repeat what I have said several times about appeals to "likelihood" or "probability," but Ewing shows clear awareness of which concept of "ought" is primary.

Let me apply what I said in the preceding paragraphs to the classic discussion of the issue. In "Duty and Ignorance of Fact" Prichard distinguishes between the terms "right" and "ought"[47] and adopts the view that what is expressed by the latter is a certain characteristic of the agent, not of the action the agent "sets himself to do." The form of a statement of obligation would be "*I* ought to set myself to do so-and-so, because I think that it—my setting myself to do so-and-so—would have a certain effect [that is, the action I set myself to do]."[48] He does not say so explicitly in this work, but presumably he still regards the rightness of an action as an intrinsic characteristic of the action. (What I shall say does not depend on whether I am right in this presumption. Perhaps Prichard meant that the notion of rightness was dispensable, and that the property of the agent that "ought" expresses supervenes on the nonethical contents of his thoughts, for example, on the contents of the thought that setting himself to shout at a man who seems to have fainted would result in reviving him.) Now, I cannot know, according to Prichard, what, if anything, will result from my setting myself to do the action, for example, whether it will be the reviving, by shouting at him, of a man who has fainted. But I *can* know what I ought to do in the circumstances, namely, that I ought to set myself to shout at the man who has fainted, because I can know that I *think* that to set myself to do so would result in my reviving, by shouting, a man who has fainted and (perhaps) also because I can know that reviving a man who has fainted is a right kind of action (in Prichard's sense of "right"). The latter knowledge, that such an action is right, is not a target of the seventh skeptic, since its object is an abstract ethical truth. Neither would the former knowledge be his target, since it is about what I *think*, and I can know what I think just as easily as I can know that I am in pain.[49]

Has Prichard answered the skeptic by granting, in effect, that one cannot know that what one will in fact do will be the *right* action (or even that one will do anything, for one might have become paralyzed!) but insisting that one can know what action one *ought* to set oneself to do? The issue does not rest, I believe, on the acceptability of Prichard's suggestion that, strictly speaking, it is not one's doing an overt action but rather one's setting oneself to do it that is one's obligation. What the skeptic would attack is rather Prichard's view that (to put it more precisely but at the risk of misrepresentation of it) one ought to set oneself to do x if and only if (1) one *thinks* that setting oneself to do x would result in one's doing x, and (presumably) (2) one *knows* that doing x is a right kind of action. Such a sense of "ought" can be introduced and, as I have remarked earlier, there is reason to think that something like it can be found in ordinary usage. When in doubt about what someone ought to set himself to do, we could say that he ought to set himself to do what he thinks is right. But probably we would mean by this nothing more than that we have no reason for supposing that he ought *not* to, and that if he faces a choice, he might as well set himself to do what he thinks is right, for then at least he would be virtuous. And the agent himself may say that he ought to set himself to do what he thinks is right, but again what presumably he would express by saying this (assuming that he is aware that he only *thinks* it is right) is his recognition of the value of virtue. If Prichard held that "ought" has only this sense, then of course he was wrong. In facing a moral decision I want to know what *will* result from my setting myself to do so-and-so, not what I *think* will result. I care not about what I think but about whether what I think is true. A natural way of expressing this is to say that what I care about is what I ought to do. Therefore, there is such a sense of "ought." But probably Prichard was not denying that there is such a sense but claiming that in that sense of "ought," we can never know what we ought to do; and he explicitly held that sometimes he knew what he ought to do. If so, he in effect agreed with the skeptic. If we can know what we ought to do only in Prichard's sense of "ought," then we have granted the skeptic all he could have wished to have.

In a thoughtful recent discussion of Prichard,[50] Ramon M. Lemos distinguishes between the concept of subjective duty, roughly, to do what one thinks is right, and the concept of absolute duty, to do what *is* right. He points out that the former presupposes, is parasitic on, the latter. Moreover, it is the concept of absolute duty that the *agent* is employing, the concept of subjective duty being essentially that of the *spectator* of the action.

Prichard insisted that one's obligation was to set oneself to do so-and-so, rather than to do so-and-so, because he was in effect a philosophical skeptic. (His ethical works should always be read in conjunction with his epistemological works. In the latter he held, following John Cook Wilson, that knowledge is not a kind of belief but rather apprehension, and that one can, by mere reflection, know with respect to any particular case whether one knows or merely believes.)[51] One could not know that one would do so-and-so if one set oneself to do it; one might have become paralyzed. But the empirical skeptic, whom we are now considering, would have no such epistemological scruples. Could he not be answered then by appealing to Prichard's (at least earlier) view that the rightness of an action is an intrinsic characteristic of the action, one that is quite independent of motivation or consequences? In chapter 2 I argued that this notion of rightness is best understood as a notion of a kind of intrinsic goodness, and called actions that have such goodness duties. But for our present purposes it does not matter whether my argument is accepted or whether rightness is regarded as a second primitive ethical concept, as it was so regarded by Prichard. Now, what I have called empirical skepticism does not deny the possibility of our knowing what intrinsic ethical characteristics our actions have. Can it not be answered then simply by saying that the rightness of an action is such a primitive, indefinable intrinsic characteristic?

No, it cannot. Once again, the skeptic would point out that the issue is not how we should use the word "right" but whether we can know of any action that it is optimizing. That an action is intrinsically good, in our sense of being a duty, or right, in Prichard's sense of having a certain primitive ethical characteristic other than intrinsic goodness, may contribute to its being optimizing, the skeptic would say, though in the revised sense of contributing greatest total value, not just goodness. But it need not suffice to make it optimizing, even in that revised sense. The consequences must also be taken into account, and their total goodness or badness may far outweigh the intrinsic goodness or value-as-rightness of the action. And it is the total goodness or badness of the consequences that we cannot know, as a matter of empirical fact. The moral agent does care about the intrinsic goodness, or the "rightness," of the action he or she contemplates. But, at least on reflection, he or she cares far more about the total value the action would contribute, through both its intrinsic characteristics and its consequences. If Prichard would have disagreed with this (I do not believe that he would have, since, like Ross, he regarded beneficence as a duty, though not the only duty), then he would have had to hold that a right action, in his sense of "right," is to be done even if as a result the heavens should fall. But what if he, or someone else, perhaps Kant, did hold this?

In chapter 2 I tried to do justice to the traditional deontological view by allowing that certain kinds of actions, those I called duties, have intrinsic goodness. The reader, even if not suspicious then, may now suspect that the strength skepticism regarding our knowledge of right and wrong seems to have exhibited in our present discussion is due to our failure to take the deontological view seriously. The deontologist, it may be said, does not claim that certain kinds of actions are good in themselves. If he did, he would indeed have to allow that their goodness is commensurable with that of their effects and therefore that the ethically crucial question is not whether the action is good in itself, but whether it is optimizing, thus allowing for the skeptical challenge of the present chapter. But, the reader may argue, the traditional deontologist would regard certain kinds of actions as absolutely obligatory, as actions that ought to be done regardless of their consequences. This sense of "ought" is quite different from that defined in chapter 2, and the skeptic's challenge does not affect such a deontological position. Indeed, this is so. And I shall not argue here that there is no such sense of "ought," one not reducible either to the sense of an action's having intrinsic goodness or to the sense of its being optimizing. My argument is simply that even if an action ought to be done in this sense of "ought," the ethically decisive question is whether it ought to be done in the sense of "ought" identical with that of "optimizing." I have already given my reasons for holding this view. An ethical theory that advocates that justice be done even if the heavens should fall is so profoundly confused morally, or even conceptually, or perhaps is just crazy, as to not merit being called ethical. However important the intrinsic "value," be it goodness or rightness, of an action may be, the consequences of the action do matter, and it would be moral, indeed conceptual, confusion to claim, perhaps on grounds of incommensurability, that it is never possible that their "disvalue" should outweigh the intrinsic value of the action. This is the truth in consequentialism that any genuine ethical theory must acknowledge. Philosophers who do not are likely to be motivated, as perhaps Kant was, by metaphysical or religious considerations that discount the importance of the consequences of our actions *in this life*.

I should make a similar reply to suggestions that the rightness of an action depends only on those of its consequences for which the agent would ordinarily be held responsible,[52] or which are intended or foreseen or foreseeable with ordinary care, or which do not involve the voluntary intervention of another person.[53] As Lars Bergström remarks concerning such suggestions, they have relevance to the question whether the agent is praiseworthy or blameworthy, but not to the question of the total normative status of the action.[54] We must not confuse the theory of right and wrong with the theory of praise and blame. This confusion lies behind the common distinction between subjective and objective rightness. There is no such *kind* of rightness as subjective rightness. When we speak of subjective rightness we simply mean virtue, in the sense of good will. If so, then we should not express ourselves misleadingly by talking about it as if it were a kind of rightness. It is a notion parasitic on that of rightness, as Ramon M. Lemos has observed.


## 6. Conclusion

It seems that the empirical skeptic has won. Neither redefinitions of the phrase "right action," most of which consist in confusions of concepts that we set out to distinguish in chapter 2, nor restrictions on the considerations relevant to its application, have affected his thesis. But there are limitations to his victory. His victory concerns mainly our knowledge of how to act so as to produce goods such as pleasure and desire-satisfaction. But there are many goods, arguably far more important, which are usually not realized, and perhaps are not realizable at all, by action. Nicolai Hartmann observed that this is often the case with what he called the moral virtues: "Such is the nature of man's moral worth that without aiming at it and by entire preoccupation with what is outside himself, he none the less actualizes it."[55] And, indeed, while we may want to achieve virtue, or for that matter, love or friendship, in ourselves or in others, we seldom regard this as achievable by any particular actions. It is more an object of *hope*. But Hartmann observed that our impotence is even more dramatic with respect to some other goods: "There are goods which one may indeed lose when one has them, but cannot gain when one has never had them, or has lost them. Of this kind are youth, ingenuousness, harmlessness; and closely related to these are certain forms of happiness, such as a cheerful disposition, healthy light-heartedness, also—up to a point—beauty, charm, natural grace and many related things."[56] We may add that, *pace* Aristotle, fortitude, whether in ourselves or in others, is hardly produced by *actions*. This is not entirely true of knowledge. There is after all the institution of education and the practice of self-education. But it is notorious that at its highest levels, knowledge, in the sense of understanding, insight, grasp, is seldom if ever imparted and is achieved not so much as the effect of actions such as teaching, training, reading, and investigating (necessary though these may be) but almost as a miracle of nature. This is especially evident in the case of a cognitive achievement that consists chiefly in its extraordinary originality. Kant is a great philosopher, not because of the logic of his arguments or his erudition, but because of his originality. And while he could have done something to improve the logic of his arguments and increase his erudition, he could not have done anything to produce or increase his originality.

Now we may not know whether in any particular case a good generally not achievable by action is unqualifiedly good, whether its consequences and relations to organic unities in which it enters constitute a contribution of more goodness than its absence, or the presence of something else in its place, would have contributed. But neither is such ignorance an ignorance of right and wrong, for it does not concern actions at all.

Indeed, this line of reasoning has some application even to goods such as pleasure and desire-satisfaction. This is more easily seen if we describe these goods generally as happiness. Contrary to the usual utilitarian assumption, happiness often is not, and often just cannot be, the result of action. Is the average Swede happier than the average Mexican? He should be, if governmental policies motivated by utilitarian considerations were effective. But *is* he happier? Our personal experiences also seem sometimes to conflict with the utilitarian assumption. "There is nothing I can do that will make him happy," "She is never satisfied," "They just don't enjoy what they have," are familiar and very common remarks in everyday life. And even with respect to the goods of existence and health, it is notorious that often there is nothing we can do to produce them or to preserve them.[57]

The skeptic may respond, of course, by saying that most of these facts may also be interpreted in a way supporting his thesis. They may be taken to show that we do not *know* how (to act in order) to produce certain goods. But I think the more plausible conclusion is that most of them show that we *cannot produce* certain goods because these are not possible effects of human actions. If so, then the facts in question indeed severely restrict the significance of empirical skepticism. But they do so in proportion to the support they lend to a position we have not considered at all: ethical pessimism. While the skeptic draws our attention to the empirical fact of human ignorance, the pessimist draws our attention to the no less evident empirical fact of human impotence.

Even though, in the light of all this, the skeptic's victory is less significant than he supposes, victory nevertheless it seems to be, whether on purely philosophical or on empirical grounds, since he questions the knowability of what *can* be consequences of actions. Of course, it is a victory only of the skeptic regarding our knowledge of right and wrong. In chapter 1 I distinguished two forms of skepticism: that which rejects realism in ethics and that which rejects cognitivism proper. My defense of realism in the previous chapters is not challenged by the skeptic we have considered in this chapter. There is such a property as goodness, there are ethical facts such as the goodness of certain abstract entities, including that of the kinds of actions I called duties, and if the skeptic grants this, he is not likely to deny that there are also ethical facts such as the virtue and the rightness of certain actions. It is no part of his thesis to deny that sometimes one is motivated by one's belief that a certain action would be right, or that as a matter of fact certain actions *are* right, that is, are optimizing. So our skeptic's victory is in no sense a victory of irrealism.

And it is only partially a victory of noncognitivism. His arguments in this chapter have not even touched our conclusion in the previous chapter that we do have knowledge of goodness itself and of abstract goods, and thus also of at least some of our duties. Nor have they touched the important corollary of that conclusion, that we do have knowledge of the concrete instantiations of goodness (and evil) in the many-faceted actual situations with which ordinary ethical thought is mostly concerned, the goodness (or evil) of the intrinsic properties, the relevant noncausal relations, and (though here the *philosophical* skeptic would demur) the more or less immediate consequences of the actions we contemplate; it is concerns with these that constitute the fabric of everyday moral life, and the realism and cognitivism underlying it remain safe from the skeptic's challenge. The latter has been directed only at our ability to know what actions are right and what actions are wrong. But they seem to have been successful. As I have argued repeatedly in this chapter, it is only an illusion to suppose that the skeptic's challenge can be met by redefining the phrase "right action," whether by making it apply to virtuous actions, or to actions the agent believes are optimizing, or to actions that are "probably" optimizing. The third possibility merely begs the question against both the philosophical and the empirical skeptic. The first and the second are merely cases of failing to face the real issue. And such are a variety of other views, that of rule-utilitarianism and those which define a right action in terms of the intrinsic goodness either of the action itself, or of the motives or character from which it issues, or of some of its known noncausal relations and perhaps more or less immediate consequences. Indeed, there is far more to the subject matter of ethics than the question which actions are optimizing. But that this question belongs to the very heart of ethics could not be denied, even if we were to use the honorific label "right actions" for something other than optimizing actions.

The skeptic concerning right and wrong seems to have won on the substantive issue before us in this chapter. Returning to the passage from Hume quoted in chapter 3, and using with clear conscience the terminology proposed in chapter 2, we must say, it seems, that we *can* find in a case of murder that matter of fact or real existence which we call "evil," the evil of untimely death, or of the very action of murder, as well as that matter of fact or real existence which we call vice, the murderer's willingness to take his victim's life, but, it would seem, we cannot find in a case of murder that matter of fact or real existence we call its being wrong, its being such that it ought not to have been committed. We can and often do know good from evil, duty from offense, and virtue from vice, but, it would seem, we cannot know right from wrong.

Yet, perhaps it only *seems* so. Epistemology has not elucidated a notion of nondemonstrative evidence that would render intelligible and acceptable the epistemic judgments the philosophical skeptic questions. But perhaps someone, some day, will elucidate such a notion. It is idle to look today to psychology, sociology, political science, and economics for an answer to the empirical skeptic. They are still in their infancy. But sometimes, though not always, infants do develop into adults, and in unexpected ways. It is also perhaps possible that a theological ethics, based solely on reason, such as the one I sketched earlier, will some day be provided.

# NOTES

## 1. Introduction

1. "The Emotive Meaning of Ethical Terms," *Mind* 46 (1937): 30. I have left out Stevenson's characterization of the truth in question as a priori, since obviously what is demanded is truth, and not mere influence, whether the truth be a priori or a posteriori.

2. *Reason, Truth and History* (Cambridge: Cambridge University Press, 1981). Robert Nozick also bases his "externalist" account of knowledge on the assumption that "we know mediately, not directly." (*Philosophical Explanations* [Cambridge: Harvard University Press, 1981], p. 203.)

3. *Realism and Reason: Philosophical Papers*, Vol. 3 (Cambridge: Cambridge University Press, 1983), especially chap. 16.

4. *Realism and Truth* (Oxford: Basil Blackwell, 1984).

5. See Michael Dummett, "Realism," in *Truth and Other Enigmas* (Cambridge: Harvard University Press, 1978).

6. *The Nature of Morality* (New York: Oxford University Press, 1977), p. 132.

7. The best attempt so far to accomplish this is Laurence BonJour's in *The Structure of Empirical Knowledge* (Cambridge, Mass., and London: Harvard University Press, 1985). But, as he seems to admit, his theory is not purely coherentist (see pp. 148–49 *et passim*); it also employs the difficult and unexplicated notion of a priori probability to connect justification with truth, a notion not obviously different from a species of the notion of justification. (See chapter 8.) For a detailed recent criticism of coherentism, see P. K. Moser, *Empirical Justification* (Dordrecht: Reidel, 1985).

8. See Keith Lehrer, *Knowledge* (Oxford: Clarendon Press, 1974), p. 188.

9. For a recent criticism of this view, and a useful review of the literature, see Arthur Fine, "Unnatural Attitudes: Realist and Instrumentalist Attachments to Science," *Mind* 95 (1986): 149–79. For a general argument against the view that reasoning to the best explanation is an alternative to inductive and deductive reasoning, see R. A. Fumerton, "Induction and Reasoning to the Best Explanation," *Philosophy of Science* 47 (1980): 589–600.

10. *A Theory of Justice* (Cambridge: Harvard University Press, 1971), p. 579. Indeed, nine years later, in "Kantian Constructivism in Moral Theory: The Dewey Lectures 1980" (*The Journal of Philosophy* 78 [1980]), Rawls wrote: "Apart from the procedure of constructing the principles of justice, there are no moral facts" (p. 519), and "rather than think of the principles of justice as true, it is better to say that they are the principles most reasonable for us, given our conception of persons as free and equal, and fully cooperating members of a democratic society" (p. 554).

11. Some of these differences are noted by Norman Daniels, who is sympathetic to Rawls's approach, in "Wide Reflective Equilibrium and Theory Acceptance in Ethics," *The Journal of Philosophy* 76 (1979): 256–82.

12. *A Theory of the Good and the Right* (Oxford: Clarendon Press, 1979), pp. 10–13, 112, 126–29 *et passim*.

13. Ibid., pp. 143–46, 217–23, 244, 331–35.

14. "Moral Explanations," in David Copp and David Zimmerman, eds., *Morality, Reason and Truth* (Totowa, N.J.: Rowman and Allanheld, 1984).

15. New York, Oxford: Oxford University Press, 1986.

16. *The Theory of Morality* (Chicago: University of Chicago Press, 1977), p. 53.

17. Alan Gewirth, *Reason and Morality* (Chicago: University of Chicago Press, 1978). Specifically, I question the derivation of "I have rights to freedom and well-being" from "My freedom and well-being are necessary goods," in the sense that "by virtue of regarding his purposes as good the agent must also a fortiori value his freedom and well-being as required for achieving any of his purposes" (p. 80). Gewirth sums up his method by saying, "from

the 'is' of the generic features of action there is logically derivable the 'ought' of moral principles" (p. 25). I regret that a detailed discussion of Gewirth's moral theory, which it very much deserves, lies outside the scope of this book. The reader is invited to consult the critical papers and Gewirth's replies to them in Edward Regis, Jr., ed., *Gewirth's Ethical Rationalism* (Chicago and London: The University of Chicago Press, 1984).

18. See, for example, David Wiggins, "Truth, Invention and the Meaning of Life," *Proceedings of the British Academy* 62 (1976); John McDowell, "Virtue and Reason," *The Monist* 62 (1979): 331–50; and especially "Non-Cognitivism and Rule-Following," in Steven H. Holtzman and Christopher M. Leich, eds., *Wittgenstein: To Follow a Rule* (London: Routledge and Kegan Paul, 1981), pp. 141–62; Sabina Lovibond, *Realism and Imagination in Ethics* (Minneapolis: University of Minnesota Press, 1983); S. L. Hurley, "Objectivity and Disagreement," in Ted Honderich, ed., *Morality and Objectivity* (London: Routledge and Kegan Paul, 1985).

19. Cambridge: Cambridge University Press, 1949.

20. Ithaca: Cornell University Press, 1958.

21. London: George Allen and Unwin, 1970.

22. Atlantic Highlands, N.J.: Humanities Press, 1979.

23. *The Moral Point of View*, p. 301.

24. *Ethical Knowledge*, p. 34.

25. See Sabina Lovibond, *Realism and Imagination in Ethics*, p. 113 *et passim*.

26. *The Methods of Ethics* (Chicago: The University of Chicago Press, 1962), Book III. The first edition was published in 1874.

27. See Robert Shope's (unintentionally amusing) survey of the trials and tribulations of the enterprise of defining knowledge, in *The Analysis of Knowing: A Decade of Research* (Princeton, N.J.: Princeton University Press, 1983).

28. Yet see Mary Midgley, *Animals and Why They Matter* (Athens: The University of Georgia Press, 1984, pp. 55–60) for a marvelous summary (by one with much sympathy with Wittgenstein's later philosophy) of the ways the Wittgensteinian attitude is *obviously* absurd.


## 2. A Conceptual Scheme for Ethics

1. There is, of course, nothing novel about the attitude toward ordinary language adopted here. One will find it defended also, for example, by John Rawls in *A Theory of Justice* (Cambridge: Harvard University Press, 1971), p. 111, and by Richard B. Brandt in *A Theory of the Good and the Right* (Oxford: Clarendon Press, 1979), chap. I. I defend it in detail, in respect to its application to epistemology, in *The Concept of Knowledge* (Evanston: Northwestern University Press, 1970), Part One, chap. 1.

2. See J. L. Austin, "A Plea for Excuses," in *Philosophical Papers* (Oxford: Clarendon Press, 1961), p. 130. Perhaps the best example so far of linguistic phenomenology in ethics is Alan R. White's *Rights* (Oxford: Clarendon Press, 1984). Nicholas F. Gier has argued in detail that Wittgenstein's "philosophy of ordinary language" is in fact a phenomenology, and cites evidence that Wittgenstein himself thought so. See *Wittgenstein and Phenomenology* (Albany: State University of New York Press, 1981).

3. Detailed discussions of the ordinary uses of (at least some) ethical terms may be found, for example, in Charles L. Stevenson, *Ethics and Language* (New Haven and London: Yale University Press, 1944); R. M. Hare, *The Language of Morals* (Oxford: Clarendon Press, 1952); F. E. Sparshott, *An Enquiry into Goodness* (Toronto: The University of Toronto Press, 1958); G. H. von Wright, *The Varieties of Goodness* (New York: The Humanities Press, 1963); Paul Ziff, *Semantic Analysis* (Ithaca: Cornell University Press, 1960), chap. VI; Zeno Vendler, "The Grammar of Goodness," *The Philosophical Review* 72 (1963): 446–65; Neil Cooper, *The Diversity of Moral Thinking* (Oxford: Clarendon Press, 1981), and the already cited Alan R. White, *Rights*. All of these works, however, have also theoretical

purposes. The limits of what can be expected from accounts of the ordinary uses of ethical terms are well illustrated by Cooper's book. He dismisses, without argument, the view that there are "objective moral properties which moral predicates designate" (p. 148). But he seems to recognize that there is plausibility to the view, defended by J. L. Mackie (*Ethics: Inventing Right and Wrong* [Harmondsworth: Penguin, 1977]), that moral judgments commit their users to accepting the existence of such properties. Yet he rejects this latter view on the grounds that it leads to the conclusion (drawn by Mackie) that all moral judgments are erroneous, which itself leads to the implausible further conclusion that antiobjectivists have always misused moral language. Cooper might have considered the analogy here with the dispute whether material objects really have the secondary qualities that of course we attribute to them. Would he have thought that this dispute could be settled by an examination of ordinary usage?

4. The example is taken from David B. Wong, *Moral Relativity* (Berkeley, Los Angeles, London: University of California Press, 1984), p. 66.

5. See *The Sovereignty of Good* (New York: Schocken Books, 1971).

6. *Summa Theologica*, Part One, Question 5, Article 3.

7. In *Tractatus Logico-Philosophicus* Wittgenstein wrote: "To perceive a complex means to perceive that its constituents are combined in such and such a way" (5.5423). This highly implausible view is required by Wittgenstein's ontology, which allows for only two categories of things: states of affairs and simple objects. That such an ontology is false is evident from the fact that complex things can have properties that cannot be intelligibly attributed to states of affairs. For example, a chessboard is complex but has a square shape. See Reinhardt Grossmann, *The Categorial Structure of the World* (Bloomington: Indiana University Press, 1983), pp. 238–59. That it has seemed plausible to many is perhaps explained by the fact that in the logic of *Principia Mathematica* complexity can be ultimately represented only propositionally.

8. For the most familiar defense of the view that events, including actions, are particulars (however complex in structure), see Donald Davidson, *Essays on Actions and Events* (Oxford: Clarendon Press, 1980), especially Essay 6. But Davidson's reasons for this view are different from, though not incompatible with, mine. For a sympathetic and useful discussion of Davidson's view, see Mark Platts, *Ways of Meaning* (London: Routledge and Kegan Paul, 1979), pp. 190–214.

9. Even Moore was not very clear about this crucial distinction. But see *Principia Ethica* (Cambridge: Cambridge University Press, 1971), pp. 77, 110, 118–19, 142, 144, where he allows that in addition to (concrete) things qualities may also be good.

10. *The Right and the Good* (Oxford: Clarendon Press, 1930), pp. 111–14, 137.

11. See Panayot Butchvarov, *Being Qua Being: A Theory of Identity, Existence, and Predication* (Bloomington and London: Indiana University Press, 1979), Appendix A; and "States of Affairs," in Radu J. Bogdan, ed., *Roderick M. Chisholm* (Dordrecht: Reidel, 1986).

12. For a detailed argument for the existence of universals, both specific and generic, see my *Resemblance and Identity: An Examination of the Problem of Universals* (Bloomington and London: Indiana University Press, 1966), and *Being Qua Being*, especially pp. 195–206. See also Nicholas Wolterstorff, *On Universals* (Chicago: University of Chicago Press, 1970); D. M. Armstrong, *Universals and Scientific Realism* (New York: Cambridge University Press, 1978); Reinhardt Grossmann, *The Categorial Structure of the World*; and, of course, virtually all of Gustav Bergmann's works, e.g., *Realism: A Critique of Meinong and Brentano* (Madison: The University of Wisconsin Press, 1966).

13. Compare Roderick M. Chisholm's lists of "intrinsically good things" and "intrinsically bad things," in his "Self-Profile," in *Roderick M. Chisholm*.

14. Moore wrote: "there is an ambiguity in the very question: What is good? . . . [It] may mean either: Which among existing things are good? or else: What *sort of* things are good, what are the things which, whether they *are* real or not, ought to be real? And of these two questions it is plain that to answer the first, we must know both the answer to the second and also the answer to the question: What is real?" (*Principia Ethica*, pp. 118–19).

15. The value of a whole need not be proportionate to the sum of the values of its parts; the presence of a part of indifferent value may contribute greatly to the value of the whole. (See *Principia Ethica*, pp. 27–30.) An example: the value of a philosophy department lacking anyone competent to teach logic would be increased greatly by the addition of a member with such competence, even if the person is a quite mediocre logician.

16. "Good and Evil," *Analysis* 17 (1956): 33–42. Also R. F. Tredwell, "On Moore's Analysis of Goodness," in E. D. Klemke, ed., *Studies in the Philosophy of G. E. Moore* (Chicago: Quadrangle Books, 1969); W. D. Ross, *The Right and the Good*, pp. 65–67; Paul Ziff, *Semantic Analysis*; Zeno Vendler, "The Grammar of Goodness." A much more moderate version of the view can be found in F. E. Sparshott, *An Enquiry into Goodness*; see especially pp. 153–54.

17. See C. D. Broad, "Certain Features in Moore's Ethical Doctrines," in P. A. Schilpp, ed., *The Philosophy of G. E. Moore* (LaSalle, Ill.: Open Court Publishing Company, 1968), Vol. 1, pp. 48–49. The sense in which a concrete good can be said to be good without qualification, that is, to be optimizing, is *analogous* to the sense in which W. D. Ross uses the phrase "actual duty." The description of a concrete good as a good F or good qua an F, or good insofar as it F's, is analogous to what Ross means by *prima facie* duty. See *The Right and the Good*, pp. 19–20, 28, 30–31, 41–43.

18. In his "Reply to My Critics," G. E. Moore suggests that the sense of "good" with which he was concerned could be explained, though not defined, in terms of "better" or "best" and gave as one example the Leibnizean statement "This is the *best* of all possible worlds." *The Philosophy of G. E. Moore*, pp. 555–56.

19. *Semantic Analysis*, p. 216.

20. Contrary to the common assumption, in *Principia Ethica* Moore seems to allow that an action may be evaluated not only in terms of its consequences but also in terms of its intrinsic nature. See pp. 24–25, 147, 149, 168. In *Ethics* (Oxford: Oxford University Press, 1977), however, he seems to hold that an action is right if and only if it is optimific. See p. 83. Compare his views on this subject in *The Philosophy of G. E. Moore*, Vol. 2, pp. 560–62. The notion of a right action as one that is optimizing, rather than optimific, was also espoused by Hastings Rashdall in *The Theory of Good and Evil* (Oxford: University Press, 1924). See, for example, Vol. I, pp. 92, 96–97, 194–95, 203. The importance for our understanding of utilitarianism of allowing that some actions may have intrinsic value was emphasized by A. C. Ewing in "Recent Developments in British Ethical Thought," in C. A. Mace, ed., *British Philosophy in the Mid-Century* (London: George Allen and Unwin, Ltd., 1957), p. 74. It was allowed also by H. W. B. Joseph, who wrote: "The rightness of a right action (which is not instrumental) is a sort of goodness" (*Some Problems of Ethics*, Oxford: Clarendon Press, 1931, p. 83), and by Brand Blanshard, who wrote: "besides the goodness of later consequences, we [should] take into account the goodness of the act itself, or, I would rather say, of the pattern of life generally, with its mass of personal relations, which this act implies" (*Reason and Goodness* [London: George Allen and Unwin, 1961], p. 158). See also Oliver A. Johnson, *Rightness and Goodness* (The Hague: Martinus Nijhoff, 1959), chap. 6.

21. Consider the following. The devil guarantees that he will produce $n$ units of goodness for any number $n$ I write on this sheet of paper. There is no number I can write such that there is not a greater number. Therefore, there is no act of writing a number on this sheet of paper that would be optimizing. See Arthur W. Burks, *Chance, Cause, Reason* (Chicago and London: The University of Chicago Press, 1977), p. 192.

22. See *Ethics*, chap. 6.

23. Compare Lars Bergström, *The Alternatives and Consequences of Actions* (Stockholm: Almqvist and Wiksell, 1966). See also his "Utilitarianism and Alternative Actions," *Nous* 5 (1971): 237–52.

24. *Principia Ethica*, pp. 148–49. Later, in order to accord better with ordinary usage, he suggested that duty is an optimizing action "which it is more useful to praise and to enforce by sanctions since [it is an action] which there is a temptation to omit" (p. 170).

25. How disorderly and murky it is can be seen from the useful examples discussed by Holly Smith in "Culpable Ignorance," *The Philosophical Review* 92 (1983): 543–71.

26. Moore denies this on the grounds that according to "popular usage" a person "may fail to do his duty, through neglecting to think of what he *might* have done." (*Principia Ethica*, p. 150.) But this is a good example of the need to regiment popular usage.

27. "Morality, Action and Outcome," in Ted Honderich, ed., *Morality and Objectivity* (London: Routledge and Kegan Paul, 1985), p. 29. See also her "Utilitarianism and the Virtues," *Proceedings and Addresses of the American Philosophical Association* 57 (1983), and the discussion of it by Samuel Scheffler in "Agent-Centred Restrictions, Rationality, and the Virtues," in *Mind* 94 (1985).

28. "Saints and Heroes," in A. I. Melden, ed., *Essays in Moral Philosophy* (Seattle and London: University of Washington Press, 1958).

29. *The Moral Point of View* (Ithaca: Cornell University Press, 1958), pp. 203–204.

30. "Saints and Heroes," p. 204.

31. See Bernard Williams, "A Critique of Utilitarianism," in J. J. C. Smart and Bernard Williams, *Utilitarianism: For and Against* (Cambridge: Cambridge University Press, 1973), pp. 116–17. See also *Moral Luck* (Cambridge: Cambridge University Press, 1981), especially chaps. 1, 2, 3, and 5.

32. See Samuel Scheffler, *The Rejection of Consequentialism* (New York: Oxford University Press, 1982).

33. John Stuart Mill, *Utilitarianism* (Indianapolis: The Bobbs-Merrill Company, 1957), p. 23.

34. These, and some related points, are discussed at great length by Derek Parfit in *Reasons and Persons* (Oxford: Oxford University Press, 1984), Part One. He writes: "It is one question whether some theory is the one that we *ought morally* to try to believe. It is another question whether this is the theory that we *ought intellectually* or *in truth-seeking terms* to believe—whether this theory is the true, or best, or best justified theory" (p. 43). See also Sidgwick, *The Methods of Ethics* (Chicago: University of Chicago Press, 1962), pp. 490ff. A valuable discussion, with much of which I agree, of the issues I have been concerned with in the last few pages may be found in David O. Brink, "Utilitarian Morality and the Personal Point of View," *The Journal of Philosophy* 83 (1986): 417–38.

35. *The Right and the Good*, p. 163.

36. "Does Moral Philosophy Rest on a Mistake?" in *Moral Obligation and Duty and Interest* (London, Oxford, New York: Oxford University Press, 1968), pp. 4–5.

37. *The Methods of Ethics*, pp. 106, 504–505. See also G. E. M. Anscombe, "Modern Moral Philosophy," *Philosophy* 33 (1958): 1–19.

38. *The Theory of Good and Evil*, Vol. I, pp. 129–30.

39. *Moral Obligation and Duty and Interest*, p. 6. The view is defended also by W. D. Ross, in *The Right and the Good*, pp. 132–33. Ross asserts, "if we contemplate a right act alone, it is seen to have no intrinsic *value*. Suppose for instance that it is right for a man to pay a certain debt, and he pays it. This is in itself no addition to the sum of values in the universe." Surely Ross must have been thinking of the physical act of handing a man some money. Paying a debt is much more than that.

40. *The Foundations of Ethics* (Oxford: Clarendon Press, 1939), p. 326.

41. Ibid., p. 307.

42. See Stephen D. Hudson, "Taking Virtues Seriously," *Australasian Journal of Philosophy* 59 (1981): 192. Hudson argues that such an action has value because it manifests a certain virtue.

43. *The Right and the Good*, pp. 47, 58, 63. As these passages show, Ross uses the term "right" (or, more precisely, "*prima facie* right" or "*prima facie* duty") in effect for what I have called an intrinsic goodness of such an action, if we assume that an action can belong to several kinds, some better than others and some even bad; and what I mean by the term "right" he in effect means by "actual duty" (or "absolute duty"). If the reader finds this implausible, he or she should note that for Ross an optimific action itself is a *prima facie*

duty, and recall that I defined a right action as one that is optimizing, not as one that is optimific. It may well be right even if it does not produce the best consequences, but only if its other qualities are sufficiently good in themselves to compensate for the insufficient goodness of the consequences. Ross was unwilling to adopt a terminology such as ours for the same reason Prichard was. I have already argued that this reason is inadequate.

44. *The Theory of Good and Evil*, Vol. I, pp. 56–59. A similar point, though from a very different perspective, is made by John Rawls when he argues that having a sense of justice is part of one's own good. (*A Theory of Justice*, chap. IX).

45. "Agent and Other: Against Ethical Universalism," *Australasian Journal of Philosophy* 54 (1976): 207.

46. In addition to the important works by Lars Bergström mentioned earlier, the following contain valuable discussions of these topics: Hector-Neri Castañeda, "Ought, Value, and Utilitarianism," *American Philosophical Quarterly* 6 (1969): 257–75; Lars Bergström, "On the Formulation and Application of Utilitarianism," *Nous* 10 (1976): 121–44; J. H. Sobel, "Utilitarianism and Past and Future Mistakes," *Nous* 10 (1976): 195–220. Of course, these are only samples of what is already an extensive literature on the questions mentioned.

47. *Moral Thinking* (Oxford: Clarendon Press, 1981) p. 95, n. 4.

48. "Ethical Consistency" and "Consistency and Realism," both included in *Problems of the Self* (Cambridge: Cambridge University Press, 1973). But see also the valuable critical discussions of these papers by Ruth Barcan Marcus, "Moral Dilemmas and Consistency," *The Journal of Philosophy* 77 (1980): 121–36; Philippa Foot, "Moral Realism and Moral Dilemma," *The Journal of Philosophy* 80 (1983): 379–97; Alan Donagan, "Consistency in Rationalist Moral Systems," *The Journal of Philosophy* 81 (1984): 291–309.

49. See especially *Ethics and the Limits of Philosophy* (Cambridge: Harvard University Press, 1985).

50. *Rights and Persons* (Berkeley and Los Angeles: University of California Press, 1977), pp. 19–20.

51. Ibid., p. 11.

52. *Animals and Why They Matter* (Athens: The University of Georgia Press, 1984), p. 63.

53. *Taking Rights Seriously* (Cambridge: Harvard University Press, 1978), pp. 335–36, also xi–xii *et passim*.

54. "Why Rights are Indispensable," *Mind* 95 (1986): 329–44.

55. *Rights, Goods, and Democracy* (Newark: University of Delaware Press; London and Toronto: Associated University Presses, 1986), pp. 66–67.

56. *The Methods of Ethics*, pp. xxv, 97–103.

57. See Sabina Lovibond, *Realism and Imagination in Ethics* (Minneapolis: University of Minnesota Press, 1983); Renford Bambrough, *Moral Scepticism and Moral Knowledge* (Atlantic Highlands, N.J.: Humanities Press, 1979); Mark Platts, *Ways of Meaning*, chap. 10, and the articles by David Wiggins, S. L. Hurley, and John McDowell cited in n. 18, chap. 1.

58. *Virtues and Vices* (Berkeley and Los Angeles: University of California Press, 1981), pp. 15–18.

59. For a succinct statement of some of these objections, see William K. Frankena, *Ethics*, 2d ed. (Englewood Cliffs: Prentice Hall, 1973), pp. 41–43.

60. *A Theory of Justice*, p. 25.

61. *Summa Theologica*, Part Two, Question 94, Article 2. Alan Donagan interprets this principle to mean "Act so that the fundamental human goods, whether in your own person or in that of another, are promoted as may be possible, and under no circumstances violated." (*The Theory of Morality* [Chicago: University of Chicago Press, 1977], p. 61.)

62. See especially chaps. 8 and 9.

63. *Ethics*, p. 44.

64. See *A Theory of Justice*, pp. 30–31.

65. Ibid., pp. 92–93, 260, 395–99, 433–34. In a more recent work, Rawls writes: "Justice

is prior to the good in the sense that it limits the admissible conceptions of the good, so that those conceptions the pursuit of which violate the principles of justice are ruled out absolutely: the claims to pursue inadmissible conceptions have no weight at all. On the other hand, just institutions would have no point unless citizens had conceptions of the good they strove to realize and these conceptions defined ways of life fully worthy of human endeavour." ("Social Unity and Primary Goods," in Amartya Sen and Bernard Williams, eds., *Utilitarianism and Beyond* [Cambridge: Cambridge University Press, 1982], p. 184.)

66. *The Theory of Morality,* p. 242.

67. *A Theory of the Good and the Right,* p. 46.

68. *Reason and Morality* (Chicago: University of Chicago Press, 1978), p. 3.

69. Franz Brentano, *The Origin of Our Knowledge of Right and Wrong,* trans. R. Chisholm and E. Schneewind (New York: Humanities, 1969), p. 18.

70. *Five Types of Ethical Theory* (Patterson, N.J.: Littlefield, Adams and Co., 1959), p. 283.

71. *The Definition of Good* (New York: The Macmillan Company, 1947), pp. 148–49.

72. "Self-Profile," in *Roderick M. Chisholm,* pp. 49–56.

73. *A Theory of the Good and the Right,* p. 112. R. M. Hare endorses Brandt's view (*Moral Thinking,* pp. 214–17), with the addition that logic includes cognizance of the logical character of concepts and sentences.

74. Ibid., p. 246.

75. Ibid., p. 17.

76. *A Theory of Justice,* pp. 143, 401.

77. Ibid., p. 417.

78. Ibid., p. 419.

79. Ibid., p. 425.

80. Ibid., p. 426.

81. Ibid., p. 332.

82. "Kantian Constructivism in Moral Theory: The Dewey Lectures 1980," *The Journal of Philosophy* 78 (1980): 549.

83. *The Philosophical Review* 84 (1975).

84. Ibid., p. 537.

85. Ibid., p. 539.

86. Ibid., p. 549.

87. *A Theory of Justice,* pp. 399ff.

88. *Realism and Reason: Philosophical Papers* (Cambridge: Cambridge University Press, 1983), Vol. 3, p. 300.

89. "Morality as a System of Hypothetical Imperatives," included in *Virtues and Vices,* p. 162.

90. *The Methods of Ethics,* p. xxiv. See also pp. 23ff, 375.

91. Ibid., p. 37.

92. In his useful recent book *Impartial Reason* (Ithaca and London: Cornell University Press, 1983), Stephen L. Darwall explicates the notion of reason he considers crucial to ethics as follows: "the content of the judgment that there is reason for one to do A is simply that *were* one rationally to consider facts relevant to doing A, then one *would* be moved to prefer A" (p. 128). By "rational consideration" he means roughly what Brandt means (pp. 95–100). And he offers this explication in order to avoid a "nonnaturalist metaphysics" such as Moore's, whether in ethics or in epistemology (p. 80 *et passim*). The connection between moral reason for action, in the sense of evidence that the action is right, and motivation for doing the action, which is Darwall's main concern, is a topic I shall discuss in chap. 3, section 2.

93. See Bernard Gert, *The Moral Rules* (New York: Harper and Row, 1973), chaps. 2 and 3; also, Derek Parfit, *Reasons and Persons,* pp. 120–26 *et passim*. But neither uses the phrase "reason discloses."

94. *Rights, Goods, and Democracy,* pp. 40–41.

95. *The Theory of Morality*, p. 220.
96. *Utilitarianism and Beyond*, pp. 12–13.

### 3. Our Awareness of Good

1. F. E. Sparshott writes: "Professor C. L. Stevenson, in *Ethics and Language* . . . ,takes as normal the nursery usage of 'good' and ignores the adult one." (*An Enquiry into Goodness* [Toronto: The University of Toronto Press, 1958], p. 170.)
2. J. L. Austin, *How to Do Things with Words* (Cambridge: Harvard University Press, 1962); J. O. Urmson, *The Emotive Theory of Ethics* (London: Hutchinson's University Library, 1968), chap. 11. See also Roger Hancock, "The Refutation of Naturalism in Moore and Hare," *The Journal of Philosophy* 57 (1960): 326–34, and John Rawls, A *Theory of Justice* (Cambridge: Harvard University Press, 1971), #62.
3. "Moore's Arguments Against Certain Forms of Ethical Naturalism," in P. A. Schilpp, ed., *The Philosophy of G. E. Moore* (LaSalle, Ill.: Open Court Publishing Company, 1968), Vol. 1, p. 89.
4. See *The Language of Morals* (Oxford: The Clarendon Press, 1952). Since then Hare's views have evolved significantly, but not in the respect I have considered.
5. *Ethics: Inventing Right and Wrong* (Harmondsworth: Penguin, 1977), pp. 44, 59, 73–76.
6. *The Methods of Ethics* (Chicago: University of Chicago Press, 1962), p. 27.
7. *Principia Ethica* (Cambridge: Cambridge University Press, 1971), p. 60.
8. *The Right and the Good* (Oxford: Clarendon Press, 1930), p. 131. See also *The Foundations of Ethics* (Oxford: Clarendon Press, 1939), pp. 23, 24, 34, on attitudes toward rightness.
9. Nicolai Hartmann, *Ethics*, trans. Stanton Coit (London: George Allen and Unwin, 1932), Vol. I, p. 189. Compare Alexius Meinong, *On Emotional Presentation*, trans. Marie-Luise Schubert Kalsi (Evanston: Northwestern University Press, 1972), especially pp. 109ff.
10. *The Emotions*, trans. Bernard Frechtman (New York: Philosophical Library, 1948), p. 52.
11. *Ibid.*, pp. 60–61.
12. *Ibid.*, p. 50.
13. *Ibid.*, p. 80.
14. *The Psychology of the Imagination* (Secaucus, N.J.: The Citadel Press, 1972), p. 39.
15. Renford Bambrough, *Moral Scepticism and Moral Knowledge* (Atlantic Highlands, N.J.: Humanities Press, Inc., 1979), p. 22.
16. *Moral Action* (Bloomington: Indiana University Press, 1985), p. 29.
17. *The Transcendence of the Ego*, trans. Forrest Williams and Robert Kirkpatrick (New York: The Noonday Press, 1957) p. 58.
18. *Being and Nothingness*, trans. Hazel E. Barnes (New York: Philosophical Library, 1956), p. 557.
19. See, for example, R. M. Hare, *The Language of Morals*; W. D. Falk, "Ought and Motivation," *Proceedings of the Aristotelian Society* 48 (1947–48), reprinted in W. D. Falk, *Ought, Reasons and Morality* (Ithaca and London: Cornell University Press, 1986); Kurt Baier, *The Moral Point of View* (Ithaca: Cornell University Press, 1958); Thomas L. Carson, *The Status of Morality* (Dordrecht: Reidel, 1984); Stephen Darwall, *Impartial Reason* (Ithaca and London: Cornell University Press, 1983). But also see the classic discussion of the topic by William Frankena in "Obligation and Motivation in Recent Moral Philosophy," included in *Perspectives on Morality*, ed. K. E. Goodpaster (Notre Dame and London: University of Notre Dame Press, 1976).
20. An excellent defense of this point can be found in Irwin Goldstein, "Why People Prefer Pleasure to Pain," *Philosophy* 55 (1980): 349–62. For an especially interesting appli-

cation of the same general idea to one's attitudes toward others' pain or distress, see Angus Ross, "The Status of Altruism," *Mind* 92 (1983): 204–18.

21. "Recent Developments in British Ethical Thought," in C. A. Mace, ed., *British Philosophy at the Mid-Century* (London: George Allen and Unwin, 1957), p. 88.

22. *A Companion to Plato's Republic* (Indianapolis, Cambridge: Hackett Publishing Company, 1979), p. 49.

23. *Metaphysics* 1072a 28–29. For a discussion of how this view accords with the *Nichomachean Ethics*, see Nicholas P. White's essay "Goodness and Human Aims in Aristotle's Ethics," in Dominic G. O'Meara, ed., *Studies in Aristotle* (Washington, D.C.: Catholic University of America Press, 1981).

24. *Summa Theologica*, Part One, Question 82, Article 2.

25. *Critique of Practical Reason*, trans. T. K. Abbott (London: Longmans, Green and Co., 1909), pp. 150–51.

26. Cambridge: Cambridge University Press, 1983.

27. *Nichomachean Ethics* 1147a 11–24. For a not dissimilar discussion of the issue in the context of current cognitive psychology, see Richard B. Brandt, *A Theory of the Good and the Right* (Oxford: Clarendon Press, 1979), pp. 58–64.

28. See J. C. B. Gosling, *Pleasure and Desire* (Oxford: Clarendon Press, 1969), pp. 14–20. Gosling does not endorse the argument, but see next note.

29. See Alan Gewirth, *Reason and Morality* (Chicago: University of Chicago Press, 1978), pp. 39–41. Gosling makes a similar distinction but then dulls it by suggesting that both senses are aspects of a "primary" sense of "want" (see *Pleasure and Desire*, chaps. 6 and 7).

30. *A Treatise of Human Nature*, ed. L. A. Selby-Bigge (Oxford: Clarendon Press, 1888), p. 469.

31. See John Leslie, *Value and Existence* (Totowa, N.J.: Rowman and Littlefield, 1979).

32. On this issue the classic work is still H. A. Prichard's "Duty and Interest," included in *Moral Obligation and Duty and Interest* (London, Oxford, New York: Oxford University Press, 1968). See especially pp. 225–26.

33. See *Being and Nothingness*, Part One, Chapter Two; Part Two, Chapter One.

34. *The Transcendence of the Ego*, p. 58.

35. *Being and Nothingness*, p. 38.

36. *The Joyful Wisdom*, trans. Thomas Common (New York: Frederick Ungar, 1960), #124.

37. See Henry B. Veatch, *For an Ontology of Morals* (Evanston: Northwestern University Press, 1971), pp. 120–22.

38. "Kantian Constructivism in Moral Theory: The Dewey Lectures 1980," *The Journal of Philosophy* 78 (1980): 559.

39. *Being and Nothingness*, p. 38.

40. *Values and Intentions* (London: George Allen and Unwin, 1961), pp. 213–26. I take this occasion, however, to express my admiration of this book. See, also by Findlay, *Axiological Ethics* (London: Macmillan, 1970).

41. *A Review of the Principal Questions in Morals*, ed. D. Daiches Raphael (Oxford: Clarendon Press, 1948), p. 42.

42. *A Treatise of Human Nature*, p. 468.

43. *Principia Ethica* (Cambridge: Cambridge University Press, 1971), pp. 9–10.

44. *Formalism in Ethics and Non-Formal Ethics of Values*, trans. Manfred S. Frings and Roger L. Funk (Evanston: Northwestern University Press, 1973), pp. 15–16.

45. Ibid., p. 25.

46. See G. E. Moore, "The Conception of Intrinsic Value," in *Philosophical Studies* (London: Routledge and Kegan Paul, 1922); W. D. Ross, *The Right and the Good*, pp. 120–22.

47. Roderick M. Chisholm, *The Foundations of Knowing* (Minneapolis: University of Minnesota Press, 1982), p. 12. Chisholm is concerned with epistemic normative terms but suggests that ethical terms can be regarded as at least analogous.

48. *A Treatise Concerning the Principles of Human Knowledge* (New York: The Liberal Arts Press, 1957), Introduction, #16. The passage was added by Berkeley in the second edition of the *Principles*.

49. On this, the exchange between G. E. Moore and C. J. Ducasse on what has come to be known as the adverbial theory of sensation is highly instructive. (See P. A. Schilpp, ed., *The Philosophy of G. E. Moore* [LaSalle, Ill.: Open Court Publishing Company, 1968]). I discuss the topic in "Adverbial Theories of Consciousness," *Midwest Studies in Philosophy* 5 (1980): 261–80.

50. *The Right and the Good*, p. 86.

51. Ibid., pp. 126–31.

52. Ibid., p. 86. But a better (though hardly conclusive) reason is that, as Ross himself notes, "the chaotic condition of aesthetic theory seems to show that it is extremely difficult, if not impossible, to specify the characteristic or characteristics of beautiful things (apart from the way in which they can affect minds) on which beauty depends" (p. 132). Unlike goodness, beauty does not seem to have generally recognized species or subgenera. But, clearly, neither is it a *specific* monadic property. To be sure, we could say that it is a supervenient property, but this would tell us as little about it as the similar claim about goodness tells us.

53. *General Theory of Value* (Cambridge: Harvard University Press, 1926), p. 29.

54. The correspondence is noted by Peter Caws in *Sartre* (London and Boston: Routledge and Kegan Paul, 1979), and by Paul Ricoeur, "Sartre and Ryle on the Imagination," in P. A. Schilpp, ed., *The Philosophy of Jean-Paul Sartre* (LaSalle, Ill.: Open Court Publishing Company, 1981).

55. *The Concept of Mind* (London: Hutchinson's University Library, 1949), p. 256.

56. *The Psychology of the Imagination*, p. 5.

57. *Being and Nothingness*, p. li. Husserl's *hyle* was not rejected in Sartre's works that were earlier than *Being and Nothingness*.

58. Ibid., p. lxi.

59. Ibid., p. 306.

60. *The Transcendence of the Ego*, p. 93.

61. *Being and Nothingness*, p. 217.

62. Ibid., p. 34.

63. *The Psychology of the Imagination*, p. 39.

64. *The Transcendence of the Ego*, p. 56.

65. Ibid., p. 49.

66. Ibid., p. 58.

67. *Mind*, n.s., 12 (1903), included in *Philosophical Studies*.

68. *Proceedings of the Aristotelian Society*, n.s., 10 (1910), especially pp. 51–55.

69. *Philosophical Studies*, p. 29.

70. Ibid., p. 20.

71. Ibid., p. 25.

72. Ibid., p. 27.

73. If consciousness is understood in the way suggested by Sartre and Moore, then the familiar distinction between objectivity and subjectivity (even the sophisticated version of it explored by Thomas Nagel in *The View From Nowhere* [New York and Oxford: Oxford University Press, 1986]) would need to be either abandoned or radically reinterpreted.

74. *Reason, Truth and History* (Cambridge: Cambridge University Press, 1981). Putnam actually speaks of magical theories of reference and seems to think that mental reference, or intentionality, is supposed to be a relation between "representations" and objects in the world. According to Sartre, as we have seen, there are no representations in consciousness.

75. See Sartre, *The Transcendence of the Ego*, and Moore, "The Subject Matter of Psychology," pp. 51–55.

76. *Being and Time*, Introduction, II, 7. Compare Sartre, *Being and Nothingness*, pp. 177–81. Sartre writes: "The knower is not; he is not apprehensible. He is nothing other than that which brings it about that there is a *being-there* on the part of the known, a presence"

(p. 177). I consider the way such remarks may be understood in *Being Qua Being: A Theory of Identity, Existence, and Predication* (Bloomington and London: Indiana University Press, 1979), Appendix Two.

## 4. The Nature of Good

1. *Principia Ethica* (Cambridge: Cambridge University Press, 1971), p. 8.
2. Ibid., p. 41.
3. "The Conception of Intrinsic Value," in *Philosophical Studies*, p. 273.
4. Ibid., p. 274.
5. See P. A. Schilpp, ed., *The Philosophy of G. E. Moore* (LaSalle, Ill.: Open Court Publishing Company, 1968), Vol. 2, pp. 582–92.
6. *Ethics* (Oxford: Oxford University Press, 1977), pp. 25–26.
7. In his important book *Color for Philosophers* (Indianapolis: Hackett, 1988), C. L. Hardin argues that the hues of the nonprimary colors have components in the sense in which a vector has components. I am not convinced that this is the phenomenologically relevant sense. I shall continue to use colors as examples, because of their prominence in the traditional literature, but nothing that I say here or later should be taken as resting on a particular theory of color. For an excellent recent argument against regarding colors as "subjective," see P. M. S. Hacker, "Are Secondary Qualities Relative?" *Mind* 95 (1986): 180–97.
8. "The Nature of Judgment," *Mind* 8 (1899): p. 183.
9. "Identity," *Proceedings of the Aristotelian Society*, n.s., 1 (1901): 123. For a detailed, even though rather unsympathetic, discussion of Moore's early ontology, see Herbert Hochberg, *Thought, Fact, and Reference* (Minneapolis: University of Minnesota Press, 1978), especially chap. IV, and "Moore's Ontology and Nonnatural Properties," *The Review of Metaphysics* 15 (1962): 365–95. See also David O'Connor, *The Metaphysics of G. E. Moore* (Dordrecht: Reidel, 1982).
10. London: George Allen and Unwin, 1953.
11. See pp. 342, 356–57, 362, 364–65, 374.
12. *Principia Ethica*, pp. 110–11.
13. Compare *Some Main Problems of Philosophy*, p. 349; but also the Appendix, p. 375.
14. *General Theory of Value* (Cambridge: Harvard University Press, 1926), p. 30.
15. *The Right and the Good* (Oxford: Clarendon Press, 1930), pp. 87–88.
16. This is how, I suggest, we should answer Simon Blackburn's argument against moral realism in "Moral Realism," included in John Casey, ed., *Morality and Moral Reasoning* (London: Methuen, 1971). See also *Spreading the Word* (Oxford: Clarendon Press, 1984), pp. 182–89. The argument rests on the assumption that moral properties would have to be supervenient on nonmoral properties and yet that their exemplification would not be entailed by the exemplification of the latter. But if "supervenience" is understood in the manner I have suggested, the entailment would hold, even though it would not be a formal entailment (as I shall argue presently). Blackburn seems to allow for this possibility in *Spreading the Word*, p. 221. I should remark that I regard "conceptual" entailment to be merely disguised formal entailment; for example, "If S is a bachelor then S is unmarried" would express a conceptual entailment because it is equivalent to "If S is an unmarried man then S is unmarried." "If S is blue then S is colored" does not express, in this sense, a conceptual entailment. Using Blackburn's term, if not meaning, we might say it expresses a metaphysical entailment.
17. *The Language of Morals* (Oxford: Clarendon Press, 1952), pp. 85–86.
18. *Reason and Goodness* (London: George Allen and Unwin, 1961), p. 269.
19. "Is Goodness a Quality?" *Aristotelian Society Supplementary Volume* 11 (1932), p. 143. This paper was Joseph's reply to a paper by Moore, bearing the same title and immediately preceding Joseph's in the cited volume, in which Moore shows singular inability to understand Joseph's views, which had already been expressed in his *Some Problems of*

*Ethics* (Oxford: Clarendon Press, 1931). I shall consider in chapter 5, section 8, the view that good is not a quality because it is in all the categories.

20. Brand Blanshard, *The Nature of Thought* (London: George Allen and Unwin, 1939), Vol. I, p. 652. The view is defended also in his *Reason and Analysis* (La Salle, Ill.: Open Court Publishing Company, 1962), pp. 402–403, 420–21. For Joseph's view, see his *Introduction to Logic*, 2d ed. rev. (Oxford: Clarendon Press, 1916), p. 83.

21. *Reason and Goodness*, p. 302.

22. *Logic* (Cambridge: Cambridge University Press, 1921), Part I, chap. XI.

23. *The Philosophy of G. E. Moore*, Vol. 2, p. 583. C. D. Broad had suggested this possibility in his contribution. See Vol. 1, pp. 59ff.

24. See *Some Main Problems of Philosophy* (London: George Allen and Unwin, 1953), pp. 315–16, 350, 364–66, 368–69.

25. *Commonplace Book 1919–1953*, ed. Casimir Lewy (London: George Allen and Unwin, 1962), p. 19, in Notebook I (c. 1919). See also pp. 20 and 50. On pp. 50–55 he describes the distinction as one between species and genera. See also pp. 204 and 225.

26. See my *Resemblance and Identity: An Examination of the Problem of Universals* (Bloomington and London: Indiana University Press, 1966), chaps. 2 and 3, and *Being Qua Being: A Theory of Identity, Existence, and Predication* (Bloomington and London: Indiana University Press, 1979), chap. 7.

27. As R. I. Aaron does in *The Theory of Universals* (Oxford: Clarendon Press, 1952).

28. On this latter point, see *Being Qua Being*, pp. 195–206; and *Resemblance and Identity*, chaps. 2 and 3.

29. Armstrong attempts to do this by identifying colors with what Moore called their physical causes, and by neglecting shapes, except for line segments, altogether. See his *Universals and Scientific Realism* (Cambridge: University Press, 1978), Vol. II, Part Six. For a criticism of his views on generic universals, see Evan Fales, "Generic Universals," *Australasian Journal of Philosophy* 60 (1982): 29–39. For an extensive argument against the view that generic identity is a partial identity, see Brand Blanshard, *The Nature of Thought*, vol. 1, chapter 16.

30. *Statement and Inference* (Oxford: Clarendon Press, 1926), Vol. II, p. 505.

31. *Logical Investigations*, VI.

32. The classic work on the topic is H. H. Price's *Thinking and Experience* (London: Hutchinson's University Library, 1953).

33. *Philosophical Investigations*, 3d ed., trans. G. E. M. Anscombe (Oxford: Blackwell, 1958), Part I, ##604, 605.

34. Etienne Gilson: "To understand something is for us to conceive it as identical in nature with something else that we already know." (*Being and Some Philosophers* [Toronto: Pontifical Institute of Medieval Studies, 1952], p. 6.) There is no infinite regress here. To understand $x$ in terms of $y$ need not presuppose that $y$ is itself understood; it is enough that $y$ should be familiar to us. (One may understand the spatial positions of other objects by reference to one's own, without having the slightest idea of what one's own spatial position is.) It should also be noted that $x$ may be similar to ("identical in nature with") $y$ either with respect to its intrinsic (monadic) properties or with respect to its relational properties. This distinction corresponds to the scholastic distinction between analogy of attribution and analogy of proportionality (see for example, Cajetan, *De nominum analogia*), as well as to the contemporary distinction between material and formal analogies. See Mary B. Hesse, *Models and Analogies in Science* (London: Sheed and Ward, 1963). Iris Murdoch writes: "The development of consciousness in human beings is inseparably connected with the use of metaphor. Metaphors are not merely peripheral decorations or even useful models, they are fundamental forms of our awareness of our condition . . . it seems to me impossible to discuss certain kinds of concepts without resorting to metaphor, since the concepts are themselves deeply metaphorical and cannot be analyzed into non-metaphorical components without a loss of substance." (*The Sovereignty of Good* [New York: Schocken Books, 1971], p. 77.) Edward O. Wilson offers the hypothesis that both the arts and the sciences "rely on

similar forms of metaphor and analogy, because they share the brain's strict and peculiar limitations in the processing of information." (*Biophilia* [Cambridge: Harvard University Press, 1984], pp. 63–64; see also p. 60.) See also Nelson Goodman, *Ways of Worldmaking* (Indianapolis: Hackett, 1978), especially chap. VI.

35. *On Being and Essence*, 2d rev. ed., trans. Armand Maurer (Toronto: The Pontifical Institute of Medieval Studies, 1968), p. 42.

36. Ibid., p. 40.

37. *Statement and Inference*, Vol. II, pp. 503–504.

38. *Logic*, Part I, pp. 174–75.

39. See Kathleen Wright, "Hegel: The Identity of Identity and Nonidentity," *Idealistic Studies* 13 (1983): 11–32.

40. *Philosophical Investigations*, Part I, ##215, 216.

41. That this is Frege's account is evident from the first few pages of "On Sense and Reference" but generally ignored, even in Nathan Salmon's recent book on the subject, *Frege's Puzzle* (Cambridge: The MIT Press, 1986). Salmon writes that "the sense of an expression is . . . a semantically associated purely conceptual representation," then uses the phrase "semantically associated purely conceptual 'mode of presentation' " (p. 47), then in a footnote says that he uses the term "concept" with "a more or less ordinary meaning" and not Frege's (p. 160, note 4), and revealingly says that singular terms "clearly and obviously do evoke concepts in the minds of speakers" (p. 65). What he seems to mean by "concept" is what Frege called an "idea," which he explicitly regarded as irrelevant to the sense of the expression. Frege nowhere characterizes modes of presentation as conceptual, or senses as conceptual representations, either in his or in Salmon's sense of "conceptual."

42. *Translations from the Philosophical Writings of Gottlob Frege*, ed. Peter Geach and Max Black, 3d ed. (Oxford: B. Blackwell, 1980), pp. 57–58. See "The Thought," trans. A. M. and Marcelle Quinton, included in E. D. Klemke, ed., *Essays on Frege* (Urbana: University of Illinois Press, 1968), p. 518.

43. *Philosophical and Mathematical Correspondence*, trans. Hans Kaal (Chicago: University of Chicago Press, 1980), p. 80.

44. Ibid., p. 152.

45. *Posthumous Writings*, trans. Peter Long and Roger White (Chicago: University of Chicago Press, 1979), p. 124.

46. *Translations from the Philosophical Writings of Gottlob Frege*, p. 58.

47. *The Foundations of Arithmetic*, trans. J. L. Austin, 2d rev. ed. (New York: Harper, 1960), for example, p. 116.

48. *Philosophical and Mathematical Correspondence*, p. 152.

49. *The Foundations of Arithmetic*, p. 73; *Posthumous Writings*, p. 255.

50. *The Foundations of Arithmetic*, p. 116.

51. Ibid., p. 73.

52. "The Thought," pp. 523, 531–35.

53. Compare J. N. Findlay, "An Ontology of Senses," *The Journal of Philosophy* 79 (1982): 545–51.

54. *Nichomachean Ethics*, 1096a 24–29, 1096b 10–30.

55. *Philosophical Investigations*, Part I, #217. If we take #215 and #216 as central to Wittgenstein's argument, as in effect I have done, then we can see that the much-discussed passages on following a rule and on private languages are essentially applications and explications of the far deeper thesis of those two passages.

56. I argue that the concept of existence can be understood in terms of the concept of identity in *Being Qua Being*, and in "Our Robust Sense of Reality," *Grazer Philosophische Studien* 25/26 (1985–86): 403–21.

57. *Reason and Analysis*, p. 406. I am indebted to Rex Clemmensen and Dennis Bradshaw for discussion of this objection.

58. The view expressed in this paragraph is defended in detail in *Being Qua Being*. See also "Our Robust Sense of Reality."

59. See Jaegwon Kim, "Concepts of Supervenience," *Philosophy and Phenomenological Research* 45 (1984): 153–76.

60. Compare A. C. Ewing, *The Definition of Good* (New York: The Macmillan Company, 1947), pp. 83–84.

61. *Ethics*, trans. Stanton Coit (London: George Allen and Unwin, 1932), Vol. 2, pp. 66–68.

62. *Principia Ethica*, p. 118.

63. Ibid., pp. 93, 142, 144, 187.

64. Ibid., p. 187.

65. Ibid., p. 189.

66. Ibid., p. 199.

67. Ibid., pp. 212, 188.

68. Ibid., p. 186.

69. According to Paul Levy, the chapter in which they are proposed was conceived and written in just a few weeks, and indeed the whole of *Principia Ethica* was written in less than a year. See his *Moore: G. E. Moore and the Cambridge Apostles* (New York: Holt, Rinehart and Winston, 1979), pp. 215, 233.

70. *Principia Ethica*, pp. 21–31.

## 5. The System of Goods

1. *Principia Ethica* (Cambridge: Cambridge University Press, 1971), p. 222.

2. *The Right and the Good* (Oxford: Clarendon Press, 1930), p. 23.

3. See Hastings Rashdall, *The Theory of Good and Evil* (Oxford: Oxford University Press, 1924), 2d ed., Vol. I, pp. 74–79, 93; and W. D. Ross, *The Right and the Good*, p. 140.

4. *Summa Theologica*, Part One, Question 47, Article 2. Compare Aristotle, *De Anima* 414a 30ff.

5. Aristotle (*De Anima* 414b 1–6) and Aquinas (*Summa Theologica*, Part One, Question 78, Article 1) seem to deny this.

6. David L. Hull, "The Effect of Essentialism on Taxonomy—Two Thousand Years of Stasis (I)," *The British Journal for the Philosophy of Science* 15 (1965): 326. In a much later paper Hull defends the view that species are to be interpreted as historical entities, and concludes that "particular organisms belong in a particular species because they are part of that genealogical nexus, not because they possess any essential traits. . . . Hence there is no such thing as human nature." ("A Matter of Individuality," *Philosophy of Science* 45 (1978): 358.) The uncertain state of the concept of species in biology is evident in three recent articles, conveniently published in the same issue of *Philosophy of Science* (vol. 51, 1984): Kent E. Holsinger, "The Nature of Biological Species," pp. 293–307; Philip Kitcher, "Species," pp. 308–33; Elliott Sober, "Discussion: Sets, Species, and Evolution: Comments on Philip Kitcher's 'Species,' " pp. 334–41.

7. It has been argued that for him this was not a contingent truth, that self-preservation was (conceptually) the standard of rationality. See Bernard Gert, "Hobbes's Account of Reason," *The Journal of Philosophy* 76 (1979): 559–61.

8. *Truth*, trans. Robert W. Schmidt (Chicago: Henry Regnery Company, 1952–54), Question 21, Article 2.

9. See, for example, Aldo Leopold, *A Sand County Almanac* (New York: Oxford University Press, 1966), and Christopher D. Stone, *Should Trees Have Standing? Toward Legal Rights for Natural Objects* (Los Altos, Cal.: William Kaufmann, Inc., 1974). See also, included in the latter, Justice William O. Douglas's dissenting opinion in the case of the Sierra Club v. Morton, Secretary of the Interior.

10. "The Concept of Natural Right," *Midwest Studies in Philosophy* 7 (1982): 146.

11. See John Leslie, *Value and Existence* (Totowa, N.J.: Rowman and Littlefield, 1979).

12. As quoted by John Passmore, *Man's Responsibility for Nature* (London: Duckworth, 1974), p. 21.

13. *Ethics* (Chicago: University of Chicago Press, 1972), p. 147.

14. Joel Feinberg, "The Rights of Animals and Unborn Generations," in William T. Blackstone, ed., *Philosophy and Environmental Crisis* (Athens: University of Georgia Press, 1974), pp. 49–50. Feinberg applies this argument also to vegetables, for obvious reasons.

15. The recent philosophical literature on "animal rights" and our obligations to the environment is enormous and cannot be canvassed here. An excellent work, which I have already mentioned, is Mary Midgley, *Animals and Why They Matter* (Athens: The University of Georgia Press, 1984). She explicitly includes in her concern "trees and forests, grasses, rivers and mountains," not just animals.

16. An excellent discussion of the role of normative concepts in biology may be found in chapter I of James D. Wallace, *Virtues and Vices* (Ithaca and London: Cornell University Press, 1978).

17. See *Mind, Language, and Reality: Philosophical Papers*, Vol. 2 (Cambridge: Cambridge University Press, 1975), pp. 65–68; also *Realism and Reason: Philosophical Papers*, vol. 3 (Cambridge: Cambridge University Press, 1983), p. 89.

18. Gilbert Ryle, *Dilemmas* (Cambridge: Cambridge University Press, 1954), p. 59.

19. See Rem B. Edwards, *Pleasures and Pains: A Theory of Qualitative Hedonism* (Ithaca and London: Cornell University Press, 1979). But Edwards does not draw the conclusion I draw from this fact.

20. See Richard Brandt, *A Theory of the Good and the Right* (Oxford: Clarendon Press, 1979), pp. 38–42.

21. An important thesis in Plato's *Philebus* is that pleasures, that is, the states we call pleasures, do not all have anything in common, do not bear to one another the sorts of similarities that would render them members of one well-defined class. See 12c–14a.

22. In the *Laws* (657c) Plato remarks that we experience pleasure when we think we are doing well. Aristotle's view (*Nichomachean Ethics*, 1174b 32–35) that pleasure perfects an activity by supervening upon it, is structurally similar to my suggestion, though only with respect to the higher pleasures, but cannot be identified with it. (I shall return to this point.) For a detailed discussion of Plato's and Aristotle's (and other Greek philosophers') views on pleasure, see J. C. B. Gosling and C. C. W. Taylor, *The Greeks on Pleasure* (Oxford: Clarendon Press, 1982). A curious feature of this book, however, is the authors' determination to impose a hedonistic interpretation on those views whenever there is the slightest excuse for doing so.

23. See Plato, *The Republic*, 584b.

24. See Plato, *The Republic*, 437d.

25. For example, Richard B. Brandt, in *A Theory of the Good and the Right*.

26. *Nichomachean Ethics*, 1113a 15–35. See also *De Anima* 432b 5 and 414b 5–6, *Rhetoric* 1369a 1–5. For an illuminating discussion of the role of this notion in Aristotle's ethics, see T. H. Irwin, "The Metaphysical and Psychological Basis of Aristotle's Ethics," in Amelie Oksenberg Rorty, ed., *Essays on Aristotle's Ethics* (Berkeley: University of California Press, 1980).

27. *Nichomachean Ethics*, 1174b 32–35, Hippocrates G. Apostle's translation (Grinnell, Iowa: The Peripatetic Press, 1975).

28. See Moore, *Principia Ethica*, pp. 191–92, where Moore makes similar distinctions regarding our consciousness of beauty.

29. They are discussed illuminatingly by Alexius Meinong, *On Emotional Presentation*, trans. Marie-Luise Schubert Kalsi (Evanston: Northwestern University Press, 1972), and by H. A. Prichard in several pieces included in *Moral Obligation and Duty and Interest*.

30. Compare H. H. Price's distinction between recognition as a source of information and recognition as an intellectual function, a manifestation of conceptual cognition. (*Thinking and Experience* [London: Hutchinson's University Library, 1953], p. 85.)

31. On p. 59 of *The Blue and Brown Books* (Oxford: Basil Blackwell, 1960), Wittgenstein says: "Our ordinary language, which of all possible notations is the one which pervades all our life, holds our mind rigidly in one position, as it were, and in this position sometimes it feels cramped, having a desire for other positions as well. Thus we sometimes wish for a notation which stresses a difference more strongly, makes it more obvious, than ordinary language does, or one which in a particular case uses more closely similar forms of expression than our ordinary language." This important aspect of Wittgenstein's later philosophy was developed, of course, by John Wisdom. Neither Wittgenstein nor Wisdom, however, seemed to see that all knowledge in the sense of understanding, whether in philosophy or in science or in the humanistic disciplines or in everyday life, consists in the perception of similarities and differences, that these similarities and differences are objective, indeed the most important, features of the world, and not at all self-contained similarities or differences among uses of words or forms of expression, that the "changes in our notation" such perception may motivate can be justified in the way a factual claim can, and that what really matters is the perception, not the notation. Compare J. L. Austin's idea of a "linguistic phenomenology," in "A Plea for Excuses," *Philosophical Papers*, p. 130; see quotation above, p. 11.

32. *Principia Ethica*, p. 199.

33. That it is a great extrinsic good is of course undeniable, and its importance for ethics has been argued in great detail by Alan Gewirth in *Reason and Morality* (Chicago: University of Chicago Press, 1978). It is also the subject of Rawls's first principle of justice in *A Theory of Justice* (Cambridge: Harvard University Press, 1971).

34. *Principia Ethica*, p. 186.

35. *The Theory of Good and Evil*, Vol. I, p. 128.

36. A useful review of the literature on friendship, especially in Christian ethics, may be found in Gilbert Meilaender, *Friendship* (Notre Dame and London: University of Notre Dame Press, 1981). But Meilaender is too confident that our everyday concept of friendship is well defined.

37. The Greek term both used in those works is *philia*, and Gregory Vlastos has argued that in some of its uses it is better translated as "love." See his "The Individual as an Object of Love in Plato," in *Platonic Studies*, 2d ed. (Princeton: Princeton University Press, 1981).

38. *Nichomachean Ethics*, 1155a 23–29, Apostle's translation. For a discussion of Aristotle on friendship, see John M. Cooper, "Aristotle on Friendship," in Rorty, *Essays on Aristotle's Ethics*; "Aristotle on the Forms of Friendship," *The Review of Metaphysics* 30 (1977): 619–48; "Friendship and the Good in Aristotle," *The Philosophical Review* 86 (1977): 290–315. An incisive discussion can be found also in Ferdinand Schoeman, "Aristotle on the Good of Friendship," *Australasian Journal of Philosophy* 63 (1985): 269–82.

39. For a detailed discussion, though not defense, of "the ethics of love," see William K. Frankena, "The Ethics of Love Conceived as an Ethics of Virtue," *The Journal of Religious Ethics* 1 (Fall 1973).

40. *Enquiries*, 2d ed., ed. L. A. Selby-Bigge (Oxford: Clarendon Press, 1902), pp. 184ff.

41. *Nichomachean Ethics* 1156b 9–10, Apostle's translation; also Book 9, chap. 9.

42. *Summa Theologica*, Part Two, Question 26, Article 4.

43. *The Theory of Good and Evil*, Vol. 1, pp. 123–24.

44. *Nichomachean Ethics* 1156b 8–1157a 20.

45. See *Principia Ethica*, pp. 203–205. In a paper read to the Society of Apostles in 1898, Moore is reported to have said: "For myself I have seen [in love] nothing but what differs in degree, and in no very marked degree, from ordinary friendship." (See Paul Levy, *Moore: G. E. Moore and the Cambridge Apostles*, New York: Holt, Rinehart and Winston, 1979, p. 202.)

46. Alan Donagan bases his ethical theory in *The Theory of Morality* (Chicago: University of Chicago Press, 1977) on the claim that the Kantian principle of respecting every rational being as an end in itself is a version of the biblical injunction that one love one's neighbor as oneself. See pp. 57–66.

47. *The Theory of Good and Evil*, Vol. 1, p. 239.

48. In what is the most vigorous recent defense of this view, Alan Donagan recognizes that the idea of a person's *being an end* has been rejected by many (for example, by Sidgwick and Ross) as unintelligible. (*The Theory of Morality*, p. 63.) But the idea that a human being has great *intrinsic value* in the sense I have explained is not only obviously intelligible but fully defensible.

49. For a valuable discussion of these attitudes, see Lawrence A. Blum, *Friendship, Altruism and Morality* (London, Boston and Henley: Routledge and Kegan Paul, 1980). Blum identifies the morally relevant sense of "friendship" to be that of "a type of regard for another person, a giving of oneself, and a caring for another for his own sake" (p. 73).

50. *Nichomachean Ethics*, 1158a 12, Apostle's translation.

51. A *Theory of Justice*, p. 191.

52. "Kantian Constructivism in Moral Theory: The Dewey Lectures 1980," *The Journal of Philosophy* 78 (1980): 528.

53. In an especially useful paper, A. D. Woozley argues that of the pair "justice" and "injustice," it is the latter that wears the trousers (in J. L. Austin's sense) and concludes that "injustice fundamentally is—the affront done to a man as a human being by not treating him in the way that he can expect to be treated . . . [the] belittling or affronting the worth of the victim." ("Injustice," in *Studies in Ethics*, American Philosophical Quarterly Monograph Series [Oxford: Basil Blackwell, 1973], pp. 121–22.)

54. *The Theory of Good and Evil*, Vol. 1, p. 240.

55. *The Methods of Ethics* (Chicago: University of Chicago Press, 1962), p. 380.

56. Compare the defense of the principle of universalizability in Alan Gewirth, *Reason and Morality*, pp. 105–107, and in R. M. Hare, *Freedom and Reason*, pp. 10ff.

57. Oliver A. Johnson seems to hold that in such a case one ought to refrain from action altogether, on the grounds that any action would be arbitrary and that arbitrariness is incompatible with morality. See his *The Moral Life* (London: George Allen and Unwin, 1969), p. 46; and *Moral Knowledge* (The Hague: Martinus Nijhoff, 1966), pp. 139ff.

58. *The Theory of Good and Evil*, p. 147.

59. "Neither intellectual nor spiritual superiority seems to constitute an intelligible ground for assigning to a man a larger share of carnal delights than his neighbour." (Hastings Rashdall, *The Theory of Good and Evil*, Vol. 1, p. 252.)

60. See Robert Nozick, *Anarchy, State and Utopia* (Oxford: Basil Blackwell, 1974).

61. See John Rawls, A *Theory of Justice*.

62. "Kantian Constructivism in Moral Theory: The Dewey Lectures 1980," p. 554. In A *Theory of Justice* Rawls is more cautious. He explains that the attribute defining the class of creatures to whom justice is owed is that of possessing the capacity for a conception of their good and for a sense of justice (pp. 504–12). But though his first principle of justice does include provision for political equality, it is justified not by reference to equality in respect to that capacity but by reference to what the parties in the original position would agree to.

63. Stripped of its alleged Kantian foundation, this conception is not at all novel. In *The Republic* Plato wrote: "Liberty, I [Socrates] said. This is what you would hear in a democracy is its finest possession and that this is the reason why it is the only city worth living in for a man who is by nature free" (562b-c, G. M. A. Grube's translation). Plato went on to argue against democracy.

64. Included in K. E. Goodpaster, ed., *Perspectives on Morality* (Notre Dame and London: University of Notre Dame Press, 1976).

65. Ibid., p. 101.

66. Ibid., p. 102.

67. Ibid., pp. 105–106.

68. On this topic, see Reinhardt Grossmann, *Ontological Reduction* (Bloomington and London: Indiana University Press, 1973), and *The Categorial Structure of the World* (Bloomington: Indiana University Press, 1983), pp. 374ff.

69. A *Theory of Justice*, pp. 331–32.

70. A *Theory of the Good and the Right*, p. 206.

71. *The Methods of Ethics*, p. 274.

72. New York: Columbia University Press, 1924, p. 94.

73. Jeremy Bentham, *An Introduction to the Principles of Morals and Legislation*, chap. X, Section 2, # X.

74. Ibid., chap. I, section IV.

75. *Hegel's Philosophy of Right*, trans. T. M. Knox (Oxford: Clarendon Press, 1965), p. 161.

76. *Ethics*, vol. II, p. 330.

77. See D. M. Armstrong, *Universals and Scientific Realism*; and more recently, *What is a Law of Nature?* (Cambridge: Cambridge University Press, 1983). But Armstrong does not allow for generic universals, for reasons unclear to me. See above, chap. 4, n. 29.

78. I have already mentioned two such valuable books: Lawrence A. Blum's *Friendship, Altruism and Morality*, and Rem B. Edwards's *Pleasures and Pains: A Theory of Qualitative Hedonism*. There are others.

79. *Philosophical Writings*, trans. Allan Wolter (Indianapolis: Bobbs-Merrill, 1962), p. 3.

80. *Ways of Worldmaking* (Indianapolis: Hackett, 1978), pp. 74–75.

81. *Summa Theologica*, Part One, Question 5, Article 1. See also *De Veritate*, XXI, 1.

82. Ibid.

83. See especially *De Veritate*, XXI, 1, 2. For an illuminating discussion, see Henry B. Veatch, *For an Ontology of Morals* (Evanston: Northwestern University Press, 1971), pp. 106–17.

84. See Aristotle, *De Anima* 412a 10ff.

85. *Summa Theologica*, Part One, Question 48, Article 5, Reply to Objection 1.

86. Ibid., Part One, Question 48, Article 5.

## 6. The Quantities and Degrees of Good and Evil

1. *Leviathan* (London: J. M. Dent and Sons, 1950), p. 125.

2. *Fifteen Sermons upon Human Nature* (London, 1726; 2d ed., 1729), Sermon 11.

3. *A Theory of Justice* (Cambridge: Harvard University Press, 1971), pp. 13–14.

4. See *A Theory of the Good and the Right* (Oxford: Clarendon Press, 1979), pp. 143–46, 331–35.

5. A glance at Aristotle's *Rhetoric*, 1362b 1–28, would suffice to demonstrate the richness of the Platonic-Aristotelian conception.

6. Oxford: Oxford University Press, 1977, p. 100.

7. *Principia Ethica* (Cambridge: Cambridge University Press, 1971), pp. 97–105.

8. *Ethics*, pp. 25–26, 73.

9. Nor is Mary Midgley an egalitarian in *Animals and Why They Matter* (Athens: The University of Georgia Press, 1984). See, for example, p. 90.

10. Compare Terence Irwin, *Plato's Moral Theory* (Oxford: Clarendon Press, 1977), pp. 53–54, 267–75; Nicholas P. White, *A Companion to Plato's Republic* (Indianapolis: Hackett, 1979), pp. 43–58; Henry Sidgwick, *The Methods of Ethics*, pp. 10–11. In a useful article, Lloyd P. Gerson argues that for Plato and Aquinas there can be no distinction, and therefore no divergence, between one's own good and the good *simpliciter*, and therefore also no divergence between one's own good and another's good. See "Plato, Aquinas, and the Universal Good," *The New Scholasticism* 58 (1984): 131–44. Aristotle's distinction between the sense in which the virtuous man may be said to be a self-lover and the sense in which to call someone a self-lover is to reproach him is also relevant to the issue under discussion. See *Nichomachean Ethics* 1168a 29–1169b 2.

11. See references in notes 31 and 49, chap. 2.

12. As well as, it seems, of many nonhuman species. See Edward O. Wilson, *On Human Nature* (Cambridge: Harvard University Press, 1978), chap. 7.

13. For an incisive modern phenomenological argument against psychological egoism, see Sartre, *The Transcendence of the Ego*, pp. 54–60.

14. *Principia Ethica*, p. 20. What I have said would also be my comment on Fred Wilson's interesting defense of Mill's ethics by appealing to what he calls the "must implies ought" principle. See his "Mill's Proof that Happiness is the Criterion of Morality," *Journal of Business Ethics* 1 (1982): 59–72.

15. See *Reasons and Persons* (Oxford: Oxford University Press, 1984).

16. For my views on the self, see *Being Qua Being: A Theory of Identity, Existence, and Predication* (Bloomington and London: Indiana University Press, 1979), Appendix Two.

## 7. Our Knowledge of Good

1. *The Right and the Good* (Oxford: Clarendon Press, 1930), p. 82.

2. *The Foundations of Ethics* (Oxford: Clarendon Press, 1939), p. 262.

3. *The Right and the Good*, p. 29.

4. "Does Moral Philosophy Rest on a Mistake?" in *Moral Obligation and Duty and Interest* (London, Oxford, New York: Oxford University Press, 1968), p. 8.

5. *Principia Ethica*, pp. viii-ix, 143.

6. Ibid., pp. 5, 17.

7. Ibid., p. 38.

8. Ibid., p. x.

9. Ibid.

10. Ibid., p. 143.

11. Ibid., p. x.

12. Ibid., p. 144.

13. H. H. Price regarded sensing as knowledge but only because he defined sensing as the awareness of sense-data, and had defined a sense-datum as that about which we could entertain no doubt in cases of perception. See *Perception* (London: Methuen and Co. Ltd., 1932), pp. 3–4.

14. *Some Main Problems of Philosophy* (London: George Allen and Unwin, 1953), p. 142.

15. Ibid., p. 90.

16. *A Treatise of Human Nature*, ed. L. A. Selby-Bigge (Oxford: Clarendon Press, 1888), p. 124.

17. Ibid., p. 70.

18. Ibid., p. 79; see also p. 69.

19. *Principia Ethica*, pp. 149–55. Later Moore modified this view in a way we shall discuss in the next chapter.

20. *Principia Ethica*, pp. 143–44.

21. I discuss this issue in greater detail in *The Concept of Knowledge* (Evanston: Northwestern University Press, 1970), pp. 69–97.

22. See, for example, *The Foundations of Knowing* (Minneapolis: University of Minnesota Press, 1982). Chisholm's remark (p. 12) that epistemic properties are "normative" and "supervenient" on nonepistemic properties, is, as we saw in chapter 4 in connection with goodness, at best the starting point of an elucidation.

23. *Epistemology and Cognition* (Cambridge, Mass., and London, England: Harvard University Press, 1986), p. 108.

24. See William P. Alston, "Epistemic Circularity," *Philosophy and Phenomenological Research* 47 (1986): 1–30. Alston argues that a vicious circularity or infinite regress arises only if one seeks "fully reflective justification," and that no belief can be fully reflectively justified. He ignores the Cartesian alternative. See below.

25. For an admirable critique of externalist theories of justification, see Laurence BonJour,

*The Structure of Empirical Knowledge* (Cambridge, Mass., and London, England: Harvard University Press, 1985), chap. 3.

26. "Level-Confusions in Epistemology," *Midwest Studies in Philosophy* 5 (1980): 135–50.

27. *The View From Nowhere* (New York and Oxford: Oxford University Press, 1986), p. 69.

28. "Self-Profile," in Radu J. Bogdan, ed., *Roderick M. Chisholm* (Dordrecht: Reidel, 1986), pp. 37–38.

29. I have already commented briefly on Laurence BonJour's recent attempt to dispel the mystery in *The Structure of Empirical Knowledge*. See above, chap. 1, n. 7.

30. "The Coherence Theory of Knowledge," *Philosophical Topics* 14 (1986): 5.

31. "The Raft and the Pyramid: Coherence Versus Foundations in the Theory of Knowledge," *Midwest Studies in Philosophy* 5 (1980): 19.

32. *Epistemology and Cognition*, pp. 99–100. For a convincing detailed criticism of coherentist theories of justification, see P. K. Moser, *Empirical Justification* (Dordrecht: Reidel, 1985), already mentioned in chap. 1.

33. *Epistemology and Cognition*, pp. 100–101.

34. Such an argument is developed in some detail by Laurence BonJour in *The Structure of Empirical Knowledge*.

35. For this objection I am indebted to Albert Casullo.

36. *Knowledge and Perception* (Oxford: Clarendon Press, 1950), p. 96. See also pp. 86–91.

37. I discuss the main point of this paragraph in greater detail in *The Concept of Knowledge*.

38. *Knowledge and Perception*, p. 97.

39. "Self-Profile," in *Roderick M. Chisholm*, p. 39.

40. *Principia Ethica*, p. 27.

41. *On Emotional Presentation*, trans. M.-L. S. Kalsi (Evanston: Northwestern University Press, 1972) p. 109.

42. *Virtues and Vices* (Berkeley and Los Angeles: University of California Press, 1981), p. 124.

43. *Groundwork of the Metaphysics of Morals*, trans. H. J. Paton (New York: Harper and Row, 1964), p. 61.

44. *The Methods of Ethics* (Chicago: University of Chicago Press, 1962), pp. 392–93.

45. Ibid., p. 402.

46. *The Republic*, 331c.

47. *Moral Relativity* (Berkeley, Los Angeles, London: University of California Press, 1984), pp. 155, 173.

48. For example, by Renford Bambrough, *Moral Scepticism and Moral Knowledge* (Atlantic Highlands, N.J.: Humanities Press, 1979); G. J. Warnock, *The Object of Morality* (London: Methuen and Co., 1971); Joel J. Kupperman, *Ethical Knowledge* (London: George Allen and Unwin, 1970). Kupperman makes the important observation that it is a contingent fact that disagreement in moral opinion is more common than disagreement in scientific opinion. It could easily have been otherwise. (See chap. 4 of his book.)


## 8. Our Knowledge of Right

1. John Rawls, *A Theory of Justice* (Cambridge: Harvard University Press, 1971), p. 30.

2. Compare Prichard, *Moral Obligation and Duty and Interest* (London, Oxford, New York: Oxford University Press, 1968), p. 23.

3. *Perceiving: A Philosophical Study* (Ithaca: Cornell University Press, 1957).

4. *The Problem of Knowledge* (London: Macmillan, 1958), chap. I, section (v).

5. "Self-Profile," in Radu J. Bogdan, ed., *Roderick M. Chisholm* (Dordrecht: Reidel,

1986), pp. 52–56. See also "The Place of Epistemic Justification," *Philosophical Topics* 14 (1986): 85–92.

6. "The Raft and the Pyramid: Coherence Versus Foundations in the Theory of Knowledge," *Midwest Studies in Philosophy* V (1980). See also "Knowledge and Intellectual Virtue," *The Monist* 68 (1985): 226–45.

7. *Epistemology and Cognition* (Cambridge: Harvard University Press, 1986). But Goldman also allows for a deontological element in epistemology, the crucial notion of justifiedness being for him deontic.

8. *The Theory of Epistemic Rationality* (Cambridge: Harvard University Press, 1987).

9. "Induction and Reasoning to the Best Explanation," *Philosophy of Science* 47 (1980): 589–600.

10. See "Chisholm and The Ethics of Belief," *The Philosophical Review* 68 (1959): 493–506.

11. Roderick M. Chisholm, *Brentano and Intrinsic Value* (Cambridge: Cambridge University Press, 1986), pp. 37–39.

12. Hilary Putnam, *Reason, Truth, and History* (Cambridge: Cambridge University Press, 1981), p. 55.

13. *Moral Obligation and Duty and Interest*, p. 30.

14. See "Recent Developments in British Ethical Thought." in *British Philosophy in the Mid-Century* (London: George Allen and Unwin, 1957), pp. 69–70.

15. *The Groundwork of the Metaphysics of Morals*, trans. H. S. Paton (New York: Harper and Row, 1964), p. 63.

16. *Summa Theologica*, Part Two, Question 91, Article 3, Reply to Objection 3.

17. Ibid., Question 91, Article 4.

18. "Dissertation II: Of the Nature of Virtue," in L. A. Selby-Bigge, ed., *British Moralists* (Oxford: Clarendon Press, 1897), Vol. I, pp. 253–54.

19. Hastings Rashdall, *The Theory of Good and Evil* (Oxford: University Press, 1924), Vol. II, p. 219.

20. For a superb discussion of these issues, let me refer the reader again to Lars Bergström, *The Alternatives and Consequences of Actions* (Stockholm: Almqvist and Wiksell, 1966).

21. *Utilitarianism, For and Against*, with Bernard Williams (Cambridge: Cambridge University Press, 1973), pp. 64–65.

22. *The Virtues* (Cambridge: Cambridge University Press, 1977), pp. 99–100.

23. *Utilitarianism and Co-Operation* (Oxford: Clarendon Press, 1980), p. 129.

24. Ibid., p. 169.

25. *Principia Ethica* (Cambridge: Cambridge University Press, 1971), p. 153.

26. *A Treatise on Probability* (London: Macmillan, 1921), pp. 309–10.

27. Keynes does not accept the principle except with major qualifications. See *A Treatise on Probability*, chap. IV.

28. See *The Theory of Morality* (Chicago: University of Chicago Press, 1977), chap. 6.

29. *The Methods of Ethics* (Chicago: University of Chicago Press, 1962), p. 131.

30. Ibid., p. 147.

31. Ibid., p. 195.

32. Ibid., p. 463.

33. Ibid., p. 464.

34. *A Treatise on Probability*, chap. XXVI. The quotations that follow are from pp. 309–12. Some of the examples are mine.

35. Hastings Rashdall, who provides one of the most sensitive treatments of the problem of the commensurability of values, held nevertheless that, "If it is a matter of indifference to me whether I enjoy one minute of one pleasure to two minutes of another, I may reasonably be said to regard the one pleasure as twice as pleasant as the other," and quotes McTaggart's assertion, "I feel no hesitation in affirming that the pleasure I get from a plate of turtle-soup is more than twice the pleasure I get from a plate of pea-soup." *Theory of Good and Evil*,

Vol. II, p. 23. For a recent discussion, see Richard B. Brandt, A *Theory of the Good and the Right* (Oxford: Clarendon Press, 1979), pp. 253–65.

36. Keynes argues in A *Treatise on Probability*, chap. III, that in many cases they are not.

37. See Alasdair MacIntyre, *After Virtue* (Notre Dame: University of Notre Dame Press, 1981), pp. 89–108; Peter Geach, *The Virtues*, pp. 104–105; and, of course, many others. In "Retrospective and Prospective Utilitarianism," *Nous* 15 (1981), Brian Ellis in effect offers an excellent defense of empirical skepticism, whether or not he realizes it. He concludes that "the basic question of how one ought to conduct one's life may not be answerable on any utilitarian theory" (p. 337).

38. David O. Brink distinguishes between (act) utilitarianism as a criterion of rightness and utilitarianism as a decision procedure and argues that if we take it as being only the former then it does not face epistemological difficulties. The agent should appeal in his decision making to rules for which there is utilitarian justification, except in unusual circumstances and in cases of conflicts between the rules. ("Utilitarian Morality and the Personal Point of View," *The Journal of Philosophy* 83 (1986): pp. 425–26.) But the empirical skeptic would question that we have genuine utilitarian justification for any rules.

39. *Utilitarianism, For and Against*, pp. 46–47.

40. Ibid., p. 41.

41. On this, there is much good sense to be found in H. J. McCloskey, "An Examination of Restricted Utilitarianism," *The Philosophical Review* 66 (1957), pp. 466–85.

42. *The Methods of Ethics*, p. 220.

43. *Proceedings and Addresses of the American Philosophical Association* 60 (1987): 509.

44. "Further on Actual Consequence Utilitarianism," *Mind* 92 (1983): 273–74. Singer's article is a reply to a criticism by Jack Temkin ("Actual Consequence Utilitarianism: A Reply to Professor Singer," *Mind* 87 [1978]) of Singer's "Actual Consequence Utilitarianism," *Mind* 86 (1977): 66–77. See also Singer's "Incoherence, Inconsistency, and Moral Theory: More on Actual Consequence Utilitarianism," *The Southern Journal of Philosophy* 20 (1982).

45. *Ethics* (Oxford: Oxford University Press, 1977), p. 81.

46. *The Definition of Good* (London: Macmillan, 1947), pp. 118, 121, 128.

47. *Moral Obligation and Duty and Interest*, p. 36.

48. Ibid., p. 37.

49. Ibid., p. 25.

50. *Rights, Goods, and Democracy* (Newark: University of Delaware Press; London and Toronto: Associated University Presses, 1986), pp. 194–97.

51. *Knowledge and Perception* (Oxford: Clarendon Press, 1950). See especially pp. 86–89, 96–98. For a discussion of this view, and an argument for the existence of such a "strong" sense of "know," see Norman Malcolm, "Knowledge and Belief," in *Knowledge and Certainty* (Englewood Cliffs, N.J.: Prentice Hall, 1963).

52. See D. D. Raphael, "The Consequences of Actions," *Aristotelian Society*, supp. vol. 30 (1956): 100–19.

53. See H. L. A. Hart and A. M. Honoré, *Causation in the Law* (Oxford: Clarendon Press, 1959), pp. 65–66; also A. C. Ewing, "Utilitarianism," *Ethics* 58 (1947–48): 103–105.

54. *The Alternatives and Consequences of Actions*, pp. 81–82.

55. *Ethics*, trans. Stanton Coit (London: George Allen and Unwin, 1932), Vol. 2, p. 40. Hartmann also remarked that "even the evil Will can bring forth good, against its own purpose" (p. 39).

56. Ibid., pp. 41–42.

57. W. D. Ross pointed out that "much pleasure, and much pain, do not spring from virtuous or vicious actions at all but from the operation of natural laws." (*The Right and the Good*, p. 134.)

# INDEX